the job of Chief Justice was the one he wanted all his life.

In nine years, he largely reorganized the Federal judicial system in the belief that he could thus stem the rising tide of democracy. He tried to make the courts more effective safeguards of private property, and to make the law a check against progressive ideas. This book explains in scholarly but simple language just how he tried to do this, and the strange paradox that his reforms helped to build the constitutional base for the judicial revolution of 1937 and a welfare state.

OTHER BOOKS BY ALPHEUS THOMAS MASON

Organized Labor and the Law, 1925
Brandeis: Lawyer and Judge in the Modern State, 1933
The Brandeis Way, 1938
Bureaucracy Convicts Itself, 1941
Brandeis: A Free Man's Life, 1946
The Rise and Fall of a Railroad Empire (with Henry Lee Staples), 1947
Free Government in the Making, 1949; 3d edition, 1965
The Supreme Court: Vehicle of Revealed Truth or Power Group, 1930–1937, 1953
American Constitutional Law (with William M. Beaney), 1954; 3d edition, 1964
Security Through Freedom, 1955
Harlan Fiske Stone: Pillar of the Law, 1956
The Supreme Court from Taft to Warren, 1958
The Supreme Court in a Free Society (with William M. Beaney), 1959
In Quest of Freedom (with Richard H. Leach), 1959
The Supreme Court: Palladium of Freedom, 1962
The States Rights Debate: Antifederalism and the Constitution, 1964

William Howard Taft:
CHIEF JUSTICE

BY

ALPHEUS THOMAS MASON

SIMON AND SCHUSTER · NEW YORK

PUBLISHED BY SIMON AND SCHUSTER, INC.
ROCKEFELLER CENTER, 630 FIFTH AVENUE
NEW YORK 20, N.Y.

First Printing
LIBRARY OF CONGRESS CATALOG CARD NUMBER: 65–11166
MANUFACTURED IN THE UNITED STATES OF AMERICA
DESIGNED BY EVE METZ

To the Memory
of
H.W.M.
and
E.L.M.

ACKNOWLEDGMENTS

THIS BOOK, the by-product of a comprehensive study of the office and powers of the Chief Justice of the United States, now in preparation, is based primarily on the massive collection of Taft papers in the Library of Congress. It also makes considerable use of Taft's books, articles, and public addresses. Mr. David C. Mearns, Chief of the Manuscripts Division, gave me access to the Taft papers and made life easier for me and my research assistant, Mr. Peter G. Fish, during the summers of 1960 and 1961. Besides the published works and special assistance from particular persons mentioned in footnotes, I drew on Mr. Michael Cole's excellent honors paper written in 1963 at Vanderbilt University and from the seminar papers of Robert H. Birkby, Gerald Garvey and David Hughes.

Mr. Sanford B. Gabin, instructor in the Politics Department, Princeton University, helped me prepare the manuscript for the printer, and the entire book profited from Professor Walter F. Murphy's careful reading. Miss Helen Fairbanks, Firestone Library, Princeton, played her customary role of tracking down hard-to-find sources, and Mrs. Helen S. Wright did the typing and retyping. The finished product was given further examination and revision after Mr. Joseph Barnes of Simon and Schuster raised pointed questions on matters of interpretation and communication. My research assistant, J. Morgan Kousser, checked the documentation and prepared the index.

The book could not have been done without the generous financial support of The Rockefeller Foundation and Princeton University. To all these persons and institutions I gratefully acknowledge my debt.

A. T. M.

Princeton
June 15, 1964

CONTENTS

CHRONOLOGY

Born in Cincinnati, Sept. 15, 1857.
B.A., Yale, 1878.
LL.B., Cincinnati Law School, 1880.
Admitted to Ohio bar, 1880.
Law reporter, *Cincinnati Times,* later of *Cincinnati Commercial,* 1880.
Assistant Prosecuting Attorney, Hamilton Co., O., 1881, 1882, 1883.
Married Helen Herron, June 19, 1886.
Practiced law in Cincinnati, 1883–1887.
Assistant County solicitor, Hamilton Co., 1885–1887.
Judge, Ohio Superior Court, Cincinnati, 1887–1890.
Solicitor General of U.S., 1890–1892.
U.S. circuit judge, 6th Circuit, 1892–1900.
Professor and Dean, Law School, University of Cincinnati, 1896–1900.
President, U.S. Philippine Commission, Mar. 12, 1900–July 4, 1901.
First Civil Governor of the Philippines, July 4, 1901–Feb. 1, 1904.
Secretary of War, Feb. 1, 1904–June 30, 1908.
Nominated for President by Republican National Convention, Chicago, June 1908.
Elected President, November 3, 1908 for term, Mar. 4, 1909–Mar. 4, 1913.
Kent Professor of Law, Yale, 1913–1921.
President, American Bar Association, 1913.
President, American Academy of Jurisprudence, 1914.
Appointed member National War Labor Conference Board, Apr. 1918; co-chairman until dissolved, Aug. 1919.
President of League to Enforce Peace, 1919.
Chief Justice of the U.S., June 30, 1921–Feb. 3, 1930.
Died Mar. 8, 1930.

PREFACE

FOR AMERICANS of my generation the conventional image of William Howard Taft is unflattering. It pictures him as a stubborn defender of the status quo, champion of property rights, apologist for privilege, inveterate critic of social democracy—the gigantic symbol of standpattism. Weighing well over three hundred pounds, avoirdupois alone made him a cartoonist's model of the bloated capitalist or political boss. This familiar portrait is blurred rather than discredited by the long and energetic campaign he waged to reorganize the Federal judicial system. In pursuit of this goal, he demonstrated singleness of purpose, a fertile imagination, and extraordinary dynamism. By streamlining the judiciary and revamping outmoded rules of procedure, he sought to make courts more efficient instruments of justice. These two drives, one reactionary and obstructive, the other liberating and forward-looking, run simultaneously throughout his career. I began this book not knowing how the two were related, but it occurred to me that somewhere Taft himself might have tried to reconcile this dualism.

The merger was attempted during his campaign for the Presidency. In a major address of August 1908 before the Virginia Bar Association, the G.O.P. candidate tied improved judicial administration to the usefulness of courts in stemming the advancing tide of social democracy. One way to undermine the social reformer's crusade was to meet his legitimate demands for evenhanded justice. Leveling gross inequalities between rich and poor at the bar of justice would remove a major source of social unrest. Improved judicial machinery would make courts potentially more effective safeguards of private property and, perhaps, help disarm its most dangerous enemies—socialists, communists, and progressives.

Taft was a judicial architect, not a social reformer. His reformism was eclectic even when confined to the judiciary. When various states began exalting the jury and curtailing the role of judges, he deplored the trend as but another manifestation of democratic idiocy. Like the Founding Fathers, our tenth Chief Justice feared unqualified majority rule. His professional career coincided precisely with the emergence of mass movements organized to influence social and political action. He was horrified by the legislation already on the statute books and even more disturbed by projected innovations. Social betterment resulted primarily from the automatic working of natural forces; judicial reform would come only with deliberate, painstaking effort.

Taft's first paper, published in 1884, struck the keynote of judicial reform. In scores of campaign speeches, special messages to Congress, law review articles, and addresses before bar associations, he kept hammering away. His titles suggest the theme—"Delays and Defects in the Enforcement of Law," "Inequalities in the Administration of Justice," "Possible and Needed Reforms in Federal Courts." To a unique degree among Presidents, Taft was conversant with the details and defects of judicial organization and procedure. No previous Chief Executive had concerned himself so profoundly or knowingly with corrective legislation. When opportunity arose in 1910 to appoint a Chief Justice, he said he wanted the office filled by "someone young and vigorous enough to revise the entire judicial procedure of this country." Yet the man he selected spurned as improper even the most modest participation in the political process. Following the ill-fated White House years, the full weight of his prestige and experience as former President guided judicial reform into Federal channels. As Chief Justice, Taft was never restrained by considerations of propriety so paralyzing to his predecessor Edward Douglass White. No other Chief Justice, before or since, worked so hard at lobbying.

An abiding concern for judicial efficiency was Taft's goad. Justice Felix Frankfurter, no friendly critic, holds that his "great claim in history will be as a reformer," crediting him with adapting the Federal judicial system "to the needs of a country that had grown from three million to a hundred and forty. . . ."

An outspoken critic of schemes for social uplift, he thought of the Supreme Court as a brake on democracy. Realizing that the decisions reached would reflect the values of the judges empowered to make them, he tried to pack the courts with men of "sound views"—"our kind." Judges of a liberal stamp, including the most eminent—Louis D. Brandeis, Learned Hand, Benjamin N. Cardozo—were suspect as destroyers of the Constitution. Taft did not always succeed either in winning the appointments he favored or in controlling the decisions of those whose selection he had approved. But his realistic stance never wavered. His spirit of unyielding resistance to the social-service state lived on into the New Deal years. In the early 1930's, it shackled the power to govern amid a national crisis that shook the foundations of our economic and political structure. The impasse between Court and Congress emboldened President Roosevelt to propose his famous Court-packing solution. Though the plan failed of enactment, it is hard to disassociate the President's stratagem from the famous "switch in time that saved nine."

Taft's worst fears are now realized. If he were alive today, he might again be provoked into saying, as he did when President Wilson appointed Brandeis in 1916 to a post he deeply cherished—*"Es ist zum lachen."*

William Howard Taft is difficult to appraise. His enduring aim was to safeguard private property—the bulwark of civilization. The Constitution, he believed, precludes social and economic experimentation. At the storm center for nearly half a century, he tried to dam the surging tide of progressivism. For him the final barrier against social disaster was the United States Supreme Court.

Taft was a thoroughgoing Social Darwinist, an outspoken critic of governmental regulation. Yet a remodeled Federal judicial organization stands as his major achievement. The irony of his career is that the revisions he sponsored and pushed through to enactment should now be helpful to causes he profoundly distrusted. Certain planks in his constitutional jurisprudence—his broad construction of the commerce power, rivaling the nationalist doctrines of Chief Justice Marshall, his firm alliance with Justice Oliver Wendell Holmes in support of the minimum wage—furnished doctrinal ammunition in the judicial revolution of 1937. Enthroned and authenticated was the dreaded collectivism he had struggled desperately to prevent. As Chief Justice between 1921 and 1930, he had stood at the crossroads of the dying old and the emerging new.

CHAPTER I

YEARNINGS

SOMEONE HAS SAID life begins at forty. For William Howard Taft it really began at sixty-four when, on June 30, 1921, he became the tenth Chief Justice of the United States. Unhappy and ineffective as Chief Executive, lifelong aspirant to the Chief Justiceship, Taft was the only man in American history to occupy both offices. The latter fascinated him; it alone promised "power without worry." Twice he declined appointment as Associate Justice; he wanted to be "C.J." Seemingly barred from this goal by the vicissitudes of fate, politics, and an ambitious wife who preferred to be First Lady, Taft persisted, finally winning the center seat in "the sacred shrine."[1]

As early as 1889, at the age of thirty-two, he had pulled every available wire leading to President Benjamin Harrison and the place then vacant on the Supreme Court. Ohio Governor Joseph Benson Foraker endorsed him, but appointment as Associate Justice of a young man of slender achievements, merely to please Ohio Republicans, was not favored at the White House. Taft himself did not take his prospects seriously. "My chances of going to the moon and of donning a silk gown at the hands of President Harrison are about equal."[2] Instead of a Court appointment, the President offered the youthful Ohio Superior Court judge the post of Solicitor General. Taft's acceptance proved important for his entire political and judicial career. The office required thorough grounding in constitutional law and procedure; it brought him into close contact with Republican bigwigs, including Theodore Roosevelt. In Washington he soon acquired "a pretty general knowledge of the persons who run things."[3]

Taft's performance of the Solicitor General's main task—arguing cases for the government before the Supreme Court—was undistinguished. He was not an impressive speaker; his presentation was marked chiefly by its soporific effect. "I have difficulty in holding the attention of the Court," he reported after his second appearance. "They seem to think when I begin to talk that that is a good chance to read all the letters that have been waiting for some time, to eat lunch, and to devote their attention to correcting proof, and other matters that have been delayed until my speech."[4] But the results belied his gloomy report. In his brief service as Solicitor General he argued eighteen cases and lost only two.

The shift from judging to highfalutin' Washington politics, though flattering, had been motivated by his wife's promptings, rather than his own ambition. She welcomed it as an opportunity for her husband to get out of the "judicial groove." Taft, on the other hand, had accepted only after "regretful glances at his beloved bench."[5] For him the position of Solicitor General was important mainly as a steppingstone. "The special feature of good fortune that I see in it," Governor Foraker had advised him, "lies beyond that office in the other position to which I clearly see that it leads—the bench of the Supreme Court."[6]

Judging was Taft's natural bent. Those close to him suspected that he had "great contempt for public life and certainly for politicians."[7] His father had been a judge in Ohio.*

---

* Secretary of War and Attorney General under President Grant, Alphonso Taft had also earned for judicial promotion. On December 7, 1874, he wrote Chief Justice Morrison R. Waite:

My dear Judge,

I have sometimes hoped, that if Judge Swayne should retire, there might be a possibility of my being thought of for that place. I should like it. The idea was suggested to me some years since, even before the death of Judge Chase, by certain persons. But I do not suppose, that anything of

"The law" was in his blood; judges were the embodiment of his ideals. "I love judges, and I love courts," he said. "They are my ideals, that typify on earth what we shall meet hereafter in heaven under a just God."[8] Yet his judicial career had begun almost by accident. Unexpectedly, in 1887 Judson Harmon, afterward Attorney General of the United States and later twice Governor of Ohio, had resigned as judge on the Superior Court of Ohio. Prominent Cincinnati lawyers of wide experience were considered, but on the recommendation of Judge Harmon, Governor Foraker appointed twenty-nine-year-old Taft.[9] With the appointment went Governor Foraker's suggestion to quit the bench after one term. Taft's father considered this "good advice," but his son did not follow it. After completing Harmon's unexpired term of fourteen months, he was elected for a full term. The Ohio Governor, not without self-serving political considerations, had initially furnished Taft an opportunity deeply gratifying "to a man of my age and circumstances."[10] It was his first step on the coveted judicial ladder. Foraker had given him the honor "from which all that I have had since has easily flowed."[11]

---

that kind is in store for me. If, however, you should think favorably of it, and should find oppertunity [sic] to encourage it, I should certainly, be under great obligation whatever the result might be.

Sincerely your friend,

/s/ Alphonso Taft

Hon. M. R. Waite,
Chief Justice of U. S.

In his reply of December 13, 1874, the Chief Justice wrote:

I need not say that, if the opportunity is given, my heart will be in the work indicated in your note of the 7th. But I have no idea that Swayne will retire at all. Certainly not for some time to come. He is as well physically as he ever was and likes his place. He used to talk about retiring, but he has not mentioned it this term.

Should he make the place vacant, I am inclined to think the Pres. would endeavor to fill it from the South. However, it [would] give me so much pleasure personally to have you with us, that I shall lose no opportunity of letting him know what a fine judge you would make. . . .

Morrison Waite Papers, Library of Congress. Box 3, General Correspondence, Aug.–Dec. 1874. For these letters, I am indebted to Professor H. M. Hollingsworth.

After a scant two years as Solicitor General, Taft resigned, against his wife's strong misgivings, to accept President Harrison's appointment to the Sixth Judicial Circuit. She had harbored doubts about a judicial career from the outset. The narrowing effects of judicial life might preclude "all-round professional development." Taft did not share these doubts. For him, appointment as a Superior Court judge of Ohio was "the welcome beginning of just the career he wanted."[12]

In 1892, at thirty-four, he was again doing congenial work—hearing motions, writing opinions, and presiding in open court at civil and criminal trials. Garbed in brand-new judicial robes, he could feel the satisfaction that comes from a sense of solid accomplishment. During one session of less than two months, he wrote twenty opinions.[13] Nor were all his time and energies given solely to judging. In 1896 he became dean and professor of property at the Cincinnati Law School, lecturing two hours a week. Part-time teaching could be used to exploit his abiding interest in judicial reform; he wanted also to raise the standards of legal education at his alma mater. His eight-year judicial stint was not only highly satisfying, but also helpful in broadening his political and legal contacts. There was still another consideration: a place on the Federal bench seemed only a short step to the highest court in the land. Yet his wife had resisted his decision to cast political ambition to the winds. "If," she had warned, "you get your heart's desire [appointment as Federal Circuit Court judge], my darling, it will put an end to all the opportunities you now have of being thrown with the bigwigs."[14] Fear of becoming "fixed in a groove for the rest of his life"[15] never troubled Taft. In 1914, with his White House experience behind him, his wife affirmed that he had enjoyed these eight years of work on the Circuit Court "more than any he has ever undertaken."[16]

Politics soon beckoned again. One January day in 1900, a telegram came from President McKinley, asking him to come to Washington on important business. The Tafts were at a loss to know what was up. Realization of his dream could not be in the offing, since no Supreme Court vacancy then existed. Nevertheless, Taft went off with high expectations. Three days later he returned, looking so grave that his wife thought he must be facing impeachment.[17] The President and Secretary of War Elihu Root had asked him to head a commission to establish civil rule in the Philippines. To Mrs. Taft the possibilities seemed boundless. Her husband was less certain. Besides his lurking doubts about the wisdom of our acquisition of the Philippines, there was a fear that acceptance of an administrative post might impede his path to the Supreme Court. Taft was hard to convince. President McKinley and Secretary of War Root went to great pains to reassure him. Surrender of his judgeship would not mean the end of a judicial career, they insisted. "If you give up this judicial office at my request," the President promised, "you shall not suffer. If I last and the opportunity comes, I shall appoint you." It was even hinted that the upshot might be "judicial promotion."[18] The Chief Justiceship was a possibility; Taft began to reconsider. Headship of the Philippine commission would enable him to test his mettle. Furthermore, the job to be done—establishing civil government—fell clearly within the lawyer's domain. For the moment, perhaps, these were rationalizations. Mrs. Taft rated her husband's resignation from the Circuit Court bench "the hardest thing he ever did."[19]

His stay in the Philippines was to have been temporary. Unexpectedly he found himself gripped by responsibilities that fully challenged him. It was not until February 1904 that Taft could be persuaded to relinquish them. Not even President Roosevelt's offer of a place on the Supreme Court could lure him away. In October 1902, when Justice George Shiras announced his intention to retire, Taft was the President's first choice for the vacancy. Offering him the post, Roosevelt said:

On January first [1903] there will be a vacancy on the Supreme Court to which I earnestly desire to appoint you. . . . I feel that your duty is on the Court unless you have decided not to adopt a judicial career. I greatly hope you will accept.

The opportunity for which he had been yearning seemed ill timed. He had just returned to the Islands after a prolonged absence. Much work still remained. Taft's strong emotional preference was to accept; yet he realized that he must not yield. Mrs. Taft recalls the decision:

This was not a question which gave Mr. Taft even a shade of hesitation because he knew immediately what he must do. All his life his first ambition had been to attain the Supreme Bench. To him it meant the crown of the highest career that a man can seek, and he wanted it as strongly as a man can ever want anything. But now that the opportunity had come, acceptance was not to be thought of. I had always been opposed to a judicial career for him, but at this point, I have to admit, I weakened just a little. . . . I yearned to be safe in Washington even though it did mean our settlement in the "fixed groove" that I had talked against for so long. Mr. Taft's plain and unmistakable duty held him in the Philippine Islands.[20]

To President Roosevelt went an unequivocal refusal:

Great honour deeply appreciated, but must decline. . . . Nothing would satisfy individual taste more than acceptance. Look forward to the time when I can accept such an offer, but even if it is certain that it can never be repeated I must now decline.[21]

The President refused to take "No" as the answer. Nearly a month after the incident was apparently closed, a somewhat playful letter came from the President:

Dear Will, I am sorry, old man, but after faithful effort for a month to try to arrange matters on the basis you wanted I find that I shall have to bring you home and put you on the Supreme Court. I am very sorry. I have the greatest confidence in your judgment, but, after all, old fellow, if you will permit me to say so, I am President and see the whole field.

The President went on to stress his high responsibility, and the necessity he was under "to yield to no one else's decision if my judgment is against it." "This is one of the cases," the letter reiterated, "when the President, if he is fit for his position, must take the responsibility and put the men on whom he most relies in particular positions in which he himself thinks they can render the greatest public good. I shall therefore about February first nominate you as I have suggested."

The matter seemed settled. Taft cabled his acceptance, but coupled with it "one more appeal" to be left at his post. "Recognize soldier's duty to obey orders. Before orders irrevocable by action, however, I presume on our personal friendship even in the face of your letter to make one more appeal, in which I lay aside wholly my strong personal disinclination to leave work of intense interest half done."

News of Taft's resignation provoked astonishment. Within a few days the Islands were placarded with cries of "We want Taft." Popular Island orators hailed Taft as a savior. "As Christ had converted the cross into the symbol of glory and triumph," one overwrought speaker said, "so had Governor Taft turned a dying people to the light and life of modern liberties." The White House response to all this clamor was a cryptic message addressed to "Taft, Manila," which said: "All right stay where you are. I shall appoint some one else to the Court. Roosevelt."[22] Both the Tafts had "a hearty laugh."

There were strong reasons for taking the judicial post. Acceptance would have immediately satisfied a longing for high judicial office; it would, moreover, pay off a little-known political debt T.R. owed Taft. In 1898 Taft had used his influence with President McKinley to win for Roosevelt the office of Assistant Secretary of the Navy, which, of course, had started T.R. on the road to the White House. This had not been easily accomplished. McKinley would have preferred to see the bumptious New Yorker somewhere else. "For the truth is," President McKinley told Taft, "Roosevelt is always in such a state of mind." Nevertheless, Taft believed his effort was successful. "We got Theodore in the Navy," Taft boasted many years later.[23]

A short six months after declining the Supreme Court appointment, the Tafts learned that Secretary of War Root was planning to retire. Despite the Governor's recent reluctance to surrender his Island responsibilities, the President practically ordered him to report to Washington as Root's successor. Acceptance would not mean abandonment of Philippine affairs. As Secretary of War he would, in fact, have a broader and more powerful field of general supervision. Mrs. Taft was elated. A Cabinet post in the rapid-fire Roosevelt administration was, she said, "in line with the kind of work I wanted my husband to do, the kind of career I wanted for him and expected him to have."[24]

Soon he was deep in the affairs of his own department, while also representing the President in various affairs of state. By 1904, President Roosevelt had come to think of Taft as President Wilson, a few years later, thought of Louis D. Brandeis—as needing him everywhere.[25] "If only there were three of you!" T.R. remarked after persuading Taft to join his Cabinet. "Then I would have put one of you on the Supreme Court . . . one of you in Root's place as Secretary of War . . . one of you permanently as Governor of the Philippines. . . ."[26] Nor were purely political assignments beyond his ken. He was a vigorous participant in the President's winning presidential campaign of 1904, but even the flush of victory did not lessen his sense of relief in having it over. "A national campaign for the presidency is to me a nightmare," he commented as the struggle ended.[27]

Taft's political stature was growing rapidly. A New York *Sun* editorial called him "the energy and force of the whole administration."

> Merely to record the movements and missions of the Secretary of War requires a nimble mind. He journeys from Washington to Manila to reassure ten millions of natives restive under an experimental scheme of civil government and turns up in Panama to speed the digging of the Isthmian canal. To give a fillip to a campaign for reform in some western State, or direct the southern Republicans in the way they should go, or enlighten the people Down East as to the President's home policy, or illuminate recesses of a problem in jurisdiction for the benefit of a bar association, is only a matter of grabbing a time table and throwing a change of clothing into a travelling bag. Such are mere relaxations and holiday jaunts for the Hon. William H. Taft.[28]

"Yet there are those," the editorial commented, "who would circumscribe his activities by investing him with the robes and immobile dignity of judicial office."

This piece fitted Mrs. Taft's image perfectly. With more than a trace of irritation, she noted that "the subject of my husband's appointment to the Supreme Bench cropped up with what seemed to me annoying frequency."[29] Cropping up also was the rapidly developing possibility that the peripatetic Cabinet officer would be the Republican nominee in the 1908 presidential election. T.R. had apparently decided to lead the G.O.P. to victory by selecting his own successor.

Serious talk of Taft as a man of presidential timber had begun while he was still in the Philippines. Colonel Theodore Roosevelt was among the first to notice his rising star. In 1901, when Taft was appointed first governor of the Islands, the editor of *Outlook* invited Colonel Roosevelt, then Vice-President, to write a feature article on the new appointee. By the time the piece was in print, the author had succeeded William McKinley as President. Uncanny words of prophecy mark the opening paragraph:

> A year ago a man of wide acquaintance both with American public life and American public men remarked that the first Governor of the Philippines ought to combine the qualities which would make a first-class President of the United States with qualities which would make a first-class Chief Justice of the United States, and that the only man

he knew who possessed all these qualities was Judge William H. Taft of Ohio.

"This statement," President Roosevelt affirmed, "was entirely correct."[30]

The Taft family took the presidential boom seriously. In Mrs. Taft's eyes, it did not seem "at all unreasonable."[31] Strongly opposed, Taft's aging mother wrote her son long dissertations on the "wisdom of his keeping out of politics."[32] These urgings appealed to nothing in him except his sense of humor. He never ceased "to regard a Supreme Court appointment as vastly more desirable than the Presidency." Besides having a distaste for politics, he considered himself "unavailable" as a presidential candidate. To be known as the inventor of "government by injunction," he commented wryly, "is not a valuable political asset."[33] Taft spelled out his thoughts to brother Charles:

> The idea that a man who has issued injunctions against labour unions, almost by the bushel, who has sent at least ten or a dozen violent labour agitators to jail, and who is known as one of the worst judges for the maintenance of government by injunction, could ever be a successful candidate on a Presidential ticket, strikes me as intensely ludicrous; and had I the slightest ambition in that direction I hope that my good sense would bid me to suppress it. But, more than this, the horrors of a modern Presidential campaign and the political troubles of a successful candidate for President, rob the office of the slightest attraction for me. I have but one ambition, and if that cannot be satisfied I am content to return to the practice of the law with reasonable assurance that, if my health holds out, I can make a living, and make Nellie and the children more comfortable than I could if I went to Washington.[34]

It seemed strange that, despite every intention to keep out of the rough-and-tumble of a political campaign, "I should thus be pitched in the middle of it."[35] Even in his own eyes Taft was becoming a creature of political destiny—and the wheel of fortune had only begun to spin. He avowed that "politics when I am in it makes me sick." Yet the fates seemed always to be pushing him higher and higher. He was, Henry Pringle writes, "the only man in American political history who can, with complete accuracy, be described as a creature of destiny."[36]

But could this be strictly true of a man so long on the public payroll, who owned to keeping his "plate right side up" when appointive jobs were being passed around? Taft's extraordinary political success, his unique accomplishment in the annals of American politics, was not solely the decree of fate. For both him and his wife, the stakes were high. Mrs. Taft kept her political eye on the White House; her husband's was fixed on the Chief Justiceship. Nor was the drive toward these goals spurred by imaginary longings. As early as July 1901, T.R., awaiting a chance to speak his mind in public, had dangled both these prizes before Taft. "If I had the naming either of President or Chief Justice," he had affirmed, "I should feel in honor bound to name you."[37]

Even before his nomination for the Presidency, Taft's friends, echoing President Roosevelt's gratuitous commitment, expressed the hope of seeing him "first, the President of this Republic, and later, the Chief Justice of its Supreme Court."[38] All this was more than rumor or idle talk. The Chicago editor and politician, H. H. Kohlsaat, tells of an incident one evening, when Secretary of War Taft and his wife dined at the White House. After dinner, the President took his guests to the second-floor library. The mood of the occasion was relaxed; as T.R. sat down in an easy chair, he closed his eyes and began:

> "I am the seventh son of a seventh daughter. I have clairvoyant powers. I see a man standing before me weighing three hundred pounds. There is something hanging over his head. I cannot make out what it is. . . . At one time it looks like the Presidency, then again it looks like the Chief Justiceship."
>
> "Make it the Presidency," said Mrs. Taft.
>
> "Make it the Chief Justiceship," said Mr. Taft.[39]

As Justice Shiras' successor, President Roosevelt appointed William R. Day, of Ohio. This was in 1902. Since then no other Supreme Court vacancy had arisen. In 1904 Taft was Secretary of War. Roosevelt's commitment to make him Chief Justice if the opportunity presented itself was still to be fulfilled. Confronted with this situation, the President inspired the White House story that Chief Justice Melville W. Fuller "may soon wish to retire and that Governor Taft would be a suitable man for the vacancy."[40] The rumor served only to stiffen the Chief Justice's resolve to hang on. Friends told him that his health "never seemed better." In response to the published report that T.R. had inspired the "news" of his approaching retirement, Fuller assured Justice Holmes: "I am not to be paragraphed out of my place."[41] Among those who encouraged the Chief Justice to stick was his good friend, Grover Cleveland. The former President wanted "to be placed among those who believe you should only 'resign when it pleases God.' "[42]

Knowledge of Fuller's stubborn resolve may have reached Taft himself. Supreme Court Reporter Charles Henry Butler, a guest at a dinner party given by the Chief Justice and his wife honoring Justice Day, remembers an incident that evening. While coffee was being served, a young officer, recently ordered to the Philippines, called to say goodbye to the Fullers. After having received her guests, Mrs. Fuller went upstairs. While the Chief Justice was making excuses for her absence, she called out to say that she could not come down, but wished to make her farewells from the banister and also relay a message to the Philippine Governor. Addressing the young man by his first name, she said firmly:

> And when you get to the Philippines, you tell Willie Taft not to be in too much of a hurry to get into my husband's shoes.

Butler recalls that the Chief Justice and his guests greeted Mrs. Fuller's parting message with "a hearty laugh."[43]

After Taft became Secretary of War, rumors of his elevation to the Chief Justiceship became more persistent. That these trial shots hit their target is evident from Chief Justice Fuller's remarks introducing Taft at the 1904 Annual Harvard Law School banquet.

When the late Governor of the Philippines arrived at Washington, as soon as I penetrated the dense thicket of laurels that embowered him, he propounded this question: "How's the Docket?" I recognized at once the demonstration of his fitness for the highest judicial station. It is very true that I knew my friend had been a professor and dean of a law school, had been a judge of a state court, had been Solicitor General of the United States and Judge of the Circuit Court of the United States, and Governor as aforesaid and had discharged the duties of all these positions to great acceptance, but I had not realized before that he felt that interest in the docket which is considered a principal qualification of Chief Justices.[44]

Though Fuller was only seventy-one, his longevity seemed to be blocking realization of a deeply felt ambition. Taft cherished the report that certain of Fuller's colleagues wished "to see me Chief Justice." Yet there was small comfort in Justice Henry Billings Brown's prognostication: "The Chief Justice is getting old and he will have to go soon. But I don't think he will ever resign."[45] Taft shared this gloomy outlook, knowing that the Chief Justice was "as tough as a knot, so that if he does not go by resignation, I shall have to whistle for his place."[46]

When Mrs. Fuller died, in April 1904, Taft mixed sympathy for the grief-stricken judge with the hope that her passing might hasten her husband's departure. "It leaves the poor Chief Justice a stricken man. I don't know whether it will hasten his retirement or not. He told me he was getting very tired of cases."[47] Warring with hopes concerning the Chief Justice's apparently slower pace were certain misgivings about T.R. himself. Encouraged by his wife's growing suspicions, Taft was not altogether certain the President, though "in honor bound," would make him Chief Justice even if the opportunity presented itself. Attorney General

Philander C. Knox was hankering for the place, and Taft surmised that T.R. might be receptive to Knox's claims. In 1904 the Secretary of War also suspected that the President had no firm ideas concerning probable Republican presidential candidates. Taft was partially ruled out "because my ambition was to be Chief Justice."[48]

Meanwhile, T.R. kept releasing trial balloons. Confusion became confounded when, in 1906, another Supreme Court vacancy occurred. The faltering judge was not, however, the Chief Justice. It was Henry Billings Brown who, only a short time before, had held out faint hopes of the Chief Justice's retirement. Once again Taft was the President's first choice. It would be hard to imagine a more awkward dilemma. By this time, T.R., having renounced third-term aspirations, was beginning to think seriously about his White House successor. In his diary of March 10, 1906, Taft recorded:

> The Supreme Court vacancy of Justice Brown I hoped I might escape, but the situation is veering around now to a position where it may be impossible. I am very anxious to go on the Supreme bench. The President has promised me a number of times that he would appoint me Chief Justice if a vacancy occurred in that position and he knows that I much prefer a judicial future to a political future.[49]

A quirk of fate and conflicting personal ambitions were among the factors that made William Howard Taft President of the United States. In 1906 he was preoccupied with "the War Department, the Panama Canal and the Philippine business," and did not want appointment as Justice Brown's successor. And Mrs. Taft was, of course, adamant. While the matter was pending, a close friend of the Taft family asked the War Secretary's son whether his father was going to be a Supreme Court Justice. "Nope," the boy answered firmly. To the further query, "Why not?" came the knowledgeable reply, "Ma wants him to wait and be President."[50]

In declining President Roosevelt's second offer of an Associate Justiceship—the post went to Attorney General William H. Moody—Taft ran the almost certain risk of being accused of aspiring to the Presidency. He pleaded not guilty. Besides lacking enthusiasm for political office and having a particular distaste for campaigning, he sensed that the President's own preference was not entirely clear. T.R. was wont "to compare Root, Moody and me, and . . . repeated the statement that I would become Chief Justice if the place became vacant."[51] Mrs. Taft alone held unambiguous views; she was vehemently opposed to any Supreme Court appointment, whether as Associate or as Chief Justice. The White House was her unshakable goal. Taft was in such a quandary that the President, following a half-hour interview with Mrs. Taft, submitted reflections faintly suggestive of the advice a father might give a perplexed son, uncertain as to his future career.

> My dear Will, it is pre-eminently a matter in which no other man can take the responsibility of deciding for you what is right and best for you to do. . . . As far as I am personally concerned, I could not put myself in your place, because I am not a lawyer and would under no circumstances, even if I had been trained for a lawyer, have any leaning toward the bench; so in your case I should as a matter of course accept the three years of service in the War Department, dealing with the Panama and Philippine questions, and then abide the fall of the dice as to whether I became President, or continued in public life in some less conspicuous position, or went back to the practice of law.[52]

As the President then analyzed the domestic situation, America posed an inviting challenge to constructive statesmanship in whatever branch of the government Taft might find himself. "I do not at all like the social conditions at present," the President observed.

> The dull, purblind folly of the very rich men; their greed and arrogance, and the way in which they have unduly prospered by the help of the ablest lawyers, and too often through the weakness or shortsightedness of judges . . . and the corruption in business and politics

have tended to produce a very unhealthy condition of excitement and irritation in the popular mind, which shows itself in part in the enormous increase in socialistic propaganda.[53]

Under the circumstances," the President rated Taft as the best "popular leader." Whether on the bench or in "active political life," he could do much—"most as President," "very much as Chief Justice," less as either Senator or Associate Justice. What Taft should do, no one, "with wisdom," could decide for him. It may be that Chief Justice Fuller's unbudging refusal to surrender the Chief Justiceship, more than anything else, kept Taft free to run for the Presidency in 1908. There were still other considerations. Acceptance of appointment as Associate Justice, though tempting, was risky. The President had repeatedly promised to elevate Taft to the Chief Justiceship if it fell vacant prior to March 1909. But one could not be sure a vacancy would occur; and even if it did, Roosevelt might make the same commitment to Root, Knox, or someone else, as inducement for his acceptance of the 1906 Court vacancy. For the moment neither fate nor Fuller was inclined to cooperate. "If the Chief Justice would only retire," Taft had moaned despairingly in 1904, "how simple everything would become."[54]

The wheel of fortune, aided by Mrs. Taft, dictated the higher prize. Brushing aside all misgivings, he finally took the realistic view: "Very few men . . . would refuse to accept the nomination of the Republican party for the Presidency, and I am not an exception."[55] Taft yielded, but not without strong doubts. He was "a most difficult candidate for his loyal and eager supporters to manage . . . and he never did cease to regard a Supreme Court appointment as vastly more desirable than the Presidency."[56]

"To be Chief Justice," Taft's father had written in 1864, "is more than to be President."[56a] The newly elected Chief Executive was uncomfortable, his ambition still unsatisfied. "I pinch myself every little while to make myself realize that it is all true," he confided to a friend. "If I were now presiding in the Supreme Court of the United States as chief justice, I should feel entirely at home, but with the troubles of selecting a Cabinet and the difficulties in respect to the revision of the tariff, I feel just a bit like a fish out of water. However, as my wife is the politician and she will be able to meet all these issues, perhaps we can keep a stiff upper lip and overcome the obstacles that just at present seem formidable."[56b]

Riding with her husband from inauguration to the White House, a privilege no previous first lady had enjoyed, was the "proudest and happiest event of Inauguration Day." At last she had "the realization that my husband was actually President of the United States."[57] In strict accord with well-laid plans, Taft had succeeded Roosevelt, and the Colonel went off to hunt big game in Africa.

In March 1909, as the frail and aging Chief Justice administered the oath, the President-elect noted the signs for which he had long been on the alert. Fuller's command that the incoming President swear to "execute," rather than "support and defend," the Constitution made it clear that he was, as Taft said, "almost senile."[58] Still in office, Fuller died the next year. Belied was Elihu Root's confident prediction that "they will have to shoot him on the day of judgment."[59]

The President sent the customary telegram and released a public statement expressing sorrow. To close friends he frankly expressed irritation.

> If the Justices would only retire when they have become burdens to the Court itself, or when they recognize that their faculties have become impaired, one could grieve sincerely when they pass away, and you would not feel like such a hypocrite as you do when going through the formality of sending telegrams of condolence and giving out interviews for propriety's sake.[60]

Taft, now in his second year as President, was on the verge of a grievous break with T.R. The Colonel's part in making Taft President had inevitably laid the foundations for the breach. Thereafter, T.R. seemed to resent any hint that his beneficiary owed his election even in small part to anyone else. Taft stubbornly refused to play the suppliant's role. He preferred to be "at odds with the Colonel and suffer from it" rather than "be on terms of intimacy and be subject to the charge of being dominated by the ex-President."[61] On August 20, 1910, Archie Butt, the President's military aide, grieved: "They are now apart, and how they will keep from wrecking the country between them I scarcely see. Possibly, after all, it may land a good Democrat in the White House. . . ."[62] When, in February 1912, the breach was complete, Mrs. Taft recalled: "I told you so four years ago, and you would not believe me."

Mixing cheerful agreement with more than a trace of acidity, the President responded: "I know you did, my dear, and I think you are perfectly happy now. You would have preferred the Colonel to come out against me than to have been wrong yourself."[63]

To appoint someone else Chief Justice would never have been easy. Now, with his administration going badly, it was intolerable. "It seems strange," the President bemoaned while the matter of Chief Justice Fuller's successor was pending, "that the one place in the government which I would have liked to fill myself I am forced to give to another."[64] Amid circumstances in which lifelong personal ambitions were deeply enmeshed, what should or could his decision be?

High in the councils of the G.O.P. was the distinguished constitutional lawyer Elihu Root. The President admired him greatly, but considered the New Yorker too old: "I don't hesitate to say to you confidentially," Taft told Chauncey M. Depew, "that if Mr. Root were five years younger, I should not hesitate a moment, . . . but I doubt if he has in him that length of hard, routine work and constant attention to the business of the Court and to the reform of its methods which a Chief Justice ought to have. This is my chief reason for not deciding to appoint him."[65]

It was rumored that Justice John M. Harlan wanted promotion "as the final ornament to his judicial career." "I'll do no such damned thing," Taft stormed. "I won't make the Chief Justiceship a blue ribbon for the final years of any member of the Court. I want someone who will coordinate the activities of the Court and who has a reasonable expectation of serving ten or twenty years on the bench."[66]

The choice finally lay between Associate Justices Charles Evans Hughes and Edward Douglass White. Hughes had made a brilliant record as Governor of New York and was on the crest of a political wave. Taft's admiration for him, long in the making, was boundless. "I always think of Hughes as a President," he commented in November 1909. "I will have a chance to offer him a seat on the Supreme Bench. . . . If he does not accept the Judiciary, I expect to see him President some day."[67] Six months later, April 22, 1910, the President had believed that Hughes was "the strongest man the Republicans can put up, . . . stronger than Roosevelt and infinitely stronger than I would be, and if party success should demand someone stronger than I am, I would gladly see it turn to Hughes." That same month the President had put Hughes beyond easy reach of political office by appointing him an Associate Justice of the Supreme Court. Fearing that the New York Governor might beg off, Taft was delighted with Hughes's acceptance.

"That is a great appointment," the President commented to his military aide. "How do you think it will be taken?"

"It will be a monument to your administration," Butt replied. "There was every political reason why you should not have made it and apparently every reason why he should not have accepted it."

"Yes," the President commented, following a thoughtful pause. "Such an appointment makes politics look petty."[68]

In appointing Hughes Associate Justice, the President had dangled before the New York Governor the most powerful judicial office in the world. "The Chief Justiceship," the President had written, "is soon likely to be vacant and I should never regard the practice of never promoting Associate Justices as one to be followed." In a postscript, Taft had added: "Don't misunderstand me as to the Chief Justiceship. I mean if that office were now open, I should offer it to you and it is probable that if it were to become vacant during my term, I should promote you to it; but, of course, conditions change, so that it would not be right for me to say by way of promise what I would do in the future. Nor, on the other hand, would I have you think that your declination now would prevent my offering you the higher position, should conditions remain as they are."[69]

Quick to reassure the President that no binding commitment had been made, Hughes replied: "You properly reserve entire freedom with respect to [the appointment] and I accept the offer you now make without wishing you to feel committed in the slightest degree. Should the vacancy occur during your term I, in common with all our citizens, should desire you to act freely and without embarrassment in accordance with your best judgment at that time."[70]

The moment for selection of Fuller's successor, so long delayed, had come sooner than either Taft or Hughes may have anticipated. In press speculations, Hughes's name figured prominently as the most likely choice. Only a few weeks earlier, Taft had told Archie Butt: "I don't know the man I admire more than Hughes. If ever I have the chance, I shall offer to him the Chief Justiceship."[71] When that chance came, the President was troubled by indecision. "I don't see how he can but name Hughes for the Chief Justiceship," Taft's aide commented immediately after Chief Justice Fuller's death. The President was committed, yet "he [Taft] expressed great doubt."[72] ". . . I am so convinced that

Hughes is the man for the post," Butt wrote, "that I would almost run the risk of his [Taft's] anger by saying so to him."[73]

On December 10, Butt went to the White House to accompany the President to the Gridiron Club dinner at the New Willard and found the Chief Executive still dressing. "Well, Archie," he began, "I am feeling better, for I have got the Supreme Court off my mind." While waiting in vain for the President's decision, Butt mused: "I cannot rid myself of the great interest I feel in this powerful man [Hughes]." The President told his aide to telephone Hughes and ask him to call at the White House at six o'clock the next afternoon. "He would have never sent for him," Butt continued, "had he not decided to pass him over, so I felt that the tinkle of the Justice's telephone bell was the knell of [his] ambition for the Chief Justiceship." These suspicions were correct. "I will have an uncomfortable half hour," the troubled President confided, "but Hughes is young enough to wait, and if he makes good on the bench, I may yet be able to appoint him."[74]

A "surge of excitement" engulfed the recently appointed Associate Justice as he hastened to dress for the White House interview. But before he was on his way, the telephone rang again. The voice was Archie Butt's. Without comment or explanation, the appointment was canceled. Of this strange turn of events, Hughes records:

> I was much embarrassed by the constant use of my name. I thought if the President was not going to appoint me he should say so frankly and proceed promptly to appoint someone else. But until almost the last moment many expected my appointment, both Justices Lurton and Day, who were close to the President, telling me that they thought I would be appointed. On Sunday evening, December 11, 1910, I received a telephone message from the White House asking me to call on the President, but within half an hour while I was dressing to go, word came canceling the appointment; and the next day Justice White's nomination was sent to the Senate.[75]

Taft had not been able to go through with it. Hughes learned of Associate Justice Edward Douglass White's promotion in the press reports.

President Taft's elevation of White shattered several precedents. White, a Southern Democrat, was a Catholic; Taft, a Midwestern Republican, was a Unitarian. White was the first Associate Justice to be advanced successfully to the center chair;* he was the first Chief Justice not of the same political persuasion as the appointing President. He was sixty-five years old, the same age as overage Elihu Root, and six years older than any other Chief had been at the time of his appointment. The promotion was made by a President who considered anyone beyond sixty practically disqualified—especially for the Chief Justiceship. The President, moreover, had made known his desire "to appoint someone young and vigorous enough to go into questions of method in equity cases, and if possible revise the entire procedure of this country and put it more in line with that of Great Britain."[76] Hughes, the picture of radiant health, was only forty-eight. No judicial reformer, the sixty-five-year-old

---

* On the resignation of Chief Justice John Jay, January 29, 1795, (Congress then in recess), President Washington gave a recess appointment to John Rutledge, of South Carolina, who had previously been an Associate Justice, having resigned to become Chief Justice of his state. Rutledge took his seat August 12, 1795. He sat as Chief Justice only during the term of August 5, 1794. Meanwhile, rumors arose as to his insanity, leading the Senate to deny confirmation.

In 1874 Justices Miller, Swayne, and Bradley were active candidates for the seat vacated by Chief Justice Salmon Portland Chase. President Grant's Attorney General, George H. Williams, himself an aspirant for the Chief Justiceship, apparently convinced the President that elevating an Associate Justice would encourage rivalries among the Justices and infuse the bench with politics. On these grounds President Lincoln had refused to promote Justice Swayne to the post vacated by Roger Brooke Taney. Justice Bradley, arguing in favor of breaking the precedent, stressed the advantage of experience. The President, he insisted, was justified in going outside for a Chief Justice only if the nominee possessed "eminence already acquired in statesmanship and knowledge of public law and public affairs." (See C. Peter Magrath, *Morrison R. Waite* [New York: Macmillan, 1963], p. 8.)

President Taft broke a precedent Bradley had denounced as "senseless and absurd."

White believed that changes in judicial organization and procedure should be taken on the initiative of Congress, not at the behest of the Chief Justice. White had fought off even the mildest pressure from the Justices. Hughes recalls that "we could have had a new building when Taft was President, as he was eager to have one provided, but Chief Justice White was strongly opposed."[77]

As the President picked up his pen to sign White's commission, he grieved: "There is nothing I would have loved more than being Chief Justice of the United States. I cannot help seeing the irony in the fact that I, who desired that office so much, should now be signing the commission of another man."[78]

What went through the President's mind when he decided to pass over Hughes is pure speculation, but certain things are incontestable. White was twelve years older than Taft; another Republican President might appoint him Chief Justice. To be the first man in American history to fill the most exalted posts in the land was a glowing prospect. Taft wanted to be Chief Justice and made no bones about it, especially in the presence of those in a position to advance his cause. The appointment of Hughes would almost certainly have precluded any possibility of ever realizing it; the elevation of White would not. Political considerations may have been a factor. The President had always catered to the Catholic vote, believing that the "Catholics elected him last time [1908] and he thinks they can do it again."[79]

It has been suggested that President Taft had "a deeply personal reason" for appointing White. "He [Taft] was looking ahead. The day might come—was coming, indeed—that brought a Democratic President. Were that Democratic Executive to be faced with the appointment of a Chief Justice, and was Mr. Taft, Republican and Protestant, available, precedent on these points of party and pew was already established. The appointment would be given him."[80] He had been among the first to suspect that by some stroke of genius Woodrow Wilson might be nominated, "and that means a pretty hard tussle."[81]

Speculation can be more charitable. Taft had a profound distaste for bigotry—sectional, partisan and sectarian. The chagrin he felt in appointing White to the position he cherished may have been mollified by the triple blow his action dealt various aspects of these hateful things. In 1924, Taft offered this explanation:

> It was because his great ability and learning, his long experience on the Bench, and his high character admirably equipped him for the position, and my judgment was vindicated by his conduct and services as Chief Justice. You intimate that I should not have appointed him because he was a devout member of the Roman Catholic Church and I was a Free Mason. Had I allowed the religious beliefs of a proposed appointee to office to exclude him from the appointment, I should have violated my oath as President of the United States under the Constitution. So far as I know, no obligation assumed by me as a Master Mason in the slightest degree conflicted with this injunction of the Constitution (Art. VI). If there had been such conflict, I would never have become a Mason.[81a]

Asked in March 1910, whether he liked being President, Taft replied: "On the whole, yes. I would rather be Chief Justice of the United States, and a quieter life than that which comes at the White House is more in keeping with my temperament." Taft realized that he had his place in history to consider; he took into account how the Presidency would affect his family. Such considerations helped to compensate "one for all the trials and criticisms he [the President] has to bear and undergo."[82] Yet the compensations were not completely satisfying. Few Presidents have the opportunity of naming a Chief Justice. That mixed pleasure came to William Howard Taft. In its exercise, he overlooked no contingency that might improve his own chances of winning the office which, in his mind, ranked above that of President.

CHAPTER II

PLATFORM

William Howard Taft reached maturity and began his professional career in the last quarter of the nineteenth century—a time of economic transformation and incipient popular revolt. Industrial trusts were rapidly replacing competing concerns; fabulous fortunes were being amassed in railroads, oil, and coal. American industry came of age and organized as the National Association of Manufacturers. Thereafter, the N.A.M. "would speak with one voice on every occasion of common concern and on all occasions pertaining to its general welfare."[1] In lawmaking bodies economic interests rather than people were the constituencies; it was not unusual to speak of "coal," "oil," or "railroad" senators.

Meanwhile, currents of popular revolt were beginning to run swiftly. These years witnessed Greenbackers, Grangers, Populists, Knights of Labor, Anarchists, and the largest Socialist vote ever cast in a presidential election. The "mere weight of numbers," that dread spectacle always terrifying to American conservatives, was given forceful justification. Edward Bellamy's *Looking Backward,* Henry Demarest Lloyd's *Wealth against Commonwealth,* and Henry George's *Progress and Poverty* were best sellers. Labor and lawmakers alike illustrated the sobering truth of Edmund Burke's words: "Liberty, when men act in bodies, is power."[2]

In response to popular protest, Congress enacted the Sherman Antitrust Act, declaring illegal "every combination in the form of trust or otherwise, or conspiracy in restraint of trade." These drastic restrictions are still unmatched. Five years later Congress passed the first peacetime income-tax law. Organized labor expressed its resentment against corporate power in a wave of strikes and boycotts. Haymarket, Homestead, Pullman, and Coxey's Army were in the headlines. When the courts intervened, usually on the side of property, protesting labor leaders promptly coined the derogatory phrase, "government by injunction."

Rarely had the country been more conscious of the Supreme Court.[3] It was rapidly becoming a crucial factor in the march of social democracy. Winning favor were the interventionist views of Supreme Court Justice David J. Brewer. In a speech before the New York State Bar Association, January 17, 1893, Brewer proclaimed Social Darwinism, the eternal verities of Herbert Spencer. "The many," he complained, "attempted to transfer to themselves through political power the wealth they lacked the ability or patience to earn in the ordinary pursuit of their business." This movement—"the movement of coercion," Brewer called it—ran counter to the primary end of free government: private property. The Justice cited "the black flag of Anarchism, flaunting destruction of property," and "the red flag of Socialism, inviting a redistribution of property." Whether in the hands of a monarch or a majority, "power always chafes at but needs restraint," he noted soberly. "Here there is no monarch threatening trespass on the individual. The danger is from the multitude—the majority, with whom is the power."

Brewer admitted that "within limits" the movement of coercion in legislative halls and in trade-unions was beneficial. Needed were safeguards against excesses. What more logical agency "to lift the restraining hand than the courts of the land?" Brewer was convinced that "the salvation of the nation, the permanence of government of and by the people rests upon the independence and vigor of the judiciary."[4]

The same year James Bradley Thayer, professor of constitutional law at Harvard and an active member of the American Bar Association, made the now classic retort to judicial aggrandizement.[5] Ignoring the inflammatory crusades so frightening to Brewer, Thayer calmly addressed himself to the nature of judicial power. The burden of his closely reasoned analysis was a solemn warning that judicial review did not imply judicial supremacy. "The judiciary may well reflect," Thayer suggested, "that if they had been regarded by the people as the chief protection against legislative violation of the Constitution, they would not have been allowed merely this incidental and postponed control. They would have been let in, as it was sometimes endeavored in the conventions to let them in, to a revision of the laws before they began to operate."[6]

So restricted was the scope of judicial review that "much which is harmful *and* unconstitutional may take effect without any capacity in the courts to prevent it. . . ."[7] In the face of Brewer's unblushing ukase—"strengthen the judiciary"—Thayer pleaded:

> This rule [judicial self-restraint] recognizes that, having regard to the great, complex, ever-unfolding exigencies of government, much which will seem unconstitutional to one man, or body of men, may reasonably not seem so to another; that the Constitution often admits of different interpretations; that there is often a range of choice and judgment; that in such cases the Constitution does not impose upon the legislature any one specific opinion, but leaves open the range of choice; and that whatever choice is rational is constitutional. . . .[8]

The judicial function was "merely that of fixing the outside border of *reasonable* legislative action. . . ."[9] Power of such modest dimension would leave courts "a great and stately jurisdiction. . . . It will only imperil the whole of it," Thayer warned, "if it is sought to give them more."[10]

The polar positions of Brewer and Thayer set the stage for Taft's entry into the fray. Profoundly conservative by instinct, Taft was a stanch Republican. A G.O.P. ticket—no matter how bad—would work less mischief than the Democrats. Certain of his views on the current unrest were reflected in his opinions as Superior Court judge of Ohio and as Federal Circuit Court judge, but he had yet to formulate them in a systematic way. His opportunity came in 1894.

Invited to address the graduating class of the University of Michigan Law School, he found it easy to select an appropriate topic. Radical thought and action now threatened our basic rights and institutions. The next year William Jennings Bryan, proclaiming the nation must not be crucified on a cross of gold, was destined to be nominated for the Presidency. Bryan was overwhelmingly defeated by the safe-and-sound William McKinley of Ohio, but the Populist party elected six Senators and twenty-five members of the House of Representatives. The restraining hand of the judiciary might still be necessary. An informed discussion of "The Right of Private Property"[11] seemed timely.

Taft shared Brewer's views. Inspired by the authoritative writings and decisions of Judge Thomas M. Cooley, Taft noted that "the ultimate tribunal"—the Supreme Court of the United States—could be counted on to uphold property's "sacred character." He applauded judicial veto of "intermittent attempts of state legislatures and of Congress" to regulate property. The Constitution made ours "a conservative government . . . strongly buttressed by written law . . . against the attacks of anarchy, socialism and communism."

From England, America inherited the conviction that the security of property and contract and liberty—the "main props of higher and progressive civilization"—are inextricably linked. We departed from the British in establishing a complicated form of government, marked by divisions and separations of powers, thus affording "substantial guaranties of those rights, much further removed from the gusty and unthinking passions of temporary majorities, than has our mother country." In England the only safeguard against legislative tyranny was the power of a free public opinion represented in Commons. America was not content to rely solely on political checks. These had to be supplemented by legal and constitutional controls enforced by judges. Herein lay the hard core of Taft's constitutionalism.

From the beginning, property and contract rights had been anchored in "the breasts of our whole people." Every individual, no matter how humble, was the beneficiary. Suddenly, in the late nineteenth century, rights formerly considered inviolable were no longer "fully appreciated by all American citizens." This alarming "change of sentiment" must be reversed; if such irreverence grew "in popular weight and intensity, our boasted constitutional guaranties of property rights will not be worth the parchment upon which they were originally written."

Taft traced the threat to "those who do manual labor for a living." Some of "the more radical" challenged the wisdom of private property; others resented the system without hoping to destroy it; still others, "not confined to the ranks of labor," gave conviction and strength to the enemies of property by voicing a strong "hatred for aggregated capital." The time had come to speak up. "Now, the institution of property is a good thing or it is not," Taft challenged. "We who believe in it must be able to give reasons for the faith that is in us."

Taft's convictions were deeply rooted. Private property had led to the accumulation of capital, resulting in lower production costs, greater comforts, and higher income for all. The "princely profits" reaped were but just rewards to "men of judgment, courage and executive ability . . . for the general good they have done."

There was, of course, a darker side. The complaint most easily documented was the corrupting influence of large corporations in politics. For this the solution was easy—"put men in political control not susceptible to corrupt influences." Just as corporations must confront in legislative halls stouthearted, incorruptible men, so labor leaders must be good Americans untainted by "Socialistic ideas which prevail among the laboring classes of Europe." Labor organizations, though advantageous, become "blinded by the new sense of social and political power which combination and organization have given them, and they fail to perceive the limitations of that power, which are fixed, not only by the inexorable law of economics, but also by the mighty force of . . . public opinion." Unfortunately, public opinion itself, particularly in farming communities of the South and Far West, had become enamored of Populist ideas.

The situation was urgent. If "the present movement against corporate capital is not met and fought, it will become a danger to our whole social fabric." For defense against "the assaults of raving fanatics, emotional and misdirected philanthropists, and blatant demagogues," Taft made specific suggestions. Spread "the truth that every laborer, and every man of moderate means has as much interest to preserve the inviolability of corporate property as he has that of his own." Call strictly to account public men "for utterances or conduct likely to encourage resentment against the guaranties of law, order and property. . . ." In legislative and executive action insist that equal and exact justice be done corporations and individuals alike. Those who believed "the best mode of a gradual elevation of the race" is security for private property "must make their views and voices heard above the resounding din of anarchy, socialism, populism and the general demagogy. . . ."

All this, however, was not enough. Times had changed. In the old days charter guarantees were given for

> the benefit of the poor and the lowly against the oppressions of the rich and powerful. Today it is the rich who seek the protection of the courts for the enforcement of those guaranties. . . . Today, if a judge would yield to the easy course, he would lean against the wealthy and favor the many. While this seems to be a change, it is not really so. The sovereign today is the people, or the majority of the people. The poor are the majority. The appeal of the rich to the constitution and courts for protection is still an appeal by the weak against the unjust aggressions of the strong.

Having reached the crux of his message, the speaker threw down his challenge. Until discussion, experience, and education enlighten the populace, the security of private property would depend upon the courts, informed and strengthened by the bar. At the threshold of their professional careers, members of the graduating class would return to their various communities and become molders of public opinion. Whether working as public figures, politicians, or private citizens, they must not cease to be lawyers; they must not forget that the Constitution they are sworn to support and defend "secured as sacred the right of private property."

As if in response to Taft's plea, the Supreme Court itself rushed to the rescue. Eighteen hundred ninety-five was the fateful year. In a single term the Justices hampered enforcement of the Sherman Antitrust Act,[12] barred a direct Federal income tax,[13] and exalted the injunction-contempt power of the Federal courts over organized labor.[14] With the development of due process as a shield against state regulation,[15] the constitutional revolution was complete. The Supreme Court had established itself as final arbiter of social and economic policy. Government at both state and national levels was stymied in its attempts to control the abuses of property. The cautionary warnings of James Bradley Thayer had gone unheeded.

Sensing the need to consolidate the Court's newly won position against the rising tide of criticism leveled at the controversial decisions of 1895, Judge Taft sprang to the defense. In an address to the American Bar Association, August 28, 1895,[16] the apostle of property took issue with the charge that the Federal judiciary had "flagrantly usurped jurisdiction, first, to protect corporations and perpetuate their many abuses, and second, to oppress and destroy the power of organized labor." The Federal courts, he explained, were "subjected to the most severe criticism without just grounds, merely because of the character of their jurisdiction." Reacting to the popular drive for regulatory legislation, corporations had turned to the Federal courts to protect their vested rights. It not infrequently became the duty of the courts to protect these rights. Understandably, Taft explained, "in a corporation-hating community" the courts were marked as "friends and protectors of corporations." In the Federal courts corporations met the same local prejudice that jeopardized their interests in state courts. State legislatures had encouraged this development, by providing for more jury trials in civil cases and reducing the judge's traditional common-law control over the jury.

Corporate abuses, he admitted, required remedy, but the cure lay with the legislatures, not with the courts. "Courts are but conservators; they can not effect great social or political changes. Corporations there must be if we would progress; accumulation of wealth there will be if private property continues the keystone of our society." Legislation to regulate the excesses of private property must be narrow in scope.

Nor could courts be properly charged with "oppressing" organized labor. Judicial action had been more effective in restraining labor excesses than corporate evils, the latter being "almost wholly beyond the reach of courts." When, on the other hand, labor trespassed on property rights, the judiciary possessed a made-to-order weapon—the writ of injunction. Taft himself, first as Ohio Superior Court judge and later on the Federal Circuit Court, had proved the usefulness of this judicial bludgeon.

Taft had effectively turned the tables on the Court's critics. Corporations were not fairly dealt with, even in Federal courts; at the mercy of prejudiced juries, they needed judicial protection. Organized labor had violated the "sacred guaranties of life, liberty, and property"; the judiciary was to be lauded for the protection afforded.

Property was a "preferred freedom"; certain other civil rights were "fetiches." Speaking to the 1905 graduating class of the Yale Law School on the "Administration of Criminal

Law,[17] Taft lamented overemphasis on procedural safeguards. "We must cease to regard them as fetiches to be worshiped without reason and simply because they are." The constitutional prohibition against compelling a criminal defendant to testify against himself seemed "in some aspects . . . of doubtful utility." So, too, did the rule against unreasonable searches and seizures, and the requirement that the criminal defendant be confronted by hostile witnesses; both guarantees tended to shield criminals from effective prosecution.

Taft's main grievance was the jury trial. In civil litigation it was an anachronism. In criminal cases, where its roots were deeply imbedded, he advocated enlarged supervision of juries by judges. Instead of following the English practice, where judges exercised substantial control, American legislatures, in the mad march of democracy, exalted the jury over the judge.

Loopholes in the administration of criminal justice soon became a monotonous refrain*—as a Cabinet member, as a

---

* One of his first papers, if not the first, written for the Literary Club of Cincinnati, and delivered on January 26, 1884, was devoted to legal reform in Hamilton County, Ohio. It was published in the February 18, 1884 issue of the *Weekly Law Bulletin;* reprinted in *Ohio Law Bulletin,* Vol. 56 (Mar. 6, 1911), 77–81.

While a Circuit Court judge, Taft, along with fellow judges Horace H. Lurton and William R. Day, all destined to occupy seats on the Supreme Court, strongly concurred in the recommendation of the Federal Commission on the Revision of the Laws to provide for but one court of first instance in the Federal judiciary. "We fully concur in your view, embodied in the proposed legislation," they wrote the Commissioners in 1899,

> that there should be but one court of first instance and we think that you have taken the wisest course in reaching that end by transferring all the jurisdiction of the existing circuit courts to the district courts.
>
> The existence of two courts of first instance has long been an anomaly, if not an absurdity, in the Federal judicial system, and their maintenance has been useful only as marking the unusual and in most respects praiseworthy conservatism which Congress has shown in dealing with proposed changes in the organization of the Federal courts. . . .

Taft, Lurton, and Day, judges of the Circuit Court of Appeals for the Sixth Circuit, to Alex C. Botkin, David K. Watson, and David B. Cuthberson, Commissioners on the Revision of the Laws. 46 *Congressional Record* 1544, Jan. 27, 1911.

G.O.P. presidential nominee, as President, and as private citizen.

Lecturing at Yale in 1906 on the "responsibilities of citizenship,"[18] Taft highlighted two basic themes: the compelling need for judicial guardianship of property; the equally urgent need for reform in judicial administration. Recalling the views he had held as a Yale graduate in 1878, the lecturer candidly stated the premises of his political philosophy:

> The tendency in my own case, and I think in that of most graduates of my time, was toward the *laissez faire* doctrine that the least interference by legislation with the operation of natural laws was, in the end, the best for the public; that the only proper object of legislation was to free the pathway of commerce and opportunity from the effect of everything but competition and enlightened selfishness; and that being done, the Government had discharged all of its proper functions.

During Taft's undergraduate years, even the Post Office was "looked upon . . . with great suspicion," and cited as "a pernicious example . . . of the extension of governmental interference and initiative into fields which ought to be covered altogether by private enterprise." A generation later, the principles he had learned in the 1870's were "still sound." Though some governmental regulation could now be countenanced, he warned against those "who yearn for an entirely different system and radical change, in which men are to be governed solely by love and not by any motive of gain." Looking the Yale men squarely in the eye, he admonished:

> The spectacle of men who enjoy all the luxuries of life, with trained servants and costly establishments of all kinds, declaiming against the social order and the injustice done to the poor and suffering in the community, is not one to attract the sympathy of sensible men.

William Graham Sumner, professor of political and social science at Yale since 1872, had been an abiding influence.

Taft had taken to heart Sumner's famous advice to Yale seniors: "Don't be a damn fool." "The truth is," Taft solemnly announced,

> . . . the law is not so carefully followed, and property rights and other rights are not so well safeguarded, and criminals are not punished with the same certainty as formerly in communities in which the jury has had the reins thrown on its back, and practically been given a discretionary power in its decisions that was wholly wanting under the common-law system.

Glorification of the jury was but another aspect of the Populist trend. The people were too impressed with the "emotional and untrue doctrine" that it is better for ninety-nine guilty men to escape justice than for one innocent man to be punished. This adage had done much "to make our criminal trials a farce."

In the following years Taft kept hammering away: protect property rights and reform the judicial system. Speaking before the Civic Forum in New York City, April 28, 1908, on "Delays and Defects in the Enforcement of Law in This Country,"[19] he pointed to one of the "gravest" defects in "our whole Government"—"our failure to secure expedition and thoroughness in the enforcement of public and private rights in our courts."

A significant count in Taft's early indictment had to do with the United States Supreme Court. Forced to review a great body of litigation, the Court was unable to perform effectively its "highest function"—that is, "interpretation of the Constitution . . . so as to guide the other branches of the Government and the people of the United States in their construction of the fundamental compact of the Union." The Court's appellate jurisdiction should "generally be limited to those cases which are typical and which give an opportunity to the Court to cover the whole field of the law upon the subject involved." One appeal from the court of first instance was "all that any litigant should be entitled to." Presaged by nearly two decades was the famous "Judges' Bill" of 1925.

Other measures were anticipated. "Much too elaborate" codes of procedure caused unnecessary delay and cost. Many people preferred to arbitrate cases out of court or, even worse, to yield to unjust claims "rather than to expose themselves to the nervous strain and expensive burden of a long-drawn-out contest in court."

> In my opinion the best method of securing expedition in the disposition of cases is to leave to the judges of the court the forming of the procedure by rules of court, imposing upon them the obligation to adopt rules making the course of litigation as speedy and as inexpensive as possible. . . .

Codes of procedure should be "simple and effective"; Britain had furnished the model.

As Republican nominee for President, Taft continued to advocate judicial reform. At Cincinnati, July 28, 1908, he insisted there be no jury trial for contemnors in injunction-contempt cases:

> The administration of justice lies at the foundation of government. The maintenance of the authority of the courts is essential unless we are prepared to embrace anarchy. Never in the history of the country has there been such an insidious attack upon the judicial system as the proposal to interject a jury trial between all orders of the court made after full hearing and the enforcement of such orders.[20]

At Hot Springs, Virginia, August 21, 1908, the nominee addressed himself to the abuses of big business. Excesses, he conceded, required "a limitation upon the use of property and capital," but social legislation must be examined with "care and caution." Advocates of radical change must recognize the difficulties of "stamping out such evils by statutory law and its enforcement."[21]

In a major campaign address before the Virginia Bar Association at Hot Springs the same month, Taft fused the two planks of his platform.[22] A tie formerly implicit was now made explicit. "The present is a time," he began, "when all our institutions are being subjected to close scrutiny with a view to the determination whether we have not now tried the institutions upon which modern society rests to the point of proving that some of them should be radically changed." "I venture to think," he asserted, connecting defense of property with judicial reform, that

> one evil which has not attracted the attention of the community at large, but which is likely to grow in importance, as the inequality between the poor and the rich in our civilization is studied, is in the delays in the administration of justice between individuals. As between two wealthy corporations, or two wealthy individual litigants, where the subject matter of the litigation reaches to tens and hundreds of thousands of dollars, where each party litigant is able to pay the expenses of litigation, large fees to counsel, and to undergo for the time being the loss of interest on the capital involved, our present system, while not perfect, is not so far from proper results as to call for anxiety. . . . The inequality that exists in our present administration of justice, and that sooner or later is certain to rise and trouble us, and to call for popular condemnation and reform, is in the unequal burden which the delays and expenses of litigation under our system impose on the poor litigant. . . .

Judicial reform could reduce the threat to private property by removing a serious source of popular unrest. Improved judicial administration must come primarily through streamlining codes of procedure. In Britain the codes, usually framed by courts, were "simple and effective." In America "every additional technicality, every additional rule of procedure adds to the expense of litigation"; the increased cost of justice fell most heavily on the poor.

Reform should begin in the courts of last resort. Judges of the Supreme Court of the United States and of the highest court of each state ought to take the initiative in revising codes of procedure. Rules should be simplified so that appellate cases turned on the merits rather than on procedural technicalities. Though empowered since 1789 to frame procedural rules in equity for Federal courts, the Supreme Court had failed to meet its responsibilities. "It has been done in England," Taft challenged, "and it ought to be done in the Federal courts." "I set a fire under that honorable body [the Supreme Court] once," Taft recalled in 1916, "and stirred them up to make an amendment of the Equity rules."[23]

By putting its own house in order, the legal profession might counteract the disruptive influence of wild-eyed reformers. This, indeed, was the link which bound together judicial reform and judicial defense of property.

For Taft and for the country, 1908 was a climactic year. Keenly aware of the perennial clash between property rights and popular power, he had formulated a solution which relied on the strong arm of a refurbished judiciary. Against growing attack, the Court since 1890 had dutifully moved—with occasional pauses—in the "right" direction. Eighteen hundred ninety-five had been a banner year for the Economic Establishment. American industry had organized; national inroads on property were effectively repulsed. Ten years later a divided Court in *Lochner* v. *New York* struck down a state law regulating the working hours of bakers, despite Justice Holmes's scathing caveat—the Constitution "does not enact Mr. Herbert Spencer's *Social Statics*."

In 1908, however, Taft witnessed an apparent judicial retreat. The brilliant Boston lawyer, Louis D. Brandeis, accepted Justice Rufus W. Peckham's challenge in *Lochner* that a relation between health and working hours of bakers could not "in fact" be established. The famous "Brandeis Brief" in *Muller* v. *Oregon*[24] helped to persuade a hostile Court that Oregon lawmakers could have reasonably believed working hours of women were *in fact* related to their health.

Despite Brandeis's successful invocation of "living law," reassuring word came the same year from Arthur Twining Hadley, president of Taft's alma mater:

When it is said, as it commonly is, that the fundamental division of powers in the modern State is into legislative, executive and judicial, the student of American institutions may fairly note an exception. The fundamental division of powers in the Constitution of the United States is between the voters on the one hand and property owners on the other. The forces of democracy on one side, divided between the executive and the legislature, are set over against the forces of property on the other side, with the judiciary as arbiter between them; the Constitution itself not only forbidding the legislature and executive to trench upon the rights of property, but compelling the judiciary to define and uphold those rights in a manner provided by the Constitution itself.

This theory of American politics has not been often stated. But it has been universally acted upon. . . . The voter was omnipotent—within a limited area. He could make what laws he pleased, as long as those laws did not trench upon property right. He could elect what officers he pleased, so long as those officers did not try to do certain duties confided by the Constitution to the property holders. Democracy was complete as far as it went, but constitutionally it was bound to stop short of *social* democracy.[25]

Hadley's "theory of American politics" had long been the essence of Taft's creed. Yet it was clearly at odds with that of Taft's sometime benefactor, mentor, and adviser—T.R.* For the Rough Rider, moreover, the Presidency—not the Court—was the locus of power for resolving the continuing conflict between "political democracy and industrial absolutism."[26] He also believed his Secretary of War could be more effective as President than as Chief Justice. Taft, whose realistic understanding of the Supreme Court's role in American politics is still unmatched, demurred.

As fate, T.R., and Mrs. Taft would have it, the critical year 1908 led William Howard Taft, against his better judgment, down the road to the White House. From that vantage point—ideal for a T.R. but ill-suited to Taft—the new Chief Executive pressed on.

---

* See Chapter I, *supra,* pp. 31–32.

President Taft's attempt to secure enactment of his program did not fail for want of effort. In his first message to Congress, December 7, 1909, he avowed that "a change in judicial procedure, with a view to reducing its expense to private litigants in civil cases and facilitating the dispatch of business and final decision in both civil and criminal cases, constitutes *the greatest need in our American institutions.*" The President recommended: union of law and equity in one form of action, reduction of the jurisdiction of the Supreme Court "almost wholly to statutory and constitutional questions," and the appointment of a presidential commission to make a full-scale examination of the Federal court system and to propose ways of simplifying procedure.[27] Taft repeated the substance of this message the next year.[28]

President Taft, rating Supreme Court appointments among his most important functions, had the good fortune to appoint five Associate Justices and a Chief Justice—Willis Van Devanter, Horace Harmon Lurton, Joseph Rucker Lamar, Charles Evans Hughes, and Mahlon Pitney, and Edward Douglass White as Chief Justice. Each appointment was a continuing source of pride. All, including the Southern Democrat White, entertained views closely akin to Taft's. In language President Taft might have accepted as his own, White wrote that "investiture of a public body with discretion does not imply the right to abuse, but on the contrary carries with it . . . the command that the *limits of sound discretion* be not transcended. . . ." The courts possess "by necessary implication . . . *power to correct wrongs done by such excess.*"[29]

As President, Taft seized every opportunity to underscore the crucial role of the judiciary. On August 15, 1911, returning to the House without approval a Joint Resolution calling for admission of New Mexico and Arizona to the union, he denounced the provision for judicial recall in Arizona's proposed constitution as "pernicious in its effect, . . . destructive of independence in the judiciary, . . . likely to subject the rights of the individual to the possible tyranny of a popular majority, . . . injurious to the cause of free government."[30] "By George, I am ready for them," the President commented gleefully. "I rejoice in the chance to give this recall business a blow."[31]

Before the end of his administration, the "recall business" had assumed threatening proportions. "Hair-trigger" reformers[32] relied on "the willingness of an inflamed majority to possess themselves of advantages over a minority, or the individual."[33] Their recklessness might lead to "confiscation and then to socialism."[34] At stake were fundamentals, including the authority of the Supreme Court—"the chief instrument in the maintenance of that self-restraint which the people of the United States have placed upon themselves."[35]

In a speech before the Chamber of Commerce, Pocatello, Idaho, October 6, 1911, the President poured out his deepest feelings. "What distinguishes this country from any other one is the Supreme Court . . . that oft has stood between us and errors that might have been committed that would have been greatly injurious to this country; and to turn on that Court and . . . to attack it seems to me to lay the axe at the root of the tree of our civilization."[36]

Judicial pre-eminence must be carefully guarded. Special precaution must be taken against any action that might destroy the popular image of identity between the judicial version of the Constitution and the document itself. It had been suggested, for example, that the 5-to-4 decision in the income-tax case of 1895 might be reversed by a mere act of Congress. Discussion of this proposal reached its height during Taft's Presidency. Though considering the Court's decision erroneous, he advised against this easy escape. "I have not considered a constitutional amendment as necessary to the exercise of certain phases of this power," the President explained, but a mature consideration has satisfied me that an amendment is the only proper course for the establishment to its full extent. . . . This course is much to be preferred to the one proposed of re-enacting a law once judicially declared to be unconstitutional. For the Congress to assume that the court will reverse itself, and to enact legislation on such an assumption, will not strengthen popular confidence in the stability of judicial construction of the Constitution. It is much wiser policy to accept the decision and remedy the defect by amendment in due and regular course.[37]

The fiction of an unchanging Constitution, save by formal amendment, had to be preserved—even when a judicial decision like that in the income-tax case exploded it. Myth and symbolism would help courts to preserve the rights of minorities against unthinking popular clamor. Realism may be all right for the select few. Taft himself recognized that in law, too, everything turns on men; but for the masses rulership should be shrouded in mystery. "It is well," Taft had observed in an address of May 30, 1908,

that judges should be clothed in robes, not only that those who witness the administration of justice should be properly advised that the function performed is one different from, and higher, than that which a man discharges as a citizen in the ordinary walks of life; but also, in order to impress the judge himself with constant consciousness that he is a high-priest in the temple of justice and is surrounded with obligations of a sacred character that he cannot escape and that require his utmost care, attention and self-suppression.[38]

Following his White House years, Taft continued to promote his judicial platform—in books, articles, and public addresses. Expounding his theory of the judicial process in *Popular Government,* the former President paid lip service to the mechanical or slot-machine theory of decision making. The test of constitutionality required only "a lawyerlike construction of the Constitution and the law in question to decide whether they are in conflict."[39] But he was under no illusion that the man who dons judicial robes thereby puts on superhuman qualities. "Judges are men. Courts are composed of judges and one would be foolish who would deny that courts are affected by the times in which they live."[40]

Far from blinking at its lawmaking role, Taft considered the shaping of law to meet new situations the Court's "highest and most useful function." "Frequently," he wrote, "new conditions arise which those who were responsible for the written law could not have had in view, and to which existing common-law principles have never before been applied, and it becomes necessary for the Court to make new applications of both." This "is not the exercise of legislative power. . . ." Rather, "It is the exercise of a sound judicial discretion in supplementing the provisions of constitutions and laws and custom, which are necessarily incomplete or lacking in detail essential to their proper application, especially to new facts and situations constantly arising. . . . Indeed it is one of the highest and most useful functions that courts have to perform in making a government of law practical and uniformly just."[41]

Though judges should not respond to the fleeting demands of popular passion, they do not live in a political vacuum. It is impossible to prevent "the influence of popular opinion from coloring judgments in the long run." The personal equation unavoidably plays a part. "There will be found a response to sober popular opinion as it changes to meet the exigency of social, political, and economic changes."[42]

Social stability through the judicial process was the primary goal. For effective discharge of this creative task, legal training alone did not suffice. Taft neither ignored the pleas of social reformers nor pretended that sociological facts were irrelevant. If "the militant social reformers and lawyers . . . don't talk exactly the same language," he observed, lawyers and judges must respond by "broadening the knowledge and studies of the members of the legal profession." "We must be able to understand the attitude of the sociological reformer," he wrote. The education of the judge "ought to include a study of economics and a study of sociology," so as to meet the reformer on "common ground." Knowledge of social needs would help judges to temper the demands of reformers, thus avoiding "radical and impractical changes in law and government."[43]

The former President's most candid expression of his distrust of the masses appears in *The Anti-Trust Act and the Supreme Court.*[44] "Those of us who insist upon the preservation of constitutional limitations upon the action of a majority . . . ," he explained, "are convinced that we are the best friends of popular government." Popular government, after all, was not an "end"; "it should not be a fetish." When men had the "capacity to govern themselves," popular government offered "greater benefit" than government by the few. When, however, that capacity was lacking, "government by one or the few is better." "What we must keep clearly in mind," he emphasized, ". . . is that the end is the pursuit of community and individual happiness, that the means is popular government." Constitutions themselves were but "checks upon the hasty action of the majority."

They are the self-imposed restraints of a whole people upon a majority of them to secure sober action and a respect for the rights of the minority, and of the individual in his relation to other individuals, and in his relation to the whole people in their character as a state or government.

Thus Taft effectively reversed the priority of values established by the framers of the Constitution. He converted judicial review, originally intended as an "auxiliary" check on the hasty action of majorities, into *the primary check.* Guardianship by the few constituted the essence of Taft's "free government." The "few," of course, was the "independent judiciary . . . a divine institution, . . . the cornerstone of our gloriously free government." "The world is not going to be saved," he observed, by the "overwhelming mass of ill-digested legislation."[45] The judiciary would see to that.

For effective discharge of its high responsibility the judicial system would have to be revised. There is "a crisis," Taft told the students of the Albany Law School in 1914, in "the life of our courts." Deeply concerned over the "flippant and sarcastic references"[46] to failures in the administration of justice, the former President diagnosed the inadequacies of the Federal judiciary in a significant address before the Cincinnati Law School.[47] Once again Britain furnished the blueprint. "Two great features" of the English system stood out: "the simplicity of its procedure and the elasticity with which that procedure and the use of the judicial force provided by Parliament can be adapted to the disposition of business." The success of the system rested on

> the executive control vested in a council of judges to direct business and economize judicial force, to mould their own rules of procedure, and also on the learning, ability and experience of the individual judges and the consequent ease and quickness with which they dispose of cases coming before them, so that in the great majority of cases the judgment of the court is pronounced at the close of the argument.

Taft made six recommendations, the fourth and fifth destined for enactment during his years as Chief Justice.

> Fourth—Authority and duty should be conferred upon the head of the Federal judicial system, either the Chief Justice, or a council of judges appointed by him, or by the Supreme Court, to consider each year the pending Federal judicial business of the country and to distribute the Federal judicial force of the country through the various districts and intermediate appellate courts, so that the existing arrears may be attacked and disposed of.
>
> Fifth—There should be a reduction of the appeals to the Supreme Court, by cutting down to cases of constitutional construction only the review as of right, and by leaving to the discretion of that court, by writ of certiorari, the power to hear such cases from the lower courts as it deems in the public interest.

Elaborating on his fourth recommendation, the future Chief Justice stressed the need for "the adjustment of our judicial force" to the disposition of its ever-increasing work load by introducing into the administration of justice "the ordinary business principles in successful executive work." He looked forward to the day when "a head" would be "charged with the responsibility of the use of the judicial force at places and under conditions where the judicial force is needed." Either through the Chief Justice or through a judicial committee of the judges, the business of the Federal courts "should be considered each year, and assignments made . . . with a view to the most economic use of each judge for the disposition of the greatest amount of business by him."

Taft pressed the fifth proposal; highlighted was the Court's "great difficulty in keeping up with its docket." If it continued to increase, as seemed inevitable, the Court would be seriously hampered in the performance of its "most important function"—"the construction and application of the Constitution of the United States." "Swamped with its burden," the Court's efficiency would falter and litigants would suffer injustice. For these reasons,

> the only jurisdiction that it should be obliged to exercise, and which a litigant may, as a matter of course, bring to the court, should be questions of constitutional construction. By giving an opportunity to litigants in all other cases to apply for a writ of certiorari to bring any case from a lower court to the Supreme Court, so that it may exercise absolute and arbitrary discretion with respect to all business but constitutional business, will enable the court so to restrict its docket that it can do all its work, and do it well.

Doing its work "well" required, above all, introduction of the "executive principle."

The details of Taft's reform platform should not obscure the philosophy which underlay it:

> We can waste money in helping individuals to a habit of dependence that will weaken our citizenship. . . . We must stop attempting to reform people by wholesale. It is the individual upon whom our whole

future progress depends. In giving and securing scope for his ambition, energy, and free action our constitutional system has its chief merit, whatever would-be reformers say.[48]

Matthew Arnold caught the essence of Taft's creed:

That elevation of character, that noble way of thinking and behaving, which is an eminent gift of nature to some individuals, is also often generated in whole classes of men . . . by the possession of power, by the importance and responsibility of high station, by habitual dealing with great things, by being placed above the necessity of constantly struggling for little things. . . . A governing class imbued with it may not be capable of intelligently leading the masses of a people to the highest pitch of welfare for them; but it sets them an invaluable example of qualities without which no really high welfare can exist. This has been done for their nation by the best aristocracies. The Roman aristocracy did it; the English aristocracy has done it.[49]

Persistent admonition to the legal profession to renew its sense of responsibility and dedication was the leitmotiv of Taft's pronouncements in 1913 as president of the American Bar Association. The British barrister was his ideal. In America, too, an elevated bar could work "wonders for politics."[50]

As Taft neared realization of a lifelong ambition, the major planks in his platform emerged with stark clarity. Use the strong arm of the judiciary, he pleaded, to resist the attacks of unrestrained popular power; streamline judicial administration. One observer, reveling in Taft's appointment as Chief Justice, likened him to Saint Peter and John Marshall:

. . . Like a Saint Peter, he will stand at the gate and call for the credentials of applicants for constitutional protection and it must be a certificate that John Marshall would have approved. So long as the spirit of the Great Marshall lives in the heart of the Chief Justice, just so long will America be the land of equal opportunity, the real essence of democracy.[51]

But Marshall had construed judicial review narrowly; he had deferred to the "wisdom and discretion" of Congress. The great Chief Justice relied on the influence constituents possess at elections as "the sole restraints" to secure them from abuse. For James Bradley Thayer, too, the Court's "great and stately" role depended on the respect it paid co-ordinate branches of government. The Court must refrain from acting like a legislature—from passing on the wisdom of legislation under the guise of constitutional construction. Judicial review, Thayer had warned, inevitably ran the risk of becoming judicial supremacy.

No such fears troubled William Howard Taft. His strong convictions, expressed repeatedly, foreshadowed a jurisprudence making property rights a preferred freedom, popular power a distrusted force, and the Supreme Court a superlegislature. The Court need not block all regulatory legislation; its function was that of a fine filter, carefully discriminating between good and bad laws. Judicial acquiescence in a small portion of the "overwhelming mass of ill-digested legislation" might placate the radicals. In this way, the socialist revolution might be averted, the excesses of democracy curtailed.

Just as Taft had fervently opposed radical social reform destructive of property, and had pitted judicial power against popular power, so he zealously promoted reform in judicial administration. Changes in the Federal rules of civil procedure, union of law and equity, reorganization of the Federal judiciary under the direction of the Supreme Court, the judicial conference, reduction of the Court's obligatory jurisdiction and expansion of its discretionary power—these measures would make the administration of justice more efficient, less costly, and less time-consuming. Judicial reform would remove a major source of popular dissatisfaction, thereby dissipating the Populist drive to abolish private property. Bereft of a clogged docket, freed from its obligatory jurisdiction over "minor" litigation, the Court would be in a stronger position to perform its "higher function"—constitutional interpretation in general, the defense of property in particular.

Taft's judicial platform had been more than twenty-five years in the making. Building up, too, were his yearnings for the center seat on the Supreme Court. The Presidency served only to spur this quest. "Presidents come and go," he commented in 1916, "but the Court goes on forever."[52] His preference for judicial office rested on solid considerations. Who, other than William Howard Taft, saw so clearly the need to maintain and consolidate the judiciary as defender of property rights? Who else saw the direct connection between the crying need for judicial reform and the Court as "Guardian Kings" of the propertied class? Who was better qualified to be Guardian Chief? Who else recognized that the impetus for judicial reform had to come from the Chief Justice? Who but Taft had such a comprehensive, magisterial conception of the office and powers of the Chief Justice? In short, who but Taft could not only do the job but do it "well"?

It had been a long time since a young Circuit Court judge addressed a graduating class of law students on "The Right of Private Property." Since then, Taft had been Civil Governor of the Philippines, Secretary of War, President of the United States, professor of law at Yale, and a prolific contributor to the literature concerning the proper role of the Court and the need for judicial reform. Far into the future was the Chief Justiceship—the ideal position from which to translate deeply held convictions into effective action.

CHAPTER III

ENTERING THE TEMPLE

THE HUMILIATION suffered in his defeat for re-election in 1912 long remained a thorn in Taft's side. Roosevelt, with whom he had freely shared his hopes and ambitions and to whom he owed the Presidency, had come roaring back, blood in his eyes, from self-imposed exile in the wilds of Africa. With withering scorn, the lion hunter attacked his old friend Will as a mossback and a bungler, mismanaging the job handed him on a silver platter. T.R.'s choice for the Presidency in 1908 became his bitter rival in 1912, splitting the G.O.P. down the middle, and thus handing over the White House to Woodrow Wilson for eight long years.

In March 1913, Taft at sixty-three was out of office for the first time in his political life. Yale, his beloved alma mater, promptly solved his unemployment problem, welcoming him back to the campus as Professor of Constitutional Law. A four-hour-a-week lecture schedule at $5,000 a year left him free to fill four lecture engagements a week at $300 each. Though his accumulated earnings were in excess of a Supreme Court Justice's salary—or even that of the Chief Justice—he kept a wistful eye on the "sacred shrine" in which, but for a compelling sense of duty and enigmatic turns of fortune, he might now be seated. But there was still time; the cherished prize might yet come.

Woodrow Wilson was hardly settled in office before he began hearing what a wonderful thing it would be for the country if Mr. Taft's lifelong ambition could be gratified at the hands of a Democratic President. William S. Bennet, a former Republican Congressman from New York, put the matter to the new President directly. Noting that Justice Holmes, then seventy-two, would soon retire, Bennet wrote:

> I imagine that irrespective of politics, a majority of voters of the U.S. would be pleased if President Taft were to go upon the Supreme Bench. He could scarcely appoint himself to succeed Judge Holmes.
>
> My suggestion, which I hope you will not deem impertinent, even though you may not agree with it, is that it would be a splendid thing if you wrote to President Taft and said to him that if he would permit the vacancy [that presumably created by Holmes's retirement] to remain until after the 4th of March, it would be a pleasure to you to appoint him to the bench.[1]

Bennet's idea was broadcast far and wide, even reaching England. "I see a story about your chief retiring and Taft succeeding him," Sir Frederick Pollock wrote his friend Justice Holmes, January 9, 1914. "But why should White want to go?" the puzzled Englishman asked.[2] On hearing this incredible story in faraway Orchard Knoll Homestead Dairy, Klamath County, Oregon, a loyal Democrat exploded:

> From a lonely cabin in the Far West I write to implore you not to do it. I have no grudge against Mr. Taft, but I believe him to be unfit for the place; that he is out of harmony with the spirit of American Liberty and the equality of the people. Born with a golden spoon in his mouth and never having had to fulfill the Divine command, "By the sweat of thy face shalt thou eat bread," it is impossible for him to sympathize with the common man, and, unconsciously, his decisions would favor aristocracy and be against democracy. The trend of his thought is backward, not forward.[3]

Organized labor had special reason for not wanting Taft on the Supreme Bench. A protesting resolution from the Central Labor Union of Indianapolis told the President:

> Whereas the said W. H. Taft has shown an opposition to labor organizations by speeches and otherwise that can readily be accepted as hatred, and
>
> Whereas there can be no justice rendered by a Court composed of men who permit their disappointments to become prejudices. . . .[4]

The Plumbers Union of St. Paul, Minnesota, cited more specific objections:

> Mr. Taft, when he was a judge, inaugurated the abuse of the injunction power of the courts in its unwarranted application to labor disputes, and invoked and used against the working people of the country other forms of judicial tyranny.[5]

One can only imagine Wilson's reaction to Bennet's fantastic proposal, but the President soon learned how an irate Denver Democrat felt.

> I see by the paper this morning (though I am far from believing all I see in the papers) that you would be pleased to appoint Mr. Taft to a vacancy on the Supreme Bench. I do not believe you would do it under any circumstances, but I wish to enter my strong protest. It would seem to me like our Saviour appointing a Judas to an apostleship after the betrayal.[6]

Stories of Holmes's and White's pending retirement were pure speculation, the wish no doubt being father of the thought. But with Justice Lamar's death on January 2, 1916, rumor took on a ring of reality. In eulogizing Justice Lamar, whom President Taft had appointed in 1910, *The New York Times* sounded the call for high statesmanship:

> President Wilson would give new strength and dignity to the court, he would recognize proved and distinguished judicial capacity by appointing ex-President Taft.[7]

"The whole country would commend the selection of Mr. Taft," the Washington *Herald* of January 12 announced. His "profound legal knowledge, fortified by broad experience in statecraft, would add greatly to the strength of the highest court." Recalling Taft's long-time ambition, the *Herald* thought that "President Wilson would serve his country well in appointing him."[8] President Taft himself had set the example of high-mindedness in 1910 when he selected White, a Southern Democrat, as Chief Justice.

Supporting messages and newspaper clippings poured into the White House. On January 10, Dudley Field Malone wrote the President about his recent visit to Buffalo,

where I spoke, with Myron T. Herrick, to twelve hundred of the most representative businessmen I have ever gathered together. They came from all parts of New York State. There was a unanimous opinion, among Democrats and Republicans alike, that it would be a most generous and magnificent thing, and pleasing to the entire country, if you could see your way clear to offer Mr. Taft the vacancy on the Supreme Court Bench. I consulted the Democratic politicians in Buffalo, like William J. Connors, Norman E. Mack, the Collector of Customs there, Mr. George Bleistein, and many others– . . . and they all said at once that they thought it would be the strongest, finest thing you could do in the circumstances. . . . I feel that the appointment of Mr. Taft would produce the most desirable results for your administration.[9]

On January 11, Hunsdon Cary, another "well-wisher and supporter" and "loyal Democrat," reminded the President of Taft's nonpartisan appointments to the Supreme Court:

He begot in the Southern states a feeling that this court was something bigger than the Republican party, that it belonged to the country; and should he now be placed upon this same court by the opposite political party, I believe it will in turn beget in the north a feeling of trust and confidence in the Democratic party that will go far toward insuring national unity. . . . I have not talked to a lawyer who does not think his appointment would be an eminently wise one.[10]

Judge Alton B. Parker, Democratic candidate for the Presidency in 1904, reported to the President on the action of the Executive Committee of the American Bar Association. Joined by the ex-presidents and the chairmen of the standing committees, the Executive Committee signed a petition endorsing Taft.

It seemed to be so unanimously the opinion that Mr. Taft was the best qualified man in the country to fill the vacancy, and the Southern men and Democrats present were so united in this opinion that it would be widely accepted in the South as a graceful and nonpartisan act on your part to appoint him who had as President appointed from the South the Chief Justice and two associates, all three Democrats and two of them ex-Confederate soldiers. . . .[11]

Though relishing the campaign in his behalf, Taft doubted President Wilson's ability to rise above political partisanship. To his Yale classmate Clarence Kelsey, the former President revealed his innermost feelings.

My dear Kels:—

I have your letter of January 15th. Wilson never made a promise to put me on the Supreme Bench, and I don't know whether I could accept if he offered it to me now. I don't say that I would not, because of course I love the Bench and would like to be on that Bench, but it would seriously interfere with plans I have for the next two years. Still, when one goes on to the Bench, he can not be a chooser as to time. . . .

I am wicked enough to enjoy the irritation that Wilson probably feels at getting those letters.[12]

Wilson lacked the "breadth of view" necessary to see the political advantage in the appointment. "I feel certain that he could not recognize a generous impulse if he met it on the street."[13]

Others envisaged "political advantage" in an altogether different light. On the day of Lamar's funeral Senator Robert L. Owen of Oklahoma suggested how the right appointment might redound heavily to the advantage of the party and its leader.

I wish to strongly urge upon your attention the importance of putting upon the Supreme Bench, in place of the late Justice Lamar, a man who has demonstrated his complete sympathy with the progressive view, and shown himself to regard the interests of human beings as superior to the interests of property holding.

I feel very strongly on this matter, and hope you will not lose sight of this vital distinction in making your nomination. We have not on the bench a single progressive man, in my point of view.[14]

"I warmly sympathize with the views expressed in your letter," Wilson replied, "and I hope with all my heart I can find just such a man."[15]

From the point of view of Wilson and his administration, the whispering campaign designed to pressure Wilson, as a gesture of generous impulse, into appointing William Howard Taft to the Supreme Court was incredibly naïve. For them the "political advantage" lay in appointing a genuine progressive. The effect might be to unite the liberal elements in both parties and thus lay the foundations for victory in the forthcoming presidential election.

On January 27, two days before President Wilson announced Lamar's successor, Congressman William Kent of California wrote the President:

> I have been doing some thinking and consulting with people concerning the vacancy on the Supreme Court and I wish to suggest to your most careful consideration our friend, Mr. Louis Brandeis. There is no one in the country better known for clear-headed, forward-looking constructive statesmanship. . . . You know, as well as I do, that the Supreme Court is the real living Constitution and therefore see clearly the necessity of having on the bench men with a vision of improving average human conditions, which is the end and the aim of democracy.
>
> I have never known Mr. Brandeis too busy to take up the cudgels for a good cause and there is no man in the country more free from suspicions of sordid motives, although the enemies of progress and friends of special privilege have made it their end and object to discredit him.[16]

One important matter remained to be settled. The man selected must have the undivided support of progressive Republican Senators. President Wilson sought and obtained this assurance from the progressive Wisconsin Senator, Robert M. La Follette. The President also learned from the Senator that the man with "demonstrated progressive views" would accept appointment. A one-word telegram addressed to Attorney General Thomas W. Gregory simply said "Yes."

Friday, January 28, 1916, found politics in the nation's capital relatively serene. Newspaper headlines featured President Wilson's preparedness speech of the day before. Suddenly Washington and the financial districts were stunned as if by a bomb from an unseen Zeppelin. Wilson had appointed Louis D. Brandeis of Boston to succeed Joseph R. Lamar as Associate Justice of the United States Supreme Court. "Impossible," certain Senators exclaimed. Wall Street's groan was like the echo of a great national disaster. Some considered it "a ghastly joke." Perhaps Sam Untermyer had "put one over."

The bitterest protest came from the man whose personal interests were deeply affected—William Howard Taft.

> . . . it is one of the deepest wounds that I have had as an American and a lover of the Constitution and a believer in progressive conservatism that such a man as Brandeis could be put in the court. . . . He is a muckraker, an emotionalist for his own purposes, a socialist . . . a man who has certain high ideals in his imagination . . . of great tenacity of purpose and, in my judgment, of much power for evil. . . .
>
> The intelligent Jews of this country are as much opposed to Brandeis's nomination as I am, but there are politics in the Jewish community. . . . Wilson has projected a fight, which with master art he will give the color of a contest, on one side of which will be ranged the opposition of corporate wealth and racial prejudice, and on the other side the downtrodden, the oppressed, the uplifters, the labor unions and all the elements which are supposed to have votes in the election. This will lead to the confirmation because of the white-livered senators that we have. . . .
>
> But as so often happens in such a well-devised Machiavellian scheme, the ultimate result is not going to be to Wilson's advantage, if we nominate any man whose conservatism appeals to the businessmen. . . . This appointment will be remembered long after the excitement of the confirmation has passed away. . . . It is too ingenious and too unscrupulous. . . . When you consider Brandeis's appointment, and think that men were pressing me for the place, *es ist zum lachen.* You know me well enough to know that my judgment on this subject is not in the slightest degree colored by the fact that men had sug-

gested me for the place. I never for one moment credited the possibility of Wilson's considering my name. The thoughts of the judges of the Supreme Court, if they could be interpreted, would form interesting language.[17]

Taft could only hope that "White will not end his judicial career with an apoplectic fit caused by the nomination."[18] At stake was "the Supreme Court as the bulwark of the guaranties of civil liberty."

The former President had special reasons for feelings of outrage. In 1910 Brandeis, as counsel for Louis R. Glavis and *Collier's Weekly* in the notorious Ballinger affair, revealed that President Taft and his Attorney General, George W. Wickersham, had predated a document in a vain attempt to exonerate Secretary of the Interior Richard A. Ballinger, caught in charges of maladministration of Alaskan public lands.[19] Coming in the middle of Taft's Presidency, the effect was to drive Ballinger from office and smear the entire Taft administration, thus setting the stage for disaster in the 1912 presidential election.

"I sincerely hope that he can be defeated in the Senate," Taft wrote his friend Gus Karger, Washington correspondent of the Cincinnati *Times-Star*, "but I don't think so."[20] The Senators were "white-livered"; and "the Senate has been La Follettized and Gomperized so that it has ceased to be the conservative body it was."[21]

Taft's hopes, though faint, were buoyed by the prospect of "a movement on foot to carry a real campaign against Brandeis." Nor was he "at all disposed to discourage the effort to bring out evidence against him, even though it shall fail of its chief purpose."[22] Through Gus Karger he kept close tabs on the Senate hearings. Every item indicating the nomination might be defeated was cherished. When A. Lawrence Lowell and other prominent citizens spoke out in opposition, the former President was "delighted."

The most lethal blow was struck on March 14, when American Bar Association President Elihu Root, prodded by

George W. Wickersham, submitted a statement of protest containing the signatures of prominent lawyers. Taft and five other past presidents signed, declaring that "Mr. Louis D. Brandeis . . . is not a fit person to be a member of the Supreme Court of the United States."[23] Heartily approving this bold step, Taft explained: "I think we owe it to ourselves and to the Bar not to be supine, growling under our breath and whispering in the closet. We should speak out."[24]

Brandeis's reaction was immediate and belligerent. "I think Taft's injecting himself into this controversy," he wrote Norman Hapgood on March 14, "gives opportunity for making clear what we omitted to make clear six years ago—the gravity of Taft's and Wickersham's act in connection with the antedating [of the Ballinger report]." Four days later Walter Lippmann's editorial in *The New Republic* declared: "One would have supposed that ex-President Taft was the last man qualified to express a judgment on Mr. Louis D. Brandeis. . . . It was Mr. Brandeis who demonstrated to the country Mr. Taft's immoral procedure in a disreputable incident."[25]

All attempts to prevent Wilson from putting "an insidious devil on the Court" failed. Brandeis was confirmed by a vote of 47 to 22.

Ahead was the 1916 presidential election—"the most crucial during my career," Taft called it. If Wilson won re-election, as seemed not unlikely, he might have as many as four Supreme Court appointments to make.

Wilson's appointment of Brandeis had been politically astute. Writing William G. McAdoo in February 1916, Amos Pinchot had enclosed excerpts from a letter received from Norman Hapgood: "Brandeis will pull a strong oar for Wilson in Wis., Minn., S. & N. Dakota and other Roosevelt strongholds. It took courage and sense to make this appointment and I take off my chapeau to the President."[26] One correspondent, John Morgan Shook, connected the

Brandeis nomination with the campaign on Taft's behalf. After warmly commending the Brandeis appointment as an "act of courage," Shook added: "While I know Mr. Taft personally, having served in the Philippine Islands under him, and while he has many lovable traits, I do not think that his sympathies are with the masses of the people."[27]

In one respect Taft and Wilson were equally realistic: both realized that the future of progressivism in America depended on the Supreme Court. Speaking at the Gridiron Club on December 9, 1916, a month after his hairbreadth victory over Charles Evans Hughes, Wilson, in a surge of optimism, thanked God "that the day of cold thinking, of fine-spun constitutional argument, is gone."

> We do not now discuss so much what the Constitution of the United States is as what the constitution of human nature is, what the essential constitution of human society is, and we know in our hearts that if we ever find a place or a time where the Constitution of the United States is contrary to the constitution of human nature and human society, we have got to change the Constitution of the United States. The Constitution, like the Sabbath, was made for man and not man for the Constitution. I have known of some judges who did not perceive that. I have known of some judges who seemed to think that the Constitution was a strait jacket into which the life of the nation must be forced, whether it could be with a true regard to the laws of life or not.
>
> But judges of that sort have now gently to be led to a back seat and, with all respect for their years and their lack of information, taken care of until they pass unnoticed from the stage. And men must be put forward whose whole comprehension is that law is subservient to life and not life to law. The world must learn that lesson, the international world, the whole world of mankind.[28]

Taft was clearly among the judges President Wilson wished to see led to a back seat, and not too gently either. Wilson's re-election in November 1916 sealed Taft's fate, so far as the Court was concerned, for four more years. After 1916, he sometimes wondered whether "so much demoralizing political experience" had not undermined his judicial temperament. More often than not the universal solvent for political scruples is ambition. So it was with Taft.

With the smashing Republican victory of 1920, entrance to the temple again became something more than a remote possibility. As the political prospects brightened, the former President again advertised his availability. A place on the High Court had long conjured up the image of "comfort and dignity," of "power without worry."[29] The Chief Justiceship would mean "realization of a dream for many years." It would provide "work in a field I love."[30] It would remove "me altogether from politics, and leave me only to consider questions from the standpoint of a just and equitable conclusion."[31]

The 1912 debacle had cut Taft deeply. In his eyes the blame rested squarely on insurgent Republicans, parading as Progressives. The Chief Justiceship would serve a double purpose: it would fulfill his ambition and at the same time provide a much-needed vindication. The 1912 nomination, rather than the election, had worried him. "If we lose the election, I shall feel that the party is rejected, whereas if I fail to secure the renomination it will be a personal defeat."[32] Elevation to the Supreme Court would provide "in one sense or another . . . [a] comeback from the status in which the campaign of 1912 left me." It would indicate that "the American people were conscious that . . . my attitude toward public affairs had been misconstrued and injustice had been done me."[33] "One can afford to wait to have such a situation remedied by time, as it usually is."[34]

In retrospect, Taft was accustomed to think and speak of his appointment as preordained, as virtue rewarded. Forgotten were the strenuous, almost bizarre, manipulations resorted to in finally bringing it to pass. After the 1920 electoral landslide, his appointment was accepted as a foregone conclusion. It was "common understanding in Washington," *The New York Times* noted, that White "intended to resign from the supreme bench . . . and that he would be willing to resign if he were certain that Mr. Taft would succeed him. . . . Chief Justice White would rather have Mr. Taft appointed as his successor than any other man."[35] The former President encouraged this belief. He liked to recall his conversation with Associate Justice White as they walked up Connecticut Avenue in the late afternoon of the day President Taft made up his mind to elevate White. "Well," the President commented with resignation, "I have decided whom I will appoint Chief Justice, and in doing so I have driven another nail in my political coffin."[36] In later years, the former President often recalled Chief Justice White's promise "that he was holding the place for me. . . ."[37]

Apparently some kind of informal understanding had been made, but Taft, on occasion, tried to make it appear that he would not insist on specific performance. Chief Justice White had "discharged his duty to me in the fullest way. I know you would acquit me of harboring the thought that my appointment imposes on him the slightest obligation to retire now in my favor." Meanwhile, the former President kept remembering that the Chief Justice ". . . in times past seemed to cherish the thought that he would show a gratitude that I expressly declined to recognize any reason for, by retiring when the time came when I could be appointed."[38] Chief Justice White had assured him "not once, but many times . . . that he was holding on to turn over the place to me."[39] That time had come. At seventy-five, White was plagued with defective hearing and impaired sight, and was eligible for retirement on a pension. Not unreasonably, Taft nursed the hope "that [White] would retire."[40]

When and if this happened, it was important that President-elect Harding be fully alerted to Taft's availability. Taking no chances, Taft and his friends labored hard toward this end. Gus Karger, Taft's former campaign manager, became the former President's lobbyist. Taft's old friend Max

Pam, corporation lawyer of Chicago, was particularly active, leading the former President wryly to suspect that "Max wishes to supervise my becoming Chief Justice."[41] Through Harding's Ohio friend and Attorney General, Harry M. Daugherty, Karger was able to make a realistic estimate of the prospects. In mid-January, 1921, Karger relayed Daugherty's understanding "that Senator Harding had told him that he didn't care what anybody else would say about it or who Senator [Philander C.] Knox's candidate might be, that he would appoint you Chief Justice of the United States."[42]

While field workers kept in close touch with Harding and his advisers, Taft himself was busy. Shortly after Harding's election, the unblushing aspirant, armed with "helpful suggestions" concerning appointments, made the pilgrimage to Marion, Ohio.[43] Taft was "non-plussed" by the manner in which the President-elect took him into his confidence, and was "nearly struck dumb" when he broached a Supreme Court appointment. Out of the blue, Harding inquired: "Would you accept a position on the Supreme Bench, because if you would, I'll put you on that Court." Taft merely repeated that "it was and always had been the ambition of my life. I had declined it twice . . . but I was obliged to say that now under the circumstances of having been President and having appointed three of the present bench and three others and having protested against Brandeis, I could not accept any place but the Chief Justiceship."[44] To disabuse Harding's mind of any thought of an Associate Justiceship, Taft wrote him a note emphasizing that his interest lay solely in the post of Chief Justice. White himself, the President-elect was told, favored this course of action.[45] The meeting at Marion had been altogether satisfying. From Harding came the reassuring word that he appreciated "fully all that you have to say concerning yourself and your ambitions."[46] His "announced purpose to put me on the Bench was abiding and . . . he sympathized with my desire to be Chief Justice only."[47]

Taft now turned his attention to the enfeebled man whom he hoped to replace. Here, too, the line of contact was Harry Daugherty. He was "the person through whom White would communicate with the President on . . . his retirement, and Daugherty would know whether White had said anything to the President on the subject."[48] After a visit with the Chief Justice, Daugherty could not report White's intention to quit, but the Attorney General did notice "that the Chief Justice looked very feeble and it seemed to him that he might soon retire, that he assumed a change in the situation would and could become a fact when the President was ready. . . ." Harry's statements "were so cordial and so unequivocal, both in interest and in the feeling and understanding that the nature of the succession had practically been understood, that there seemed nothing to do but wait."[49]

But Taft had been waiting for months; winter passed into spring. In mid-March he felt "it reasonable to expect that he [White] will do nothing formal and open before March 25th."[50] That date came and went; nothing happened. Yet the President had promised he would "keep in touch with the situation" and that matters would develop "in a reasonable time."[51]

Taft's concern began to border on alarm. With White, a "reasonable time" threatened to run on indefinitely. When told that Taft's friends were advocating him for the bench, the Chief Justice bluntly replied that there was no vacancy.[52] Other members of the Court were annoyed by the pressure for White's resignation. Justice Day did not understand the constant reference to various persons as candidates for the bench when no positions were open.[53]

To ascertain the likelihood of a forthcoming vacancy, Taft decided to determine more precisely the state of White's health. A visit with the Chief Justice in mid-March, 1921, proved discouraging. Though White referred to his illness, he said nothing about retiring. Despite a cataract condition, he could still read. The only cheering note was the Chief Justice's complaint about the burden of work.[54] Suspecting that White might be nearer the end than appeared on the surface, Taft consulted White's physician, Dr. J. J. Richardson.[55] Any hopes based on the doctor's report were dampened in early April, when Justice Day told Max Pam "that the Chief Justice [had] indicated to no one any intention of resigning or retiring and that in his opinion no such intention exists." Day ventured the further opinion that the Chief Justice is now in good physical condition, except that "he does not see very well." Hopefully, Karger added that he was "told by others that he does not hear very well either."[56]

A month before the Chief Justice died, Taft despaired of ever reaching the goal. He was now "getting on" himself. That summer he would be sixty-four, and he felt it would be unwise "to appoint a man to that bench at such an age that he has to serve long after seventy to make up the ten years after which he can retire."[57] Taft himself later indicated that, if appointed, he would retire after ten years and take his wife on a trip around the world.[58] But Edward Douglass White was giving no sign of stepping aside. "As a man comes to the actual retirement, after he is seventy years of age," Taft remarked dolefully, "he seems to regard it as an admission of weakness, a singing of the *Nunc Dimittis,* and he satisfies himself with many reasons why the time has not come."[59] Rationalizing disappointment, he reflected: "If the position, which I would rather have than any other in the world, is not to come to me, I have no right to complain, for the Lord has been very good to me."[60]

On May 18 the clouds parted a little; Dr. Richardson then informed Taft that "the Chief is still alive, but the end is only a question of a few hours."[61] The next day White died. Almost anticlimactic, "the unexpected" had finally happened.[62]

Over seven months had elapsed between Harding's election and White's death. Meanwhile, the path to the Chief Justiceship became cluttered with other contenders. Aware that the President-elect was not a decisive man, Taft's friends anticipated that Harding might use the claims of others as an excuse for delay. "I pray to Heaven," Karger had written Taft, "that Senator Harding will be quite as positive and firm when the time for action in the matter shall arrive."[63] The time had arrived, but there was no action. At the 1920 conference in Marion, Harding had mentioned that Charles Evans Hughes would like to be Chief Justice, but that threat was removed when the New Yorker accepted appointment as Secretary of State. Another possible delay was suggested by the rumor that the President was waiting until he could reward former Senator George Sutherland of Utah, Harding's astute presidential-campaign adviser.[64] Sutherland was known to harbor Supreme Court ambitions. The President had promised him an appointment; he knew also that the former Utah Senator was "crazy" to be Chief Justice. The President-elect had told Taft, "I am going to put him there," adding the reassuring comment that the Senator "could wait."[65] But Harding did not tell the former President that he, too, might have to wait.

Apprehensive lest Republican insurgents put up a hue and cry if he nominated Taft alone, the harassed President pursued a watch-and-wait policy. Harding "hates to offend anybody," Connecticut Senator Frank B. Brandegee explained. "His nature is to arrange compromises and ways by which everybody can be pleased."[66] "He seemed to believe that in every way it was desirable to couple [Taft's] name and Sutherland's in the nomination."[67] Such was the strategy, despite "a distinct promise to make me Chief Justice."[68]

Matters were further tangled by rumors that Harding planned to promote aging Justice Day to the Chief Justiceship on a temporary basis.[69] Taft exploded: "I don't know what he [the President] is going to do. I don't favor any such arrangement. I don't want to be a party to it."*[70] Various considerations, not all of them disinterested, bolstered Taft's opposition to this weak-kneed scheme. "No one should go into office . . . under an obligation to lay it down at a particular time. The office is too exalted. . . . More than that, I venture to think that Day's memory of the understanding will grow as dim as the Chief Justice's frequent statement to me that he wished to retire as soon as I could be appointed."[71]

At the very moment the prize came within reach Taft trembled "to think whether I can worthily fill the position and be useful to the country."[72] Characteristic misgivings were reinforced by the stress he had always placed on the age factor in Supreme Court appointments. Anyone beyond sixty was suspect. President Taft had ignored this test in appointing Lurton and White, both of whom he considered eminently qualified by judicial experience. Perhaps an equally strong case could now be made for him. In the remarkable postscript to a letter sent Gus Karger, May 19, 1921, the former President listed his qualifications in the fashion of a fledgling lawyer seeking his first job.

> . . . I have had federal judicial experience, too. 1. Three years on the State bench. 2. Two years solicitor general, U.S. 3. Eight years presiding judge, U.S. Circuit. 4. Four years Court of Appeals, Sixth Circuit. 5. Four years secretary of war. 6. Four years president. 7. Eight years Kent professor, Yale University, five hours a week Federal Constitutional Law, except one year Chairman National War Labor Board and one year arbitrator in case between Canadian government

---

* This was not the first time this maneuver had been broached. In 1873, Benjamin F. Butler, influential "rascal" in the Grant administration, had suggested that Justice Caleb Cushing be given a "temporary" appointment as Chief Justice. The matter was discussed at a Cabinet meeting December 1, 1873. Secretary of State Hamilton Fish, feeling the force of "the objection to Cushing's age [74], and the question of the propriety of dispensing an office of that character on a conditional tenure," argued against it. The Cabinet agreed and President Grant abandoned the idea. (See C. Peter Magrath, *Morrison R. Waite,* pp. 9–10.)

and Grand Trunk Railway. That would seem to indicate pretty continuous service in the line of judicial and other duties preparing one for service on the Supreme Court.[73]

History affords no certain clue as to the best type of training for Supreme Court justices.[74] Some have had backgrounds in practical politics, others in academic careers or as practitioners; still others came to the bench after judicial service at lower levels. The record indicates that all these types of experience have value.[75] Taft, encompassing all three, seemed to possess unique qualifications.

All the unforeseen obstacles thrown up after White's death made Taft "a good deal discouraged over the matter, because [he] had supposed it was so clearly understood that there would not be any hesitation."[76] From the unfailingly loyal Karger came word that he would attempt to see the President "to get an expression from him, if it can be done without making myself officious." Prodded by Taft to press for action, Karger resisted: "I don't believe more than that can be done by anyone. His [Harding's] assurances are of such a nature that they must be accepted; to bring pressure to bear on him now would indicate suspicion." To make certain that no stone was left unturned, however, Karger advised: "If you see an opening for action, let me know and I shall do all that is within my power."[77]

Working through Attorney General Daugherty, Karger learned that the plan to give Day a temporary appointment had been shelved. But Harding still saw no need for a quick decision, as the Court was about to adjourn for the summer recess.[78] Harry Daugherty, destined to spend four years as inept head of the Justice Department, now stressed the difficulties he encountered in enforcing the law. Courts were congested; there was compelling need for additional judges on the Federal circuits. Taking his troubles to President Harding, the harassed Attorney General urged Taft's immediate appointment. Prompt action would mean that the country's leading advocate of judicial reform would be available to advise and guide him.[79]

By June 1921, Taft's tireless drive was beginning to pay off. Pressing for a decision before July 1, Daugherty drew from President Harding a promise to send "pipelines out to secure a retirement. . . ."[80] The President sounded out Holmes and Day, but without success.[81] Hearing that Harding could not " 'jar loose' either Holmes or [Joseph] McKenna," Taft hit upon the idea of making retirement more attractive to Holmes. The Disarmament Commission would be just the place for him. Holmes "loves England," Taft noted, and, of course, the Commission could conveniently meet there. Of course, there were other advantages. The "Great Dissenter's" resignation would be a real boon to Taft's ambition to "mass the Court" in line with his own beliefs. "The Bench would be well rid of him," he commented summarily, "for his influence is not good on the Bench. He is always or generally with Brandeis."[82]

In mid-June, Harding finally abandoned any hope of naming Taft and Sutherland simultaneously. With pressure mounting, he finally told Karger on the fourteenth: ". . . say to the Big Chief that there has been a wonderfully fine expression with regard to him."[83] "Tell the Big Chief," Harding advised a week later, "that I'm going to put that [appointment] over about the first of July. Somewhere between the first and the fifteenth."[84] Two days later, another potential obstacle was removed. Taft then learned that Sutherland was slated for appointment to the Shipping Board.[85] On the twenty-ninth, Karger conveyed the welcome news that "Mr. Harding is beginning to inform people that he intends soon to announce your appointment." Senator Henry Cabot Lodge, who had just seen the President, "told me that he was the custodian of some secrets which he could not divulge."[86] The next day the secret was out. Taft was named Chief Justice.

Only one last hurdle remained—Senate confirmation.

Hopefully Taft recalled that this body had immediately confirmed his nomination of White, without reference to the Judiciary Committee. But Taft doubted whether his "enemies in the Senate would permit this, and any one by an objection could block it."[87] On the day of White's death, Taft had tried to ascertain the strength of the opposition, requesting Karger to find out "how the Democrats stand." "It would be the grossest ingratitude," he said, ". . . if they were to oppose me, in view of the fact that I gave them three Democrats out of six appointments to that bench."[88]

All these neurotic fears proved groundless, the nomination being promptly confirmed over the votes of four insurgents. Taft was naturally curious to know "who the four were who voted against me." "I can guess," he commented knowingly.[89] Speculation was short lived. The next day an admirer told him that the four dissenting votes had been cast by "the 'bitter-enders,' [Hiram] Johnson and [William E.] Borah, the Pro-German [Robert M.] La Follette, and the rank Socialist [Tom] Watson. . . ."[90]

Public reaction was generally favorable, blighted only by the outcries from the "nonconstructive" elements—the reckless promoters of social reform. The private opinions of at least one Supreme Court Justice were negative. Preferring the appointment of former Associate Justice Hughes, Holmes said of Taft: "I never saw anything that struck me as more than first-rate second rate."[91] In Holmes's eyes Taft's overweening ambition had been unworthy and belittling. The former President had "marked a fundamental difference in our way of thinking by saying that this office had always been his ambition."[92] For Holmes the only valid ambition was "the aspiration to touch the superlative in one's work."[93] Holmes soon relented, finally admitting that Taft's appointment was the best that could have been made.[94]

Press opposition came primarily from "disreputable" publications—*The New Republic, The Nation,* and the Socialist *Call.* The *Call* denounced the new Chief Justice as a tool of capitalism, who "can be depended upon to stand for property rights whenever they come into conflict with human rights."[95] The New York *Herald's* failure to give its endorsement came as a surprise. The "*Herald's* article," brother Horace noted erroneously, "was the only uncomplimentary one published." The most likely explanation was that the Hearst papers, like *The New Republic,* were "vicious."[96] Certain criticisms gave the new Chief Justice pause. *The Nation* wondered whether he was really intellectually equipped for an office which wields an enormous influence upon our national life and development. Taft had not been actively engaged in the law for thirty years, *The Nation* noted, and he was now approaching retirement age. Such doubts hit a tender spot. "You will observe," Taft wrote his wife, "that Borah attacked my legal qualifications. He did not seem to get very far with it, tho' perhaps there is more of truth in it than you and my friends would be willing to admit."[97]

In the face of opposition primarily from the "lunatic left," Taft could be philosophical: ". . . we must take the bitter with the sweet. . . ."[98] The chorus of praise so overwhelmed "the bitter" as to convince him that "no man has ever been appointed Chief Justice with so many approving as in the present case."[99] Buried under two thousand congratulatory telegrams and letters, Taft had good reason to suppose that his appointment had the wholehearted support of a grateful nation.

The appointment of Taft as Chief Justice has been cited as "the most distinguished thing that President Harding ever did."[100] Julia B. Foraker called the former President's elevation "an ideal consummation. One of those rare, quite perfect things that could not possibly be brought about by human maneuver."[101] Mrs. Foraker's own speculations suggest human intervention. There had been "intricacy . . . in President Taft's attitude toward the appointment of a Chief Justice when the matter came before him in 1910."[102] In appointing White, President Taft had covered every possible contingency. If the office fell vacant during the incumbency of a Democratic President, he had set a precedent for the appointment of a Republican Chief Justice. With a Republican President in the White House, the aging Chief Justice White could easily discharge his oft-repeated promise and give the office back to the Republicans—and to William Howard Taft.

While a professor of law at Yale, Taft used to tell of the Kentucky Republican Aleck Carter, who, in a rare year when the G.O.P. controlled the state house, came down from the hills to apply for a job. It would be, Aleck felt, his reward for faithful party service. He was told, however, that the new administration believed in reform and that under the new policy, the "office must seek the man." Aleck waited patiently for an office to seek him, but after a few weeks his money ran out and he started home. As he was leaving, a friend called out: "Aleck, where are you going?"

"I am going home," Carter replied. "I've heard tell, since I've been here, a good mite about an office seeking a man, but I hain't met any office of that kind. My money's gin out, and I'm bound for the mountains."

Then a hopeful thought seemed to strike him: "But if any of 'you-uns' see an office hunting a man, tell 'em that you just seen Aleck Carter on his old mare 'Jinny' going down the Versailles Pike and he was going damn slow."[103]

Taft's progress toward the Chief Justiceship had been "damn slow." The goal was reached only after more than thirty years of dreaming, pining, skillful planning—and a dash of luck.

CHAPTER IV

JUDICIAL REFORMER

By the second decade of the twentieth century, the Federal courts were in dire need of modernization. Decentralized and encumbered by a staggering variety of outmoded procedures, including automatic appeals to the Supreme Court, the Federal judicial system had become characterized by clogged dockets and delayed judgments.

> The system was without direction and without responsibility. Each judge was left to himself, guided in the administration of his business by his conscience and his temperament. The bases for informed public judgment and self-criticism were wanting, since adequate judicial statistics were unknown.[1]

Popular dissatisfaction with the administration of justice had begun to express itself at the turn of the century. In America, however, neither state nor nation has any official comparable to the Lord Chancellor of England, charged with the duties and opportunities of a Ministry of Justice.[2] Except for the initiative President Taft had provided, leadership in the movement for judicial reform had been largely private. Roscoe Pound sounded the alarm in 1906.[3] Taft had been voicing complaints since his years as a Circuit Court judge; he had continued to urge reform as a member of President Theodore Roosevelt's Cabinet. In 1908, before his successful bid for the Presidency, he had singled out the legal system as the most grievous among America's shortcomings. "If one were asked," he remarked, "in what respect we had fallen farthest short of ideal conditions in our whole Government, I think he would be justified in answering, . . . it is in our failure to secure expedition and thoroughness in the enforcement of public and private rights in our courts."[4] Rules of procedure were unnecessarily elaborate and complex; the time and energies of the nation's highest court were being frittered away on inconsequential issues rather than devoted to providing guidance to other branches of the government and the people of the United States.

As President, Taft made his criticisms and recommendations official. In 1921 he was Chief Justice. To a far greater extent than any of his predecessors, Taft was determined to translate his ideas into law. Some remedial legislation had been enacted, the most significant being the Act of September 6, 1916,[5] enabling the Court to keep more nearly abreast of its docket by cutting down on cases of minor importance. By 1921 this advance merely indicated a step in the right direction.

A mounting volume of litigation compounded organizational troubles. Increased government participation in the nation's economic life made a bad situation worse. Anti-narcotic and smuggling laws, auto-theft and white-slave statutes, income-tax violations—all this swelled the volume of litigation and swamped Court dockets.

World War I had an impact. From the First Circuit to the Ninth, Espionage Act cases crowded the criminal calendar. A marked rise in civil litigation occurred as wartime contracts were canceled; the shipping industry battled with the Shipping Board, and bankruptcy overtook businessmen in the jolting financial readjustment.

Ratification of the Eighteenth Amendment in 1919 administered the *coup de grâce* to an already harassed judiciary. In a wave of patriotic fervor the National Prohibition Enforcement Act, commonly known as the Volstead Act, became law. Thereafter, brew containing more than one half of one per cent alcohol by volume was illegal. "Near beer," as the authorized concoction was called, failed to satisfy the craving for hard liquor. Bootleggers, rumrunners, and hijackers strove to meet the demand; an unprecedented era of lawlessness ensued. The dangers Taft had long deplored attained ominous dimensions. Even normally law-abiding citizens ignored National Prohibition. Yet neither the states nor the Federal government provided adequate enforcement machinery. Meanwhile, astronomical profits in racketeering stimulated the growth of criminal elements. Equipped with war-surplus firearms and the automobile, aided by corrupt police, organized crime enveloped the country on an unparalleled scale.

The ultimate solution lay with Congress. Over the years, however, that body had demonstrated little inclination to do any hard thinking about law enforcement and judicial reform. Ensnared in a web of partisan politics, and jealous of its own authority over the judiciary, Congress tended to follow the path of least resistance. The lawmakers had turned a deaf ear to President Taft's repeated recommendations of specific corrective measures. During four disillusioning years he had stood by helplessly while a combination of Democrats and insurgent Republicans tore his program to pieces. Pathetically he had written his White House predecessor:

> It is now a year and three months since I assumed office and I have had a hard time—I do not know that I have had harder luck than other Presidents, but I do know that thus far I have succeeded far less than have others.[6]

Hope, nevertheless, sprang eternal. During the years following his ill-starred Presidency, Taft rarely missed an opportunity to point an accusing finger at Congress. His sense of frustration was deepened by the prevalent view that administration of the law fell within the exclusive province of the judiciary. The assumption was that "where the law fails and peace and order are not maintained, and the rights of parties are not promptly settled, the judges are responsible." Taft demurred. He conceded that "while the judges of our courts have their faults, they may rightly excuse themselves in a large degree on the ground that the fault lies with the legislative power, which does not provide them with adequate machinery for the prompt and satisfactory dispatch of business." The new Chief Justice "could point to instance after instance in which judges have worn themselves out" in the vain effort to win legislative relief.[7]

Firm determination to overcome congressional apathy and neglect of the Federal courts was partly motivated by an abiding conviction "that the danger to this country is in the enlargement of the power of Congress. . . ."[8] More than a trace of irritation runs through Taft's observation that overloaded jurisdiction of courts was incidental to the exercise of "heretofore dormant powers." The Federal government had "poked its nose into a great many fields where it was not known before, for lack of congressional initiation." "Something must be done," he pleaded, "to give the Federal courts a judicial force that can grapple with unconscionable arrears."[9]

Still fresh in mind were the frustrations of the Presidency. Leading Senators, including La Follette, Dolliver, Burton, Clapp, Beveridge, and Borah—all members of his own party—had joined hands not only to hamstring his legislative program, but also to defeat his renomination. Taft never completely forgave those who had stomped out of the furnacelike 1912 Republican Convention with his political benefactor, Theodore Roosevelt. The party split remained a continuing source of irritation, and, after 1921, of grave and immediate concern. Roosevelt's example in breaking up the Republican party had "created a disregard of party loyalty," permeating the rank and file. "We are short in leaders," Taft said, "still shorter in followers."[10]

As Chief Justice, more intent than ever on remodeling the judicial system, he discovered that those who had once led the Bull Moose movement now sat securely in the Senate. The triumph of Progressives in the 1922 congressional elections supplied a solid core of radical discontent. In the Senate a handful of irreconcilables were on the rampage. His own Court, especially during the years 1922 to 1924, came in for harsh condemnation. A rash of magazine articles fanned the flame of discontent. "Shall We Curb the Supreme Court?" "The Supreme Court as Legislature," "Is the Supreme Court too Supreme?" "To Shear Supreme Court Powers"—these were among the inflammatory captions under which irreverent commentators discussed the "main buttress of civilization." Leading the attack, Senator La Follette charged that five Supreme Court Justices "are actually the Supreme rulers, for a bare majority of the Court has repeatedly overridden the will of the people as declared by their representatives in Congress, and has construed the Constitution to mean whatever suited their peculiar economic views."[11] In response to La Follette's charges, the 1924 Progressive platform favored a constitutional amendment providing that Congress may, by re-enacting a statute, make it effective despite a judicial veto.

In his address at the unveiling of a monument to Chief Justice Salmon Portland Chase,[12] Chief Justice Taft took public notice of these onslaughts. The Court had always been "the stormy petrel of politics," he observed. In Chase's day there had even been proposals for the Court's abolition. Nor did these attacks subside. In 1895 Taft himself, noting the barrage of criticism hurled at the *Pollock, Debs,* and *Sugar Trust* decisions, had welcomed critical comment.

> Nothing tends more to render judges careful in their decisions and anxiously solicitous to do exact justice than the consciousness that every act of theirs is to be subject to the intelligent scrutiny of their fellow men, and to their candid criticism. . . . In the case of judges having a life tenure, indeed, their very independence makes the right freely to comment on their decisions of greater importance, because it is the only practical and available instrument in the hands of a free people to keep such judges alive to the reasonable demands of those they serve.[13]

In the 1920's the Chief Justice seemed somewhat less charitable toward criticism. "I think," he commented in

1922, "we are facing now another of the half-a-dozen attacks in its history which have been made upon the Supreme Court and its powers under the Constitution. La Follette is to lead it."[14] Taft accused "blatherskites," such as George W. Norris, of "joyfully" abusing the opportunity and immunity offered them by the floor of the Senate to advance their nefarious goal. Commenting on the ill-tempered attack of certain Senators on President Coolidge's nomination of Attorney General Harlan Fiske Stone as an Associate Justice, Taft declared that in the Senate "there is less appreciation of what the people really think than anywhere else that I know of."[15] Three years later, the Senate had become a "Bolshevik body."[16] Class voters—farmers and laborers—exercised wide influence. Labor, in particular, was a "class . . . distinctly arrayed against the Court."[17]

Ironically those now casting themselves in the role of critics gained a hearing partly because of Taft's inability to win approval of specific proposals going back more than a quarter of a century. Finding himself in an advantageous position effectively to advance the most ambitious reform program in the annals of the judiciary, he was face to face with his severest critics. Certain of them were firmly entrenched in the Senate Judiciary Committee, whose endorsement his measures must win. Borah, Norris, Walsh, and Shields, all members of that committee, were spokesmen for the class the Chief Justice profoundly distrusted.* Small wonder he considered it "a very poor committee, consisting mostly of radicals and progressives. . . ."[18] Chiefly responsible for this unhappy state of affairs was "supineness,

---

* In 1921 the full membership was: William P. Dillingham, Vermont; Frank B. Brandegee, Connecticut; William E. Borah, Idaho; Albert B. Cummins, Iowa; LeBaron B. Colt, Rhode Island; Thomas Sterling, South Dakota; George W. Norris, Nebraska; Richard P. Ernst, Kentucky; Samuel M. Shortridge, California; Charles A. Culberson, Texas; Lee S. Overman, North Carolina; James A. Reed, Missouri; Henry F. Ashurst, Arizona; John K. Shields, Tennessee; Thomas J. Walsh, Montana.

Members of the subcommittee were: Brandegee, Sterling, Ernst, Overman and Shields.

lack of real interest and patriotism of the entire body of the Republican party as represented in both Houses of Congress. . . ."[19] Sound party members had become thoroughly "buffaloed," allowing "these yahoos of the West and crafty damage lawyers like [Thomas J.] Walsh of Montana and [Burton K.] Wheeler of that same State and [Clarence C.] Dill of Washington to accomplish what they choose apparently in the matter of any kind of legislation that is sought for."[20]

The regular Republicans, instead of resisting this boring from within, had "permitted the Judiciary Committee to sink to a collection of so-called lawyers who have no conception of Federal court procedure or the importance of Federal courts, and only entertain the deepest hostility toward them." "So far as the Senate is concerned," he charged, "it puts the Federal courts at the mercy of their enemies."[21]

Conspicuous among the wrong kind of men on the Judiciary Committee was John K. Shields of Tennessee, "one of the narrowest, meanest men from a partisan standpoint that I know."[22] Taft remembered Shields disdainfully as "the man from Tennessee who voted against the League."[23] On the committee also was Montana Senator Thomas J. Walsh, "one of the most narrow-minded men I know, not a useful legislator, because he [never] looks for progress. He is always looking for criticism and condemnation."[24] To Justice Brandeis, the colleague perhaps closest to the carping Montana Senator, the Chief Justice poured out his troubles. Walsh, he declared, "belongs to that character of lawyer who is obstructive and not constructive. He gives an appearance of constructive views by suggesting changes that there is no possibility of having, but when there is anything practical, he is against it, and that is because he is against the Federal courts."[25]

For sheer "subversiveness" Senator George W. Norris of Nebraska topped the list. Less than a year after Taft's appointment, Norris told the Senate that there was "something fundamentally wrong with our judicial system." Life tenure was "not good for the people," tending to make some judges "forget the common people, the common run of humanity." Norris charged that "our judicial system is not doing justice to rich and poor alike"—a fact the Senator said he could prove "by testimony as high as your desk, Mr. President. . . ."[26] The Nebraska Senator would "abolish every United States District Court in America," and the entire system of United States Court of Appeals, leaving "nothing of our judicial system except the Supreme Court of the United States." State judges and state courts should, he said, take over "all the jurisdiction now held by United States judges and United States courts."[27] Among the "enemies of the Federal judiciary, willing in every way to obstruct its usefulness,"[28] Norris emerged as the one most to be feared. Running Norris a close second was William E. Borah of Idaho, of whom the Chief Justice remarked: "If he ever pushed a bill for the reform of anything, I don't know it, and the same is true of the rest of them."[29]

"The wretched personnel of the Judiciary Committee"[30] had not come about by accident. The men "least fitted for the Judiciary Committee" had sought places on it because they could not enhance their "reputation as lawyers in any other way."[31] Their self-seeking had succeeded only too well. Something must be done about it, or else all Taft's plans for judicial reorganization would be doomed to failure.

It seems "too bad," the Chief Justice wrote Republican Senate leader Henry Cabot Lodge in early 1922, "that two of the leading lawyers of the Senate should not be on that [Judiciary] Committee, to wit, Frank Kellogg and George Pepper."[32] Both ought to be assigned to it. But the situation was worsened when Senator Kellogg of Minnesota, bitter foe of Senator Robert M. La Follette, went down to defeat in the November election. Ironically, Kellogg was beaten by Farmer-Labor candidate Henrik Shipstead. Four years later, distinguished Philadelphia lawyer George Wharton Pepper failed in his bid for renomination as the Republican candidate for Senator. So ended Taft's efforts to reorganize the Senate Judiciary Committee.

Disaster struck in 1926. Norris, of all people, then became head of the Senate Judiciary Committee. A worse fate could hardly be imagined. To Taft's profound dismay, the man who "attacked me very much during my Presidency" and took occasion "to criticize my appointment to the Bench and my acceptance of some dinners after I came on to the Bench," had now "by right of seniority come to be the Chairman of the Judiciary Committee in the Senate, with whom I must have direct relations in any legislation which I seek for the Court."[33] The Chief Justice's only hope lay in the Senator's own sense of self-restraint—a very faint prospect.

Without Senators Brandegee and Cummins he might not have had the heart to make the fight. Writing to Brandegee in 1923, Taft said:

> I am glad you have come to the head of the Judiciary Committee, and I hope that you will find it possible to give much time and energy to helping the administration of justice in the Federal Courts. I think a great deal can be done there, and that the people will be very grateful if you can initiate it and carry it through. I would like to talk with you on the general subject when I reach Washington.[34]

Cummins of Iowa, who had forsaken President Taft in 1912, was now the Chief Justice's staunch supporter as ranking member of the Judiciary Committee. It was a sad day in 1926 when, on Cummins's death, Norris became chairman of the committee.

Such were the untoward circumstances under which Chief Justice Taft embarked on his campaign to reorganize the Federal judicial system. His indictment of the political complexion of Congress struck at the foundations. The people, acting through the usual electoral procedures, had elevated Norris, Shields, *et al.* to positions of authority. Power, thus conferred, enabled men of this stripe to legitimize, confirm, and perpetrate their alleged class prejudices. For Taft this meant that the best of our society was at the mercy of the worst. Yet the very system which Taft, by implication, deplored as subversive had elected to the Presidency a singularly mediocre man—the man to whom Taft owed his appointment as Chief Justice.

Taft's strong distaste for his own particular brand of mediocrity was of long standing. He had felt its frustrations keenly while occupying the most powerful office in the world. Now he was Chief Justice, the head of a body in a position to checkmate the legislative product of "yahoos" from whatever quarter. In furtherance of this task he was determined to incorporate in legislation the "executive principle," thus making the efficiency of the Court commensurate with its high responsibility. At long last, he was beginning to feel the "joys of leadership." From the vantage point of the Supreme Court and as Chief Justice, he resumed leadership in the campaign he had waged as President and later on as publicist and law professor at Yale.

The first year of his appointment Taft campaigned tirelessly, making speeches before the American Bar Association at Cincinnati and San Francisco, the Canadian Bar Association, and the Chicago Bar Association.[35] He presented his case to Congress, making statements and testifying before the House and Senate Judiciary Committees. Motivating these intense and far-flung activities was his determination to secure effective "teamwork" in the judiciary.[36] Soon to be demonstrated and implemented was an altogether novel conception, long in the making, of the prerogatives and duties of the Chief Justice. "If the Chief Justice is to have the duty and responsibility for the Federal judicial force of the country," he had challenged in 1914, "he should have an adequate force of subordinates to enable him to discharge it."

"Three needed steps of progress" were envisaged. First, an increase in the judicial force; second, a systematic distribution of that force by a council of judges. Two district judges at large—eighteen in all—would be added to each circuit. These judges would be assigned to any district in the circuit where needed and by the Chief Justice to any district in any other circuit. Needed also was a judicial conference of the senior judges of the nine circuits, annual meetings in Washington or elsewhere at the bidding of the Chief Justice. Scheduled judicial conferences were considered the "kernel" of progress. Heretofore, each judge had "paddled his own canoe." He had been subject to little or no supervision. Recognizing that judges, like other men, "needed the stimulus of an annual inquiry," Taft advocated a yearly accounting of the condition of the docket in the various circuits. Reports would be required from district judges and clerks, concerning the business in their respective districts, with a view to making a yearly plan for massing the judicial force in those districts where arrears had accumulated.

"Judges should be independent in their judgments," Taft explained, "but they should be subject to some executive direction as to the use of their services, and somebody should be made responsible for the whole business of the United States."[37] His image was that of "a General Director who shall be able to mass judicial force temporarily at places where the arrears are greatest and thus use what is available to do the whole judicial work."[38]

The Chief Justice's promotional activities were facilitated by easygoing Harry M. Daugherty, head of the Department of Justice. Before the Senate Judiciary Committee, Harding's Attorney General introduced himself as "less experienced in that office than any of my predecessors." But Daugherty promptly put the nation and the courts in his debt. "I began," he told the Senators, "to figure out some plan that would give relief to the country and give relief to the Judiciary."[39] Toward this end the Attorney General had appointed a committee to work out a specific proposal.[40] Keenly aware of the value of Taft's advice, the Attorney

General had made reform "an excuse for demanding my immediate appointment because he wanted to use me in this matter."[41] It was all part of a carefully conceived plan—presumably Harry M. Daugherty's. Taking the committee into his confidence, Daugherty announced: "About two months ago, or probably less, the Chief Justice was chosen, and I asked him to meet this commission and myself for the purpose of going over this situation, and I found him enthusiastically willing to render any assistance."[42]

The Chief Justice's informal account of what went on in the committee put Daugherty in a less favorable light. Taft came away from the first committee meeting unimpressed with the Attorney General, but satisfied and relieved that their views coincided.[43] Daugherty, and indeed the entire committee, seemed inclined to follow the Chief Justice's lead. "We had a long session," Taft reported to his wife, "and agreed substantially on my plan."[44] A week later, Daugherty, puzzling over Taft's idea of a judicial conference, asked its originator to "draw up a tentative bill with regard to the annual meeting of the senior circuit judges with yourself and myself."[45]

Testifying before the Judiciary Committee on October 5, 1921, the Chief Justice referred to his appearance as "an opportunity. . . . I have always been and am now very much interested in rendering the Federal courts more efficient in the dispatch of business." The story he told was one of rapidly increasing congestion. Enforcement of the Volstead Act, usually viewed as the factor creating the crisis, was only partly to blame. Crowded Federal dockets had long been chronic judicial disease. Liquor litigation was in fact responsible for only 8 per cent of the cases. Needed was a corrective for a situation certain to grow worse.

"The principle of this bill," Taft told the Senators, "is the executive principle of having some head to apply the judicial force at the strategic points where the arrears have so increased that it needs a mass of judges to get rid of them."[46]

He kept insisting that you have to have an *executive principle* in the dispatch of judicial business. Besides increasing the number of judges, a judicial conference consisting of the nine senior judges, one from each district, meeting together each year with the Chief Justice was necessary. This was not a power grab. The proposed conference would not "do anything," Taft declared, "but take up and consider and deliberate on . . . what shall be done with reference to meeting the arrears of the particular court. The assignment is left completely to each circuit judge and the Chief Justice."[47]

No one could reasonably deny "that an increase of the judges of first instance in the Federal system [was] absolutely necessary."[48] The Republican-controlled Congress stood ready and willing to approve new judges appointed by President Harding. Yet a howl of protest greeted Taft's recommendation that eighteen new judges be appointed as district judges at large, to be assigned to any court in the country.[49] Accustomed to the traditional concept of judicial localism, Congress objected to delegating the assignment power to the Chief Justice, the Attorney General, and senior circuit judges. Mobility of judicial personnel ran counter to traditional notions of judicial organization. Judges must be kept independent not only of the President and Congress but also of each other.

Senator Norris, leading the way, fiercely attacked the provision, making what Taft later called a "wild speech" against all Federal judges.[50] "As it adds to my powers of usefulness," he explained, Norris "was naturally against it."[51]

Giving the Chief Justice direction of the Federal judicial force conjured up in Senator Shields's mind "the Chief Justice as Commander in Chief." The Senator noted that Taft himself, testifying before the Judiciary Committee of the House, had presented himself as "the executive head of the Judiciary."[52] "Now the Lord High Chancellor of England," Shields went on, "is both a judicial and political officer. . . . Are we not somewhat copying after the system in England in creating a political as well as a judicial head of the Federal Judiciary?"[53]

"We would not stand for that bill at all," North Carolina Senator Overman declared, "and I do not think that any man in the Senate would stand for such a bill as that—to have eighteen roving judges to be sent around at the will of the Chief Justice and his staff here in Washington, coming here once a year to send them around all over the country. It is fundamentally wrong."[54]

Especially serious misgivings arose in connection with enforcement of National Prohibition, risking assignment by the Chief Justice of a judge out of contact with local mores. Consequently, in addition to those "gentlemen of communistic and socialistic tendencies who are opposed to any enforcement of the law at all," Taft noted that the assignment proposal had "attracted opposition of those who oppose enforcement of the liquor laws. . . ."[55] Since both the Anti-Saloon League and the Chief Justice supported the measure, Senator Shields suspected a "corrupting relation between [Wayne B.] Wheeler, congressional lobbyist for the Anti-Saloon League, and . . . me in sending dry judges into wet territory."[56] Expanding on his theme, Senator Shields predicted that the measure would invite swarms of agents financed by the League, the whisky interests, industry, labor, and the farmers to encourage him to assign judges favorable to their selfish interests.[57]

Deeply aroused, Shields predicted that the power to assign judges would provide an unparalleled opportunity "for political influence and power over the judiciary of which a designing man could avail himself in times of great political turmoil."[58] He did not relish the thought of "giving this great and unlimited and dangerous power to the Chief Justice."[59] "It is personal government," Senator Thaddeus H. Caraway, of Arkansas, exploded, "so far as the Chief Justice is concerned. It is wrapped up in the bosom of the Chief Justice to determine whether or not he ought to send judges to certain districts. . . . To send out," Caraway wailed, "a horde of judges all over this country" would concentrate "in his power the whole judicial system."[60]

Senator Cummins, taking a more relaxed view, explained: "So far as the power of the Chief Justice is concerned, . . . there is no considerable or appreciable addition to that power."[61]

> We have not . . . enlarged the powers of the Chief Justice further than to give him the right to designate or assign district judges to any of the circuits of the United States, precisely as in 1913 we gave him the power to assign district judges to any point in the second circuit. That is the substance of the additional power we have given to the Chief Justice.[62]

The Chief Justice was not, in fact, given a completely free hand. He could not move judges across the judicial chessboard at will. Exercise of his assigning authority was contingent on certification of need by the senior circuit judge of the congested district and a certificate of dispensability from the circuit judge of the releasing district.

Senator Cummins's words did not satisfy. The idea of judges at large, without local attachments or responsibilities, evoked the image of "eighteen roving carpetbag" judges under the direction of the Chief Justice, "like the head of an army, a chief of staff."[63] Quick to realize that his proposal was doomed, Taft endorsed House bill H.R. 9103, introduced November 14, 1921. Additional judges were provided but assigned to specific districts. As finally passed, the act[64] added new judges to twenty-one districts. The suggestion of a "flying squadron of judges," Taft commented philosophically, "did not meet with approval in the House and their Judiciary Committee preferred to add local district judges for the congested districts."[65]

The "judicial conference" provision, embodied in the same bill, also aroused strong opposition. Designed to make comprehensive surveys of Federal court business and draw up plans for assigning judges, the conference had long been the Chief Justice's pet reform measure.[66] The conference would provide centralization of judicial power and judicial mobility; it would secure "effective teamwork." In the eyes of certain Senators, no such serious purpose motivated the proposal.

"You will note today and perhaps during the week," Taft wrote brother Henry, "some roaring by Borah, Norris, La Follette and perhaps Johnson, as well as some Democrats against me as seeking power instead of attending to the high and lofty duties of my great office. . . ."[67] The blast came on April 6, when Senator Norris portrayed the Chief Justice's conference idea as a sort of annual social binge.

> When these judges come to Washington at the expense of the taxpayers, . . . what will they do? They will meet with the Chief Justice. They will be dined every evening somewhere. They will be run to death with social activities. . . . I do not believe there is any man who can stick his legs under the tables of the idle rich every night and be fit the next day to sit in judgment upon those who toil. Honest though he may be, . . . it will affect him and get him in the end.[68]

Senator Shields, alluding to Taft's crowded social calendar, charged that the conference would be nothing more than "a great social function of the judiciary of the United States, presided over by the Chief Justice, here in Washington or at any other place—at times it may be at White Sulphur Springs in Virginia or at San Francisco, or at Colorado Springs in Colorado, or any other nice place—to meet and talk over the judicial affairs of the United States and such other matters as they may enjoy."[69] The Senator insisted that "The Chief Justice has no more to do with the judges of the district courts of the United States, and with the trial of cases, and procedures in those courts, or the congestion of business in them, than does King George. . . ."[70] Shields considered the presiding officer of the Supreme Court "vested with as much power as any officer in our government, and there should be no extension of it."[71]

Senator Shields objected not only to the substance of the measure, but also to the prominent part the Chief Justice played in promoting it. Taft's appearance before the Senate and House committees "violated the spirit if not the letter, of the constitutional separation of powers of government. . . ."[72] Said the Tennessee Senator:

> The Chief Justice wanted this legislation . . . , he did go before the committees of both Houses . . . he came before the Senate committee twice, . . . he did talk to Senators outside of the committee. . . . The propriety of all this is a question for the Chief Justice.[73]

In the House, Representative Clarence F. Lea of California charged that the conference was a "publicity-seeking propaganda effort" designed to create a "judicial machine." "If," he argued, "the Federal judges of the United States were members of a legislative body, if they were a boosters' organization, or if they were a fraternal order, such an arrangement . . . might be appropriate, but I believe this scheme is wholly inappropriate for the Federal judges of the United States."[74] The basic argument against the conference stressed the proposed transfer to the Supreme Court of the assignment power over inferior Federal courts. Stating the time-honored legislative position, Shields observed:

> The power of assigning judges is not a judicial power and does not in the remotest manner concern the exercise of the jurisdiction of the Supreme Court. The judicial power is the power to try and determine controversies. . . . The power to establish courts and provide them with judges and other officers is a legislative power. Congress alone has this power. . . .[75]

What the Chief Justice wanted from Congress was a delegation of this power. Reluctant to comply, certain Senators predicted that authorization of a judicial conference would yield sinister consequences. Senator Overman had visions of a judicial system modeled on the Prussian military organization. The proposed legislation partook "of a military feature, in that we have a staff and a chief of staff for the judiciary, and provide for the staff to be called to Washington to meet and the chief of staff, the Chief Justice, will assign these men."[76] Shields charged that enhanced power delegated to the "chief of staff" constituted "a sort of entering wedge with regard to the independence of the judiciary."[77] Such interference could "grow and grow and sap and undermine that independence."[78]

Congressman Lea, trying to get the conference provision eliminated altogether, met strong and reasoned opposition from Chairman Andrew J. Volstead of the House Judiciary Committee: "I think we ought to retain this provision. This is one of the provisions that the Chief Justice is very much interested in, and so is the Attorney General and the commission that was appointed by the Attorney General for the purpose of trying to see if we could not get some system into our judicial machinery."[79]

The lawmakers' suspicions were not altogether groundless. Taft was accustomed to regret the absence in America of a responsible law officer like the Lord Chancellor in England. Envying the British official's authority to take the lead "in framing measures and pushing them through," Taft sometimes simulated the role. "It gives me pleasure," he told a 1921 assemblage of lawyers meeting in Cincinnati, "to say that I am coming to meetings of the American Bar Association. And, when I am not shut off by the previous question, I am going to discuss those subjects in which I have an interest, and in which I can make suggestions."[80]

In response to a note of thanks from the president of the Chicago Bar Association, the Chief Justice wrote:

I am grateful to the Association for the honor it did me and also for the pulpit it afforded me for saying some of the things in a public way in respect to the legislative needs of the Court and the Federal Judiciary system. The auspices under which I made the remarks gave them publicity which I valued, for the purpose of bringing to the attention of the public and Congress the reforms I have much to heart.[81]

Such utterances, often made in the context of high admiration for the Lord Chancellor of England, clearly delineate the image he had of the Chief Justiceship, its duties and responsibilities.

While the Act of September 14, 1922, fell short of granting the all-encompassing power so repulsive to Senators Shields, Overman, and others, it did enlarge the Chief Justice's stature as head of the Federal judiciary. Inferior judges would thereafter look to him for relief from crowded dockets and for guidance in conducting judicial business. Judicial statistics would now be available for a more effective execution of this task. The conference, headed by the Chief Justice, was authorized to suggest and promote needed legislation, including the revision of rules of procedure.

With this power finally wrenched from Congress, Taft could, at the very least, "promote the strategic massing of the judicial force of the country at the points of congestion."[82] But he still could not relax. Remembering the fate of the Commerce Court, created by Congress on his recommendation in 1910 and abolished three years later, Taft knew only too well that what Congress gave, Congress could take away. Moving judges over long distances caused "a considerable drain on the fund for the payment of the traveling expenses of the Federal judiciary." Any extravagance offered an unsurpassed excuse for clipping Taft's newly acquired power. Therefore the Chief Justice ordered senior circuit judges to "exercise . . . discretion to prevent abuse, not only because it is right, but also because it is of the highest importance that we retain the power of transfer and should not lose it by Congressional objection or repeal of the law."[83] He protested vigorously when, without his approval, one of Harry Daugherty's Assistant Attorneys General transferred a district judge.[84] Reasonable complaint could be made, Taft pointed out, if the Justice Department, charged with prosecuting criminal cases, selects its own judges. Objections could also be raised by defendants convicted by these judges. They will, he warned Daugherty, "incline Congress, properly sensitive to the slightest possibility of unfairness in the machinery of justice, to take away their most useful power of transfer."[85]

The Act of September 14, 1922, marks a new chapter in the administration of the Federal judicial system. Previous legislation had been *ad hoc* and temporary, difficulties growing out of an ever-expanding docket were met by increasing the number of judges or districts, or lengthening the term. Without disturbing the autonomy of district judges, the 1922 Act enabled judges from various parts of the country to meet and work out means of eliminating defects in the administration of justice. Above all, it embodied the "executive principle." Congress finally recognized

> that effective and economic adjudication is to no small measure dependent upon the ways in which the federal courts transact business. Hundreds of judges holding court in as many or more districts scattered over a continent must be subjected to oversight and responsibility as parts of an articulated system of courts. The judiciary, like other political institutions, must be directed. But it must be self-directed. An executive committee of the judges, with the Chief Justice of the United States as head, is a fit and potent instrument for the task.[86]

Against formidable odds, Taft had scored a great victory. He now turned to the problem of congestion in the Supreme Court's docket.

When Taft took his seat as Chief Justice of the United States, the august tribunal over which he presided had some of the attributes of a small-claims court. The Justices held the power of life and death over state and national legislation, often the final word in controversies between huge competing private interests, but they had comparatively little control over their own docket. A die-hard lawyer, astute in the labyrinthine ways of procedure, could appeal his client's case, no matter how picayune or devoid of public interest. Too often matters of grave constitutional import bided their time, while the nine Justices wrestled with a host of minor disputes. In 1922, Justice John H. Clarke, appointed to the Court by President Wilson in 1916, estimated that "more than one half of the cases are of no considerable importance whether considered from the point of view of the principle or of the property involved in them."[87] This freedom of appeal was a luxury the nation could ill afford. In 1922 the average interval between the filing of a transcript in the Court and its hearing was more than fourteen months. The Chief Justice appealed to Congress "to help us and relieve us from a good deal of burden so that we might write better opinions and less of them."

"The situation is rendered critical," Taft observed, "by the accumulating mass of litigation growing out of the war, and especially of claims against the Government which, if allowed to come under the present law to the Supreme Court, will throw us hopelessly behind." "The use of the Supreme Court," the Chief Justice reiterated,

is merely to maintain uniformity of decision for the various courts of appeal, to pass on constitutional and other important questions for the purpose of making the law clearer for the general public. Litigants . . . can not complain where they have had their two chances, that there should be reserved to the discretion of the Supreme Court to say whether the issue between them is of sufficient importance to justify a hearing of it in the Supreme Court.[88]

No specific steps to provide a corrective had previously been taken. In response to a request from Taft, Justice Van Devanter recalled:

No committee having anything to do with legislation was appointed during Chief Justice White's incumbency. He was unalterably opposed to any action along that line by the Court or even by its members. I drafted the act of 1915 and submitted it to him. He approved it, but particularly requested that it be turned over to a legislator who would make it his own and in no way connect the Court or any member of the Court with it. Justice [James C.] McReynolds drafted the act of 1916 and submitted it to Justice Day and myself, some changes were made, and it was introduced and passed during a summer recess. When Chief Justice White returned in the fall, he was much disappointed at what had been done—so much so that he never became reconciled to that act.[89]

At the suggestion of Senator Cummins, Chairman of the Senate Judiciary Committee, Chief Justice Taft appointed a committee consisting of Day, Van Devanter and McReynolds to assist in drafting the 1925 bill. At the committee's request, Taft served as a member,[90] and Justice Sutherland, though not on the committee, assisted in presenting the measure. Justice Van Devanter testified that the Court had merely responded to a request from the Chairman of the Senate Judiciary Committee. But Taft's letter to Cummins indicates that the bill originated in the Court.

We are preparing a bill which we hope to bring before your committee, to reduce the obligatory jurisdiction of the Supreme Court in cases from the District of Columbia and in a good many instances where a direct review by the Supreme Court is given quite out of keeping with the present system of certiorari. . . . The bill to which I refer is one which has been under consideration by the Supreme Court for some time and which they wish me to go before the Committee and present at the request of the Supreme Court.[91]

The House Report of the Committee on the Judiciary declared that the bill (H.R. 8206) was one prepared by the Justices of the Supreme Court, not as volunteers, but in answer to a proper request. A committee of Justices carefully considered the subject for a long time and then framed a tentative measure, submitted to all the Justices and approved by them.[92] The Committee Report concluded with words of "deep obligation to the Chief Justice and Justices of the Supreme Court for their help not only in preparing this bill but explaining it thoroughly."[93]

Taft opened his campaign with high hopes. The Congress was dominated by Republicans, and word reached him that opposition to the main purpose of the bill was practically nonexistent. But his prominence in the battle for the Act of September 14, 1922, had stirred bitter enmities. Friends of the measure therefore advised the Chief Justice to remain out of the spotlight. Taft, so far as possible, gracefully subordinated himself.

> I gather from what Cummins told me, that I ought to rely on members of our Court, who are on the Committee—rather than myself—that some of my old enemies rather resent my being prominent in pressing legislation. They want me to be "shinny on my side." I am delighted to escape the friction of that kind of contact, and in compassing legislation one cannot afford to ignore the irrelevant reasons and prejudice of the small-minded. The small-minded, if not in the majority, are at least a sufficient minority to create serious obstruction to real advance where the matter excites their littleness.[94]

The maneuver worked perfectly. "You certainly made a good choice in Mr. Justice Van Devanter," Thomas W. Shelton reported. "Without drawing invidious comparisons, he was the only substitute for you. It placated Senator Cummins for your absence."[95]

But victory was not yet assured. The measure was highly technical, containing few provisions that might excite popular protest or attention. The main handicap was timing; 1924 was an election year. Besides the presidential campaign and election, Congress was preoccupied with other legislation, including the war veterans bonus bill and amendments to the Railroad Act. Furthermore, an unforeseen contingency required the Chief Justice to curtail his activities; in February, 1924, he suffered a mild heart attack. Taft cleverly turned this setback into an additional reason for legislative limits on the Court's obligatory jurisdiction. In a mood of helplessness, he wrote:

A man cannot do all the work there is to do, and if Congress refuses to furnish the means by which our Court can keep us [abreast] we shall just have to let the work sag. We could do the work if Congress would give us an extended jurisdiction in certiorari. In that way we could eliminate a lot of cases that do not deserve the time that we have to spend on them.[96]

This was the measure for which Taft had labored so relentlessly.[97] By reducing the Supreme Court's obligatory jurisdiction and extending discretionary review, he hoped to reroute many cases on appeal to the Circuit Courts.

The principal arguments against expanding the Court's certiorari jurisdiction were: (1) Making the writ of certiorari the only writ from the Circuit Courts of Appeals to the U.S. Supreme Court cast aspersions on the state supreme courts. (2) Constitutional rights might go unprotected. Enactment of this measure, Oklahoma Senator John W. Harreld contended, would tempt the Court to put too many cases in the certiorari category.[98]

Granting the Supreme Court power to review the merits of a case before hearing oral argument was especially alarming to Thomas J. Walsh.[99] "To deny," Walsh asserted, "a litigant a right to present to the Supreme Court a question arising under the laws of Congress . . . , except by writ of certiorari to be issued upon written application supported by briefs, but without oral argument, is all but to compel him to abide by chance alone, with the odds all against him."[100] Taft's proposal exemplified, Walsh protested, the ancient "truism, half legal and half political, that a good court always seeks to extend its jurisdiction, and that other maxim, wholly political, so often asserted by Jefferson, that the appetite for power grows as it is gratified."[101] On learning that former Associate Justice Hughes shared the Montana Senator's constitutional doubts, Taft fumed: "Hughes is a small-minded man; . . . it is perfectly characteristic of Hughes."[102]

To combat the growing opposition, Taft, with the loyal support of Thomas Shelton, set in motion the powerful machinery and organization of the American Bar Association. A persistent campaign waged in Walsh's home state moved the Montana bar to censure him. The effort, though telling, was not enough. At times even Shelton despaired. Sharing Taft's sense of frustration, he confessed having "almost lost my faith in Congress." He was tempted to abandon the law and "take up journalism" and thus "smoke these people out. I'm trying not to let indignation get the better of common sense in the matter of the campaign before Congress. There are days yet to come."[103]

Trying to bolster Shelton's faltering spirits, the Chief Justice pointed out that "everything is ruled by politics just now, and there will be more chance for useful legislation in the next session."[104] But he was disinclined to let matters drift. "I asked the President to help us and he told me to write him something, which I did. I'm afraid he won't put in all I have written, but if I can get him started, it will perhaps attract the support of party members."[105] Extending the range of this pressure, he worked directly on governors and other state officials. To Senator A. Owsley Stanley of Kentucky went words of sweet reasonableness:

> For two years our Court has been very anxious to secure the passage of a bill to give us greater power of certiorari. We wish to put into one statute the grounds and methods of appeal both to the Circuit Courts of Appeals and to us. . . . The bill is opposed by Senator Thomas Walsh and Senator Shields on the ground that they do not believe in giving to our Court greater jurisdiction in certiorari. They think they shouldn't give us too much discretionary power. I am sorry they think so, but the truth is that there is no other way by which the docket in our Court can be reduced so that we can manage it. We are now a year and three months behind.[106]

To undercut opposition, Thomas Shelton resorted to an unusual strategy. Reporting on it to the Chief Justice, he wrote:

An earnest effort was made to convince members of the House, particularly the Steering Committee, that this bill was of such a highly technical order that the Bar Association did not feel itself prepared or qualified to act. . . . The Bar Association therefore suggested to the members of Congress to adopt the bill promptly and watch its operation. If any hardships should happen, the Supreme Court would be the first to give notice of it and Congress might feel assured that in such an event it would hear mighty voices of complaint from all over the United States and that was the best way to study the jurisdiction bill and understand it.[107]

On the last day of December 1924 victory seemed certain. "I am looking forward to the New Year with a tremendous interest," Shelton wrote. "It is difficult to understand how the procedural bill and the jurisdiction bill can be defeated. I have before me the signatures of 84 Senators and over 80 per cent of the members of the House." By this time support included forty-six state bar associations, the Conference of Appellate Judges, American law-school deans, and various national, civic, and commercial organizations.

Taft's realistic approach had finally paid off. "The way to get legislation through is to continue to fight at each session and ultimately wear Congress out."[108] "I have been writing letters to a lot of Democrats to interest them in the Supreme Court," he had written in mid-December. In response to Taft's plea, President Coolidge "made a direct invitation to Congress to pass the two bills."[109] The cumulative effect was irresistible.

In February 1924 Thomas Shelton reported that he found no objections of any consequence to the jurisdiction bill.[110] Walsh could not stem the onrushing tide. "We met Walsh, who has always been opposed to the bill," Taft wrote shortly before it passed the Senate, "but for some reason or other he has been friendly. . . ."[111] Said Walsh:

. . . I have been accused of standing in the way of a good many of these proposed statutes that are asked for by the Supreme Court of the United States, and I do not feel like standing alone on the matter.[112]

"We made our preparation with care," Taft gloated, "and it proved to be easier than we supposed."[113] In the final vote, February 13, 1925, Borah and Walsh lined up in support, while Norris, La Follette, and Shields failed to appear. Picturesque Senator J. Thomas Heflin of Alabama cast the lone dissenting vote in a 76-to-1 landslide.[114]

Two major aspects in the Chief Justice's three-pronged program had now been enacted into law. The judicial millennium had not, however, been achieved. Even the "Judges' Bill," as it was called, fell short. Justice Van Devanter had spoken of the goal as "a revision and restatement—a bringing together in a harmonious whole—of the statutes relating to the appellate jurisdiction of the Circuit Court of Appeals and the Supreme Court."[115] This objective, for practical reasons, had not been realized. A complete revision of the whole Judicial Code would have been better, as the Chief Justice said, but such a revision would require a corps of assistants exclusively devoted to it.[116] There was still work to be done.

Not every measure met the generally favorable reception accorded the "Judges' Bill." While President and later as law professor, Taft had been in the vanguard of the drive to empower the Supreme Court to unify Federal rules of procedure in law and equity. In 1910 he had informed Congress: "One great crying need in the United States is cheapening the cost of litigation by simplifying judicial procedure and expediting final judgment."[117]

With almost a hundred different systems of procedure plaguing state and Federal courts, the average litigant, in order to get in and stay in a Federal court, needed the services of an expert "Federal Practitioner." An unwary counsel might even then be submerged in the miasma of writs, pleadings, forms of process, motions, and procedure in civil actions at law. Compounding his difficulty, as well as his client's and ultimately the court's, was the maintenance of the historic separation of civil actions at law and those in equity. Existing rules of procedure, defined or undefined by many different statutes and special acts, had become, as Taft put it, "almost a trap to catch the unwary."[118] No one understood more clearly than he the great benefits to be gained from unifying the various procedures used in the Federal judicial system. Needed was a single form of civil action.[119]

In his testimony before the Senate Judiciary Committee on October 5, 1921, the Chief Justice had eagerly seized an opening created by Senator Cummins to harp on a favorite theme. The Iowa Senator wanted to know whether the bill proposing to shift judges to circuits other than their own might not require greater familiarity with statutes, rules of pleading and practice than most judges were likely to possess. The Chief Justice rose to the Senator's query with alacrity: "I am very strongly of the opinion that there ought to be a law making the practice in the Federal courts a code, including both equity and law." With this refom "you can have one form of action so simple that it does not need any knowledge of the local practice."[120] "We still retain," Taft observed in another forum, "the distinction between suits at law, suits in equity and suits in admiralty. . . . There is no reason why this distinction, so far as actual practice is concerned, should not be wholly abolished, and what are not suits in law, in equity and in admiralty, should not be conducted in the form of one civil action, just as is done in the code states."[121]

Taft made the revision seem easy. "It is not a delegation of great power to the Supreme Court," he explained somewhat defensively. "The Court, in formulating the rules, will of course consult a committee of the Bar and a committee of the trial judges. Congress can lay down the fundamental principles that should govern, and then the Court can fill out the details." Concluding on a deferential note, the Chief Justice observed: "Reforms of this character should begin in Congress and the state legislatures, and I am glad to say that

I think Congress is ready to undertake the reform, if it be clearly outlined."[122]

The task was obviously one for the technically trained lawyer. Legislators had neither the time nor the experience to frame an effective code of Federal procedures.[123] As President Taft had declared, "the best method of improving judicial procedure at law is to empower the Supreme Court to do it through the medium of the rules of the Court, as in equity."[124] A decade later his opinion remained unchanged. He regarded the judicial conference as an admirable vehicle for such reform.[125] "The judges," he reasoned, "are constantly engaged in applying rules of procedure, and they more than anyone else are advised of the defects in an existing code, and with power to amend rules originally adopted by them, they can mold the code as actual work under it shows the necessity."[126]

From the beginning, Congress had committed to the Supreme Court the power and duty of making the rules in equity, in admiralty and in bankruptcy. Said the Chief Justice:

> There would seem to be no reason why, where the more difficult work of uniting legal and equitable remedies in one procedure is to be done, the Supreme Court, or at least a committee of Federal Judges, should not be authorized and directed to do it.[127]

England had pointed to the way. British lawyers had laid down certain general principles and then vested in courts of justice the power to prescribe the details of the procedure. All that is needed, the Chief Justice concluded, "is to vest the same power in the Supreme Court with reference to the rules of the common law and then give that Court the power to blend them into a code, which shall make the procedure the same in all [civil cases] as simple as possible."[128]

In May 1926 the Senate Judiciary Committee unanimously reported Senator Cummins's procedure bill.[129] Chances of passage glowed brightly, only to be clouded by the rumor that Holmes, Brandeis, and McReynolds intended to communicate their doubts to Senator Walsh. Despairing of the bar and the bench as instruments of reform, Holmes thought it futile for the Supreme Court to waste time and energy revising the Federal rules of procedure. The Chief Justice was more optimistic. Admitting the impossibility of attaining perfection, he contended that, with appropriate legislation, some improvement was possible.[130] Taft failed to overcome Holmes's doubts, but, through the intervention of Van Devanter, Sutherland, and Stone, Holmes was persuaded not to send "a letter . . . of opposition to the whole business."[131]

McReynolds was dissuaded from overt protest, less perhaps by Taft's entreaties than by his own distaste of being quoted in the *Congressional Record*.[132] Brandeis troubled the Chief Justice profoundly. Taft was uncertain exactly where his colleague stood, but he was quite sure Brandeis was on the wrong side. Rather than deal with him directly, Taft requested the chairman of the Bar Association Committee on Uniform Judicial Procedure to interview him a second time and "press [him] not to send a letter against the bill."[133] Writing Shelton in May, 1928, the Chief Justice was still in the dark about Brandeis: "I don't know what Brandeis's opinion was, or whether he had much of an opinion."[134] With open hostility among the Associates subdued, the Court was ready to present its case to Congress.

In sponsoring this legislation, as in his effort in behalf of other reform measures, the Chief Justice did not minimize the disaffection among his colleagues, nor did he try to ride over them roughshod. At one point in Taft's support of pending legislation designed to relieve congestion, Senator Brandegee interrupted to ask whether the Chief Justice spoke for his colleagues. Taft's reply was scrupulously accurate. "One or two of the Justices have written me favoring it," he replied, "but the Justices of the Supreme Court have not taken any action about it at all, and I would like to disavow assuming any representative character for the Court. I do not appear here in that capacity." Concluding his testimony, Taft repeated: "I would like to emphasize that I speak for myself only and not for my colleagues."[135]

The rules-of-procedure revision Taft advocated never became a reality during his lifetime. Almost singlehandedly, Senator Walsh beat back all attempts to pass it. For him such reform appeared to be part of an insidious plot to concentrate further power in the hands of Federal courts, at the expense of the state courts. Walsh, considered by many one of the most distinguished lawyers in the Senate, argued that under the Judiciary Act of 1789, procedures in district and circuit courts must conform to those prevailing in the state courts. Uniformity of Federal procedures would, of course, wipe out this similarity—so convenient for small-town lawyers whose practice never took them outside their state of residence.[136]

Not only would the proposal enhance the stature of the Federal courts, but the new rules would be written by judges rather than by Congress. Latent jealousy of the traditional power over rulemaking stimulated in some lawmakers the fear that this was the first step in a gigantic offensive against congressional authority. If successful, future raiders like the Chief Justice would use this victory as a precedent for "any delegation of legislative authority to that tribunal, at least any authority to enact rules in relation to the courts, as, for instance, what inferior courts should be constituted, what jurisdiction they shall have, how causes shall be removed from the State to the Federal courts, what salaries the judges shall have. . . ."[137]

With characteristic doggedness the Chief Justice persisted. In calls and letters, he bombarded the Montana Senator with the names of eminent supporters throughout the country. When it became clear that the battle was lost, Taft appealed to Walsh's sense of responsibility. The Chief Justice professed to be "constantly grateful" that the opposition rested "in such capable and trustworthy hands." Despairing of all success, he wrote:

I do not believe that there exists one who could have controlled the destiny of this sacred legislation as you have been able to do. By and by, . . . I shall have but one criticism of your course . . . I believe . . . that the spirit of representative government has been violated. . . . The will of the majority has been violated.[138]

Walsh's cries of "Wolf" did not go unnoticed. When, in 1928, Charles P. Taft, then chairman of the American Bar Association's Committee on Jurisprudence and Law Reform, went before a subcommittee of the Senate Judiciary Committee to advocate passage of a Federal Declaratory Judgment Act, Senator William H. King of Utah warned him to delete the provision enabling the Supreme Court to adopt rules for the enforcement of the act.[139] Its inclusion might serve to "excite opposition to the bill, because I think there are a number of Senators who may oppose this bill because of their opposition to the theory and proposition of giving to the Supreme Court the right to provide rules with respect to procedure in common-law actions."[140]

Nothing could allay the lawmakers' suspicion of judicial aggrandizement. The Chief Justice's impassioned plea that the grant of the authority he desired was "not a delegation of great power to the Supreme Court" echoed through empty corridors.[141]

It was cruel fate. On no other reform had Taft worked so long or so persistently. During his Presidency a commission had been appointed to revise the procedures in the United States courts.[142] In aid of this enterprise he and Judge Lurton spent the summer of 1922 in England studying the British system. The changes recommended in equity rules were based largely on the information they assembled.[143] Nothing specific was accomplished. After leaving the White House, he gave the weight of his influence to the American Bar Association's program for reforming the Federal rules of procedure. On its behalf, he had appeared, February 27, 1914, before the Judiciary Committee of the House of Representatives. Not until 1934 did Congress authorize the changes Taft had so long advocated.[144] When, in 1938, the Federal Rules of Procedure Act became law, Chief Justice Hughes noted that Justice Brandeis was still in dissent. "I am requested to state," the Chief Justice wrote, "that Mr. Justice Brandeis does not approve of the adoption of the rules."[145]

Despite this failure, Chief Justice Taft's place in history as a judicial reformer is firmly established. One of his harshest critics, at the time of his appointment, accords him rank next to Oliver Ellsworth, who originally devised the judicial system.[146] For Taft, administration was the key to effective law enforcement. Yet none of his predecessors had assumed such a large responsibility for the functioning of the Federal judiciary. William Howard Taft brought to the Chief Justiceship an almost majestic conception of its prerogatives, duties, and responsibilities. Without awaiting directives either from the profession or from Congress, he seized the initiative. Effective "teamwork" through vigorous application of the "executive principle" was his motto.

CHAPTER V

LOBBYIST

PIERCING THE legislative barrier is not easy for a Chief Justice, even for one like Taft, uninhibited by the traditional proprieties. In overcoming his theoretical isolation from partisan politics, he utilized and exploited an intricate web of vast personal relations. With the skill of a legislative draftsman he combined the qualities of a lobbyist, keeping tabs on his measures at every stage. When the Supreme Court Jurisdiction Bill[1] and the Federal Uniform Procedure Bill[2] began to bog down, the Chief inquired of Thomas Shelton anxiously: "What is the situation with respect to Cummins and his procedure and jurisdiction bills?"[3] Retention of these measures in committee could not be explained.[4] Worse still was the news that Senator Walsh was "waging relentless war against them in every manner in his power."[5] Needed was more pressure, not less.

The chairmen of the House and Senate Judiciary Committees were special targets,[6] but non-committee members were also alerted. When the "Judges' Bill" reached the floor, a typical reminder went out to Senator Royal S. Copeland of New York: "For two years our court has been very anxious to secure the passage of a bill to give us greater power of certiorari. . . . I hope that when the question comes up you will give attention to it."[7] The Chief Justice attended hearings, and lobbied on Capitol Hill.[8]

Conceiving of himself as guardian of the entire Federal judiciary, he promoted beneficial legislation concerning the lower courts. In 1921, Harry Daugherty recommended that Congress create nine additional judgeships. The Chief Justice engaged in various backstage manipulations to obtain twice that number. By requesting a modest addition Daugherty had hoped that intense partisan feelings, which had wrecked similar proposals during Wilson's administration, could be averted. Taking his own soundings, Taft learned from Senator Kellogg of "a disposition to put a new judge in every district."[9] "This," Taft bluntly told the wavering Attorney General, "would seem to indicate that now is the time to get additional judges. . . ."[10]

Daugherty was doubtful: "I am a little afraid that we cannot get it through."[11] But he was ultimately convinced.

Taft's strategy won. A week later, the chairman of the Senate Judiciary Committee introduced S. 2433 providing for eighteen district judges at large. Working closely with aging Knute Nelson, Chairman of the Senate Judiciary Committee, Taft advised Daugherty to change the eighteen-judges bill in conformity with suggestions made by the Chief Justice's strong supporter, Circuit Judge Arthur C. Denison of Michigan.[12] Nelson readily acquiesced. Thanks to the former President's tireless efforts, the essential form of the measure was fixed by the fall of 1921. During the remainder of that year and the following spring all attempts to alter its contents were blocked.[13] By mid-September 1922 a bill providing for twenty-four new judges, a judicial conference, and the all-important power of assignment bore President Harding's signature.

Taft's intervention in the legislative process provoked varied reactions. Many Federal judges, scattered in the far corners of the nation, considered him omnipotent. One judge, desiring a change in the proposed measure to permit assignment of judges, wrote him "knowing that your counsel and advice will have great weight, and in the hope that you may find it possible to suggest that the bill be amended."[14] Taft's name, in support of the bill authorizing transfer of district judges from one district and circuit to another, sufficed to win Representative William D. Boies's support:

"If we had no other information," the Iowa Congressman told the House, "it seems to me that those gentlemen are of such high character that we could without much alarm follow their advice and suggestion."[15] When Taft conveyed to Congressman George S. Graham of Pennsylvania, Chairman of the House Judiciary Committee, his thanks for support of the "Judges' Bill," the Congressman replied: "Not only because of my personal regard but because of the value I place upon any suggestion that you may make, I would be very much influenced by any request emanating from you."[16] With good reason Taft could tell the Chicago Bar Association that

> Congress has shown itself in the past quite willing to follow suggestions with reference to [changes in the Supreme Court's jurisdiction] as may enable it to keep up with its work, and I hope that we shall find Congress in the same attitude of mind when this bill is perfected and introduced.[17]

Not all legislators encouraged his promotional activities. But when critics pointed an accusing finger at the Chief Justice, others promptly came to his defense. Senator Shields objected heatedly to the way Taft pressured G.O.P. Senator Shortridge of California outside the committee room. To this charge the California Senator responded: "It so happens that he did not, but it would have been very proper for him to have done so."[18] "Every man has his own conception of judicial propriety," Shields mused.[19]

By 1926 Taft's influence with legislators seemed presumptuous. Following the annual judicial conference, the Chief Justice, presenting its recommendations to Congress, "simply called the chairman and the ranking member of each Judiciary Committee in to ask them to take up the subject and see if there could not be some plan devised."[20] One Congressman criticized the Chief Justice's interference in the legislative process. But Congressman Graham brushed all objections aside, declaring: ". . . perhaps ethically the gentleman is correct, and I am not going to dispute that proposition. . . ."[21]

Earlier, Taft had been more sensitive to resentment and took steps to allay it. At the hearings on the bills he sponsored, Justice Van Devanter assured Senators that no member of the Supreme Court had ever harbored any "wish to step into the legislative field or . . . presume to suggest a course of legislation.[22] . . . We want the Committee to feel that we merely wish to help, if we can, and that we have no disposition to press any legislation or any particular form of legislation."[23]

Congressional hearings on his legislative proposals were, of course, crucial. "Teamwork" was as important here as in the judicial process. Opposition among his associates had to be appeased, and a united front presented. But Taft did not pretend the measures he promoted enjoyed the Court's full endorsement.[24] Brandeis had misgivings about the sweeping Supreme Court jurisdiction bill, querying whether it might "not be desirable to introduce a bill lopping off some odds and ends of jurisdiction. . . ."[25] A limited approach, he thought, might avert frontal congressional opposition. Taft, on the other hand, favored an all-or-nothing policy. Compromise, he realized, might ultimately be necessary. Meanwhile, the Sixty-eighth Congress had to be organized and the membership of the Judiciary Committees determined. Not until he had conferred with the chairmen of both the House and Senate Committees should any thought be given to "piecemeal bills."[26] A year later the Chief Justice confessed to the House Judiciary Committee:

> There may be one member—I do not think there are more—who is doubtful about it or, I should say, doubtful as to its efficacy; but he said to me that I could say the whole court were in favor of the bill.[27]

After passage of the "Judges' Bill," the elated Chief Justice gloated: "We have been three years at work on this and it represents really a great effort. Brandeis was reluctant, but we ran over him."[28]

The Chief Justice's appearance at the hearings was not always welcome. After one hearing, he reported: "My old friends Borah and Norris and La Follette [not a member of the Judiciary Committee] and Shields—and others turn up against whatever I desire." He was never sure of the reasons for their opposition, whether it was because "I wish it that they oppose or because we look at things so differently. I think perhaps there is a trifle of both in their opposition."[29] Senator Walsh, in particular, resented Taft's practice of rendering an opinion on every conceivable topic.[30] Walsh had suggested that separate Federal police courts be created in order to relieve district court congestion. The Chief Justice objected, arguing that the effect might be to lower the prestige of the entire Federal judicial system. "The matter was dismissed," Walsh complained, "with such contumely by the Chief Justice and the committee that I did not press it."[31] Yet the more Taft reflected on its merits, the more acceptable the Senator's idea became. Three years later Taft himself recommended a similar plan to the chairman of the Senate Judiciary Committee.[32]

Some of the Chief Justice's troubles were of his own creation. Speaking in 1921 before the Judiciary Section of the American Bar Association, he bitterly attacked failure to provide a judge for the Middle District of Tennessee, contending that it was due to a "fear that if the bill went through, one faction or one party would be successful in securing an appointment of its candidate."[33] Two months later, the Chief Justice appeared before the Senate Judiciary Committee to advocate the creation of a judicial conference. Inferring from Taft's pronouncements that he had been judged derelict in his duty, Senator Shields accused the Chief Justice of falling into a "political error." Not only had the speech been used against him in the Democratic primary, but the Senator contended it was wholly false.

Thrown off balance, the Chief Justice replied: "You do not mean to say that I had you in mind?" Hesitating for a moment, Shields answered: "Oh no, but that is the fact." Beating a hasty retreat, the Chief Justice remarked jovially: ". . . my interest in that part of Tennessee is in the Republican party."[34] A burst of laughter ended this partisan wrangle.

Ended but not forgotten. In a private letter, Taft criticized Shields for his "evasion and obstruction to the creation of a new judge in Middle Tennessee, . . . so badly needed there, because he did not want a Republican appointed. . . ."[35] The Tennessean did not have a short memory either. On the Senate floor, he questioned:

> whether or not it was proper for the Chief Justice of the Supreme Court of the United States to appear before a committee of the judiciary and advocate a bill to give him very great and unprecedented power over the judiciary of the United States. . . .[36]

Shields's attack struck at the very core of Taft's lobbying activities. He knew, moreover, that such charges might jeopardize his entire legislative program. "I have some more legislation I am pressing," he noted cautiously, "and expect to clash again with the obstructionists of the Judiciary Committee of the Senate. . . ."[37] Later on, when the chairman of the Senate Judiciary Committee recommended a secondary role at the hearing on the "Judges' Bill" and the procedure bill, Taft readily acquiesced.[38] Thereafter, George Sutherland, James McReynolds, and Willis Van Devanter presented the Court's case. Sutherland, a former president of the Bar Association, had long supported legislation to unify Federal rules of procedure. As a Utah Senator, moreover, he had been a respected member of the "club" as well as of the Senate Judiciary Committee. McReynolds, Wilson's Attorney General and a Democrat from Tennessee, would, Taft thought, deflect opposition from the Democrats, and especially from Senator Shields.

Formal responsibility for pleading the Court's case for the

"Judges' Bill" lay with Justice Van Devanter, "one of the most forcible of our Court and most learned on questions of jurisdiction."[39] Even when not in evidence, however, the driving force was the Chief Justice himself. Four days before Van Devanter's scheduled appearance at the Judiciary Committee, Taft briefed his "chancellor" in detail, with the reminder that "Senator Cummins is anxious that you should present the argument as fully as possible."[40]

A similarly circumspect selection of personnel characterized Taft's campaign for improved Federal court libraries. Circuit Court and District Court library facilities were a glaring example of "outrageous" neglect.[41] In 1926, an opportunity arose to purchase the Boston Bar Association law library. Instead of going alone before a subcommittee of the House Appropriations Committee, Taft invited Holmes and Brandeis to join him. Both were from the Bay State, and the First Circuit was assigned to Holmes. The Chief Justice hoped "that with such big guns from Massachusetts, we can impress the Committee with the importance of this comparatively small item."[42] The Chief Justice's strategy paid off; the second deficiency bill for the fiscal year 1926 included the full $20,000 asked for.[43]

Uninhibited by the Supreme Court's tradition of isolation, the Chief Justice occasionally communicated directly with newspaper editors. Press support was enlisted in 1928, when Senator Norris, once again "off the reservation," campaigned vigorously for the withdrawal from Federal courts jurisdiction of diversity-of-citizenship cases.[44] Such a reform, Norris believed, would assist impoverished farmers hailed into Federal courts by wealthy out-of-state corporations. Taft was adamantly opposed. Six years before, he had told a meeting of the American Bar Association that "no single element in our governmental system has done so much to secure capital for the legitimate development of enterprise throughout the West and South as the existence of Federal courts there, with a jurisdiction to hear diverse-citizenship cases."[45] He had often accused "Brother Norris" of seeking to destroy the Federal courts. It looked now as if the Senator might succeed. The measure had slipped out of the Judiciary Committee without dissent and reached the floor without discussion. Much alarmed, the Chief Justice notified Casper Yost, editor of the St. Louis *Globe-Democrat,* of approval in Congress of "the most radical bill that has been introduced in either House. . . ."[46]

The Chief Justice himself could not declare war on the proposal, but, he told the editor, "you can, and I invoke your influence in maintaining the protective power which citizens may secure from the Federal judiciary in defense of their rights."[47] Responding favorably, Yost published two editorials "very much in point."[48] Through Henry Taft, the Chief Justice tried to secure other newspaper support: "I think it ought to be called to the attention of the *Times* and of the *Tribune.* I think you ought to go to the New York *Times* and to the *Tribune* and explain the effect of the bill and have editorials printed on the subject. . . . Opposition to it ought to be made a plank in the National Republican platform."[49] Two weeks later the first of two editorials on Norris's bill appeared in the *Times.*[50]

The Chief Justice's influence was felt in other areas. An editorial in the *Florida Times-Union* noted "emphatic protests against the bill including that of the Chief Justice of the United States Supreme Court, who is reported to have said that this bill has features that can be regarded only as most undesirable and harmful."[51] These inspired howls of protest, along with other voices of opposition, forced Norris to postpone the proposal indefinitely.

Taft may have realized that this measure could never be enacted. His long-range strategy was to use this merely as an opportunity to inform the lawmakers and the public and thus stave off future assaults. "We ought to make such a showing," he explained, "so as to have it understood that it cannot be undertaken, even in a Democratic administration, without a very profound kick on the subject."[52]

Early in his tenure, Taft had foreseen the likelihood of an all-out war on the Federal judiciary in general and the Supreme Court in particular. "From the attacks made on the Court by the labor unions and by La Follette," he anticipated "active agitation against the Court, and an effort to reduce its functions. . . ."[53] These assaults would "probably last a decade,"[54] but the Chief Justice was confident that "those who advocated depriving the Supreme Court of its power to declare laws unconstitutional would find arrayed against them a conservative strength that in their blatant mouthings they do not realize the existence of."[55] Power within conservative ranks needed only to be "startled into activity."[56]

Among the stabilizing forces in the United States, none was so powerful, so disposed to uphold the Federal courts, or so receptive to appeals from their distinguished former president, as the American Bar Association. Taft had long been a faithful attendant at its annual meetings. "I come," he told the assembled lawyers on one occasion, "just to register the presence of our court and to have you know that we are humbly waiting for your assistance as the body which probably needs that assistance most. . . ."[57] The American Bar Association was central to his reform effort. "I deem this one of the most important extracurriculum things that I have to do as Chief Justice," he said.[58] The Chief Justice was not content merely to put in an appearance. An activist, he spared no effort to enlist the Association's highly effective support.

When Senator Norris's "radical bill" to deprive the Federal courts of diversity jurisdiction reached the Senate floor without a hearing, it was no accident that Senator Copeland of New York berated it so fiercely. Dr. Copeland had been "advised by the attorneys who have spoken to me that the Chief Justice of the Supreme Court feels that the bill is not a good bill in some respects."[59] "We ought to tackle John W.

Davis and Hughes," Taft had written brother Henry.[60] Together, these influential members of the New York bar had "worked on" Copeland, who, taking his cue from them, forced Norris to admit failure to hold hearings because "the class of attorneys who will object to this proposed legislation will be attorneys for railroad companies, insurance companies, and other big corporations whose business takes them into several different States."[61] In the end, the Nebraska Progressive capitulated, agreeing to consider objections.[62] After all, he said, "I do not want to shut anybody off from any proper discussion of the bill."[63] Taft was elated. "I think that Norris has heard a good deal about his proposed changes," he wrote Henry, "and that he does not find them so easy to push through as he thought he would, in view of the agitation you have all stirred up on the subject."[64]

Taft also succeeded in blocking passage of the Caraway bill, designed to take away "the power of the Court in helping the jury to a right conclusion in the way in which it was done at common law."[65] Introduced by Arkansas Senator Thaddeus H. Caraway, this measure would prevent Federal judges from commenting on the testimony of witnesses in civil or criminal trials. Restricting the judge's comments on the weight of the evidence in state courts and the resulting leniency toward criminals was, the Chief Justice thought, "one reason for the demoralizing verdicts which [were] reported to the press."[66] When, in late March, 1924, the measure[67] passed the Senate and came before the House Judiciary Committee, Taft considered it unconstitutional, and said so. The outraged Chief Justice conferred with President Coolidge and furnished him a long statement of his reasons for opposing the Caraway plan. Taft worked closely, as always, with Thomas Shelton of the American Bar Association, urging on him the necessity of having "the various Bar Associations, who will act in this matter, apply to the committee to be heard upon this bill in opposition to it. . . ."[68] Conferring with Wade Ellis, a member of the American Bar

Association's Law Enforcement Committee, the Chief Justice "made him wise to the situation."[69] Following this meeting, Ellis visited Nicholas Longworth, the Republican floor leader. With Longworth, a 1912 Taft supporter, Ellis reached an informal understanding. On Taft's insistence, the floor leader and the Bar Association's spokesman had gotten "the thing fixed so that the bill can not come up until next session."[70]

The Chief Justice not only stimulated the bar's opposition to measures he detested, but encouraged its support for bills he favored.[71] The announcement of a new rules-of-procedure bill was made, shortly after his appointment, to the Judicial Section of the Bar Association. Attorney General Daugherty caused the measure to be introduced in the Senate,[72] but it met its doom in the Senate Judiciary Committee. The next year at the 1922 Bar Association convention, Taft gave a major address, urging the appointment of a presidential commission authorized to prepare and recommend to Congress legislation on uniform procedure.[73] While the bill was pending in the House, the Chief Justice learned that Representative Wells Goodykoontz, of West Virginia, needed a car. Taft graciously put his own limousine and chauffeur at the Congressman's disposal, coupling with it the not too subtle suggestion that the Congressman "get behind" the Bar Association's proposal for a commission to survey practices and procedures in Federal courts. "I hope you will get a report on this bill on Tuesday; then push it through the House. We can assure you a majority in the Senate."[74] Taft was too optimistic; in this instance his *quid pro quo* lobbying failed to achieve the desired result.

In 1926 when the Senate Judiciary Committee favorably reported this long-sought legislation, the majority report noted that "the demand for the enactment of this legislation is of such magnitude as to set a precedent in the history of jurisprudence, if not in legislation. It is the first time in the history of jurisprudence that the organized lawyers and judges have unanimously agreed upon the manner of perfecting the procedure of the courts."[75] Enactment, however, was still far in the future.

Conditions in the Second Circuit in particular needed attention. Located in an area crowded with "speakeasies" and rumrunners, entailing difficult enforcement problems, the Second Circuit Court of Appeals struggled with an incredibly clogged docket. Taft considered the delays "perfectly dreadful" and "a disgrace to the administration of Federal justice."[76] Efforts to assign judges were unavailing, but Taft admonished Circuit Judge Henry Rogers: "We must not be discouraged but continue at the work, and you can count on me to assist you in every way."[77] The Chief Justice, supported by the President and the Attorney General, joined in demanding increase of personnel for the Southern District of New York, but a bill providing for two additional district court judges failed in the House by a slim ten-vote margin.[78] To forestall repetition of this upset, Taft wrote Charles Evans Hughes: "You and my brother Harry, as the President or recent President of the Association of the Bar, and a number of other influential men, should organize a movement to attack the Judiciary Committees of Congress and compel them to pass a bill giving us three new district judges in New York City and money enough to equip three new courts." "It is a desperate situation over there," he urged, "and if you could come over with a heavy delegation—I mean in matter of influence and importance—early in the session of the next Congress, I think we could do something."[79] The Special Committee on Congested Calendars, with Henry Taft as its chairman, suddenly materialized. Two months after the Chief had first called on the bar for support, a report urging more judges in the Second Circuit was on its way to Congress. This time the measure received more friendly consideration in the House. By a comfortable margin the Federal courts in New York received three additional judges.[80]

The most striking example of Taft's effectiveness as a lobbyist was the campaign he waged for a new Supreme Court building. As the Court's administrative head, the Chief Justice allocated quarters to his colleagues and to the Court's staff. Then located in the old Senate chamber, the Court was dependent on that body for release of needed space.

"We do think," Taft told Senator Charles Curtis, of Kansas, in 1923, "you might be willing to keep your Senate committees within space which is reasonable in view of the real needs of the judicial branch of the government. . . . With the very large Senate Office Building," he went on, "you ought to be willing to let the Supreme Court have at least breathing space. The room which you propose to give us is an inside one. It really is not fair. In our conference room the shelves have to be so high that it takes an aeroplane to reach them."[81] Grudgingly accepting a room he did not want, Taft gave warning that he would "continue to protest against the fact that you do not allow the Supreme Court to have space enough for its records."[82] This barrage had the desired effect. "Personally," Curtis conceded, "I am in favor of erecting a new building for the Supreme Court."[83]

Though he had long favored a new building, Taft gave little serious attention to it until 1925, when a Senate bill authorized expenditures of fifty million dollars for new public buildings.[84] Taking advantage of this opportunity, the Chief Justice pressed Senator Reed Smoot, of the Senate Committee on Public Lands and Surveys: ". . . I would like to invoke your attention to and your introduction into the bill of, a provision for the purchase of land and the construction of a building for the sole use of the Supreme Court. . . ."[85] Taft inspired New Hampshire Senator George H. Moses's report that the Court had "expressed themselves . . . very vigorously in the hope that this amendment would be agreed to."[86] The proposal was defeated 50 to 22, thanks largely to the opposition of Smoot and Norris.[87] Since the

Senate appropriations bill conflicted with the House version, it went to conference. There Taft worked on the chairman of the House Public Buildings Committee, who doubled as conference manager of the bill.[88] While the measure was still pending, Taft negotiated at length with members of the House committee.[89] His lobbying was successful. The conference report, issued a week later, called upon the Secretary of the Treasury to acquire a site for the Supreme Court.[90] Both the House and the Senate approved it, and the following week President Coolidge's signature made the measure law.[91]

The next step was to find a suitable site, the legislative hurdle being the Senate Public Lands and Surveys Committee, whose membership included Progressives and Democrats. Undaunted, Taft wrote Senator Moses, requesting him to "stir up" Chairman Smoot "to pass the necessary resolution and institute the proceedings to condemn the lot we wish for the Supreme Court."[92] By 1928 the plot, partly on the site of the old brick capitol, had been purchased; still to be determined was membership of the commission authorized to plan the building. Of crucial importance was the selection of an architect of national reputation.[93] As chairman of the Lincoln Memorial Commission, Taft had taken steps to make certain that the Architect of the Capitol played a secondary role. "That is the way we built the Lincoln Memorial," he pointed out, "and the way, I think, we ought to build this building."[94] This opinion was not shared unanimously. In fact, a measure had already been introduced making the Architect of the Capitol, David Lynn, both a commissioner and executive officer, with authority to select consulting architects and to have custody of the building after its completion. Under this plan the Court would have no supervision over its own building. "I think that was unfair," the Chief Justice complained to Senator Claude A. Swanson of Virginia. "I don't think the Architect of the

Capitol occupies such a position that he ought to be both commissioner and executive officer."[95]

Particularly irritating was the fact that the original bill, drawn, presumably, by someone in the House Appropriations Committee at "the instance of the Architect of the Capitol," had been introduced without the Court's notice.[96] Refusing to allow the Capitol Architect to take over, the Chief Justice, accompanied by Van Devanter, called on Senator Henry W. Keyes of New Hampshire, Chairman of the Senate Committee on Public Buildings and Grounds. The upshot was a request "that we draft a bill making such amendments as we thought ought to be made."[97] Both the amended bill and the original were submitted to the Saturday conference of the Court. Approving the former, the Justices authorized Taft to say that they were "very anxious to have the bill go through as we have recommended it."[98] This flurry of activity got results. As reported two weeks later, the amended bill provided that "the Architect of the Capitol shall serve as executive officer of the Commission and shall perform such services . . . as the commission may direct."[99]

Substantial progress toward enactment was made in December 1928 at a dinner Taft gave for the chairman and ranking member of both the House and the Senate building committees.[100] Shortly thereafter Congressman Richard N. Elliott, a dinner guest, introduced, and the House passed, a bill providing for inclusion on the building commission of two representatives from the Court.[101] President Coolidge signed the measure, making Justice Van Devanter and the Chief Justice members of the building commission,[102] thereby shifting the balance of power in the Court's favor. With Lynn's influence thus diminished, the Chief Justice was able to exercise almost absolute power over the commission, including selection of Cass Gilbert, an architect of national reputation.

Taft's dream of a Supreme Court Building, independent of

the other branches of the government, had not been easily realized. Chief Justices Fuller and White had opposed it. Certain members of Taft's own Court resented a "marble palace" as a regrettable departure from sacred tradition. Unable to understand such opposition, Taft surmised that they were men who "would not really enjoy the amplitude and comfort of such a building. . . ."[103] "They did not," he reflected, "look forward or beyond their own service in the Court or to its needs."[104] "Those of us who have responsibility," he told Senator Charles Curtis of Kansas, "ought to look after the welfare of those who come after us."[105] Throughout 1929, construction plans moved forward at a slow pace. By December, Taft, rapidly failing in health, knew he would never live to see the new Court building started, much less completed. Nevertheless, he resolved "to devote [himself] to lobbying."[106] A week later Congress allocated $9,740,000 for the new Court building. On December 17, 1929, President Hoover affixed his signature to the measure.[107]

The steps taken were irretrievable and could not be changed. "This has been a great week for me," the aging Chief commented ecstatically. "I was really deeply gratified to find how much interest there was in pressing the matter."[108] Two months later Taft was dead. "My prayer is," he had said in 1927, "that I may stay long enough on the Court to see that building constructed. If I do, then I shall have the right to claim that it was my work, for without me it certainly would not have been taken up at this time."[109]

All obstacles had been overcome; the budget-slashing orgies of the Coolidge era, the antagonism of members of the Senate, the misgivings of colleagues, and the lack of widespread popular support for the new building—all these had fallen before the Chief Justice's vigorous lobbying. At the cornerstone ceremony, October 1932, Chief Justice Hughes declared: "For this enterprise now progressing to completion . . . , we are indebted to the late Chief Justice William

Howard Taft more than anyone else. This building is the result of his intelligent persistence."[110]

Taft's lobbying has no precedent in Supreme Court annals. Few of his predecessors were either prepared for or capable of plunging into the shifting congressional tides. Chief Justice White had spurned any suggestion of transgression on the legislative domain. Years of public service had educated Taft in the ways of party politics. After leaving the White House, he canvassed the nation in quest of support for judicial reform. By the time he ascended to the bench, thousands of influential Americans knew that he favored far-reaching correctives. Bringing to the Court a definite program, he launched it within days after his appointment. He drafted legislation, exerted vast influence on individual legislators, pressed his program at congressional hearings, enlisted the support of the American Bar Association members and newspaper editors. By utilizing in various combinations these instruments of power, he got much of what he wanted.

CHAPTER VI

PRESIDENTIAL ADVISER

BECAUSE OF wide interests, ranging from the appointment of district judges in faraway Idaho to protection of the smallest entrepreneur, Chief Justice Taft found it advantageous to establish cordial relations with the President and various members of his official family. He often dealt directly with Presidents Harding, Coolidge, and Hoover. On occasion, however, he achieved better results, or thought he could, by working through executive officers with easy access to the President. Though the Chief Justiceship did not encompass formal policy making, Taft's invaluable experience as a former President not unnaturally made him feel that any White House incumbent would welcome his help. Warren G. Harding clearly needed it, as he himself frankly confessed.

Known as a "lodge orator—a silver tongue," Harding had been chosen in 1912 to nominate President Taft at the Republican National Convention. Yet Harding's nomination as the party's standard bearer in 1920 had generated little enthusiasm. Disappointed with the candidate and the party's weak platform endorsement of the League of Nations, Taft resigned himself, believing that "on the whole, . . . what was done at Chicago is about as good a result as we could have expected. . . ."[1] Misgivings soon accumulated. After the convention, the Republican nominee, surrounded by the Senators who had secured his nomination, promptly returned to Washington. Concerned about the baneful consequences, Taft thought the best thing for Harding was "to get out of Washington and go home to Marion and stay there."[2]

As the pre-election summer wore on, Taft became increasingly apprehensive. "I regret to hear that Harding is surrounded by such influences as you indicate," he wrote Gus Karger, "but a man in his situation needs education and he is going to get it. . . ."[3] Taft, of course, stood ready to help. The best way to begin was at the policy level. Less than two weeks after his appointment as Chief Justice, Taft went with Harry Daugherty to the White House. "The President read us his [war veterans] bonus message for our comment and criticism," the Chief Justice reported. "We induced him to change it some so as not to commit himself to the bonus later when we are in funds."* "I think we improved it," he concluded with satisfaction.[4]

In addition to advising the President on the contents of his public addresses, Taft encouraged Harding to deal aggressively with disruptive elements in the socioeconomic fabric. The summer of 1922 found the nation in the grip of a paralyzing coal and railroad strike. After nonstriking miners had been massacred by a mob at Herrin, Illinois, Harding went before Congress. To spontaneous and prolonged applause, he stated his resolve "to use all the power of the Government to maintain transportation and sustain the right of men to work."[5] "It is fundamental to all freedom," he declared in the best conservative tradition, "that all men have unquestioned rights to lawful pursuits, to work and to live and choose their own lawful ways to happiness. . . . These rights have been denied by assault and violence, by armed lawlessness. If free men cannot toil according to their own lawful choosing, all our constitutional guarantees born of democracy are surrendered to mobocracy. . . ."[6]

Convinced that Harding would stand fast against the bonus and other attacks on business interests, Taft ap-

---

* Taft probably referred to Harding's suggestion that a general sales tax be imposed to provide sufficient funds for the bonus. See "President's Message: Veto of Bonus," *House Journal,* 67th Cong., 2d Sess., p. 605.

plauded the President's message.* "I felicitate you," he wrote, "on the sharp and properly emphatic words in which you called the attention of the country to the tyranny which coal miners and railroad unions claim the right to exercise in choking the people into conceding what terms they choose to exact. . . ."[7] The former Ohio Senator received these communications with warm appreciation. He needed advice and all the support his friends could give him.

Since Harding's unexpected nomination, Taft had been aware of his inherent weaknesses as a leader. Not one to ignore obvious receptiveness to advice, the Chief Justice sought to enlist White House influence on his program for judicial reform. One of the most logical contacts was Solicitor General James M. Beck.[8] Taft, seeking to enlist Beck's support for the Supreme Court's jurisdiction bill, sent him a copy of it. Beck, disagreeing with the Chief Justice's purpose, and having in readiness a bill of his own, merely directed one of his Assistant Solicitors General to review it for errors in drafting. Taft persisted; he wanted the Solicitor General's active participation in support of his own measure and urged him to "press the matter at once, because the Court is very anxious to have me go before the Senate Judiciary Committee and have the bill introduced."[9]

Favor-seeking acquaintances soon began to turn the tables. Taft, like Civil War politician Salmon P. Chase, discovered that even the Chief Justiceship does not insulate a public figure from friends who conclude "that the Chief Justice is a good man through whom to reach others."[10] Taft

---

* He had recently expressed sentiments not unlike Harding's: "Within recent years, a dangerous disposition has been manifested in organized labor to threaten a general strike in a field of activity like transportation, or coal mining, the continuity of which is essential to the life of the country, in order to choke the country and Congress into a compliance with the economic demands of this particular class of labor. This is the selfish and Bolshevistic use of a combination of a minority to compel a majority to yield to its demands. . . ." W. H. Taft, *Representative Government* (New York: New York University Press, 1921), p. 26.

had either to turn aside his friends or else urge them to appeal to those who possessed patronage channels. To one office seeker, he bluntly stated:

> I regret in my present position, I have no patronage and no opportunity to control its exercise. Indeed, the position of the Chief Justice is one that precludes the incumbent from taking part in such matters. For that reason, your appeal to me is not to one who has the power to grant it.[11]

This plea of powerlessness was traditional. Yet Taft, with few offices to distribute, exerted considerable influence on the first Republican administration since his own. Learning that Max Pam, a close friend, aspired to an ambassadorship, the Chief Justice wrote: "I . . . shall be glad to see the President in respect to him. . . ."[12] Charles H. Cottrell, appointed by Taft to a position in the Internal Revenue Bureau, wanted to be Registrar of the Treasury. "That is one of the positions to which I appointed a colored man in Washington," the Chief Justice informed Harding. "I am in accord with your general policy of honoring the colored race in national positions; it seems to me this is an opportunity to appoint a man admirably qualified. . . ."[13]

By 1922 the "Ohio Gang" held sway; they, not the Chief Justice, began to prevail. When Taft's candidate for the Tariff Commission lost out, the President told him: "I am obliged to write you that I have already committed myself concerning this appointment."[14]

The President might turn a deaf ear to him, but Taft could unfailingly depend on Harry Daugherty. Niles Mosely of Mississippi needed a Federal job—the only kind of political office open to a Southern Republican like himself. His father, the former President warmly recalled, had been a "loyal and consistent Republican . . . when it cost something to be a Republican."[15] Transmitting his request to the Attorney General, Taft dulled its edge by assuring Daugherty that he did "not wish to interfere in any way with the patronage of your office. . . ."[16] The next month Mosely became an assistant United States Attorney in Mississippi.

Taft did not hesitate to call at the State Department or to dispatch messages to Secretary Charles Evans Hughes, whom he had elevated to the Supreme Court in 1910. In 1924 the Chief Justice wrote Hughes about a vacancy on the International Joint Commission between the United States and Canada. Taft maintained a summer home at Murray Bay, Quebec; he naturally considered himself in a position to advise. Furthermore, he wanted to see Brigadier General William H. Bixby on the Commission. Conveying this thought to Hughes, Taft confessed to "butting in," but explained, "I have known something of the work of this Board."[17] So did Hughes. He thanked the meddlesome Chief Justice, noted his suggestion, but hedged on the appointment.[18] Bixby never became a member of the Joint Commission.

Nineteen hundred twenty-four was Calvin Coolidge's first full year in office. Slight contact with Harding's Vice-President left Taft with a relatively favorable impression. Taft described the wizened Vermonter as "very self-contained, very simple, very direct, and very shrewd in his observations."[19] But "Coolidge is Coolidge," he confessed, "and he does the pumphandle work without much grace. . . ."[20] Not inclined to complain, Taft confidently predicted that "there will be no great departure from Harding's policies. . . ."[21] Coolidge would adhere to ". . . Mr. Harding's purpose to defend the institutions of the country against wild radicals."[22] To assure himself of the direction of Coolidge's program, Taft called on the President. The conference went well, and Taft came away ". . . very much pleased with his views of things and his attitude."[23] Most consoling was Coolidge's approach to the chronic postwar farm depression.

The President's strategy in dealing with the clamorous Western Senators also met with Taft's approval. "He is letting these gentlemen from the West expound at great length methods by which the price of bread can be put up and the

Treasury opened so as to support people who continue to plant wheat . . . even though the land is hopeless as a source of profitable agriculture."[24] "With approaching and present prosperity," the Chief Justice told Coolidge, "the people wanted to be let alone." They were "confident that with him in the White House, nothing would be done for effect, and quiet would be maintained if there was no reason for affirmative action."[25]

Future conferences with the President brought mixed results. When the Caraway bill, designed to restrict the role of Federal judges in charging juries, threatened to become law, the Chief Justice hastened to the White House.[26] Coolidge proved receptive. "I enlisted the assistance of the President in suppressing the bill," Taft told brother Henry, "because he is very much opposed to it, and I think I could induce him to veto it."[27]

Less successful were the Chief Justice's efforts to put Coolidge behind the movement for higher judicial salaries. Despite Taft's lurid description of the dire financial plight of inferior Federal judges, the frugal Vermonter refused to lend a hand. "The first thing he said to me, showing the trend of his mind," the Chief Justice recounted, "was that an increase from $7,500 to $12,500 [for district judges] was a pretty big jump."[28] On the defensive, Taft argued for such a sharp rise "because Congress had been so contemptible in keeping down the salaries of the district judges."[29] This line made no impression; Taft came away empty-handed. The conference did not, however, represent a total defeat. Coolidge agreed to remain neutral; he would neither balance the budget by vetoing the increase nor "do a great deal to press it through the House."[30] This proved sufficient. Even without White House support, a $2,500 hike in the salaries of hard-pressed district judges passed Congress.

Throughout Coolidge's tenure, Taft maintained continuous correspondence with the President—with steadily diminishing results. A few months after Harding's death, the

New Englander assured Taft that "When your notes come to me, sometimes I put them aside in my desk for my private information, so that I am afraid that they do not get the proper acknowledgment."[31] Undaunted, Taft continued to bring pressure, especially in connection with the President's power "to grant reprieves and pardons for offenses against the United States. . . ." In 1923 he intervened in behalf of Charles L. Craig, Comptroller of the City of New York. Four years before, Craig had published a letter to the Public Service Commissioner, assailing United States District Judge Mayer for refusal to act in several pending receivership cases. Speaking for the Supreme Court, Justice McReynolds upheld the contempt conviction and its stiff sixty-day sentence.[32] The Chief Justice concurred, reasoning that such criticism of judges before adjudication of the case under consideration tended to impair the impartiality of their verdicts.[33] Taft had been annoyed by Craig's failure to appeal the questions of fact and law to the Circuit Courts instead of going to the overburdened Supreme Court with a habeas corpus petition.[34] Both Holmes and Brandeis differed. Dissenting, the former contended that Craig had allegedly misstated only past matters of fact which might belittle Judge Mayer but hardly obstructed justice.[35]

Holmes did not stand alone; within days a storm of protest arose against the verdict. Worried Republican leaders began to press Coolidge to pardon the Comptroller. Even Taft began to entertain doubts. Joining the rising chorus demanding executive clemency, he told the President: "I can't keep my mind off the Craig case."[36] By now Coolidge was also pondering an escape and Taft was eager to assist him. Little more than a week after the Court had acted, he recommended to the Chief Executive an explicit three-point rationale: "You may well base your action first," he advised Coolidge, "on the severity of the sentence in view of the close and doubtful question of fact and law . . . second, on the fact that no reviewing court has had an opportunity to pass on the merits of that question, and third on the fact that execution of the sentence will take the defendant away from his duties as Comptroller two months. . . ."[37] Several days later, Coolidge remitted Craig's jail sentence allegedly on the recommendation of Attorney General Daugherty.[38]

Scarcely had Taft finished advising the President on the intricacies of executive clemency than he was out scouting for potential Cabinet officers. Senator Walsh had launched a vicious attack on Harding's Cabinet. The smell of government-owned oil gushing into Harry F. Sinclair's pipes began to permeate the Navy and Interior Departments, reaching sensitive nostrils on Capitol Hill. With Walsh relentlessly digging up dirt, Interior Secretary Albert Fall vacated his post the year Harding died. Fall was followed in 1924 by a fellow conspirator, Navy Secretary Edwin Denby. Finally Harry Daugherty, implicated in the mounting scandals, departed in humiliation. Taft busily began rounding up replacements. "I have been trying to help the President get an Attorney General and a Secretary of the Navy," he told brother Horace.[39] "The man for the Navy is Fred Delano. . . . the other man for Attorney General is an appointee of mine, George Carpenter, whom I made a judge in 1910."[40]

Even Horace was struck by his brother's brashness. "It seems to me," he reflected, "that you and the President are a good deal closer than most Presidents and Chief Justices."[41] To Taft's chagrin, it became a somewhat one-sided affair. From Columbia Law School came Harlan Fiske Stone instead of George Carpenter to head the shattered Justice Department. The Navy Department had a new Secretary too, but not Fred Delano. The honeymoon was over. By the spring of 1924 Taft's advisory letters reached the President, but they apparently went into his private file—perhaps unread. The White House had to be reached by more subtle means.

Never before had the Chief Justice been more anxious to have his views heard and followed. In April 1924 a pall hung over the once clear political and economic skies. Lining up outside Andrew Mellon's Treasury Building were "class" voters—farmers, veterans, widows, and laborers. In Congress their most vociferous spokesmen, Democrats and insurgent Republicans, were busily hatching plots to wreck the economy. "Utterly reckless" in the matter of expenditure, they would merely "pile up wrath against a day of wrath."[42] A pervading spirit of Progressivism in the halls of Congress accentuated the danger. Coolidge represented the last hope —if only he stood firm in his defense of sound money and basic constitutional principles.

The strongest defense was the presidential veto, which would enable the thrifty President to "stand out in the landscape against these groveling demagogues of both Republicans and Democrats that have no conception of the welfare of the country."[43] Moreover, it would endear him to the commercial interests, then at the zenith of power. "Where all the businessmen of the country are for the candidate of one party," Taft observed with satisfaction, "that candidate has heretofore prevailed."[44] Obtaining their support at the polls in November depended upon negating certain senatorial machinations.

The apprehensive Chief Justice went into action. Andrew Mellon's views carried extraordinary weight with Coolidge; no better "broker" existed in Washington. Consequently, the Chief Justice "wrote quite a letter to the Secretary of the Treasury . . . urging that he induce the President to veto a lot of the bills which threaten to burden the Treasury."[45] Taft's letter embodied a catalogue of specific recommendations, a master outline for pending and potential executive treatment of nonjudicial legislation. The first recommendation dealt with the annual attempt to foist a soldiers' bonus on the taxpayers. Taft's opposition was well known to the President. "I assume, of course," the Chief Justice reminded Mellon, "that Mr. Coolidge will veto the bonus bill."[46] Seventeen days later the measure was returned to Congress—vetoed.

The Bursum bill, a fifty-million-dollar windfall for veterans and widows, "had no more justification than the bonus," Taft protested.[47] He advocated the veto not because the bill was excessively expensive but because "the policy manifested in vetoing it will find a warm response in the heart of all the businessmen in the country in condemning this demoralizing method of largesse for a particular class, at the expense of the rest of the citizens."[48] The Bursum bill had already passed both Houses. Nevertheless, a week after Taft's letter reached Mellon, Coolidge dealt the measure a death blow. "I haven't read anything in public that has given me more satisfaction than the President's veto of the Bursum bill," Taft wrote exultantly.[49]

Then there was the projected $150,000,000 for Post Office employees.[50] The Chief Justice confessed that "they probably deserve the increase, but now the increase ought not to be paid unless special provision, by increasing the receipts of the Post Office Department through an increase in charges, should accompany that increase."[51] In June 1924 the measure was approved by both the House and the Senate only to be killed by President Coolidge's veto.

Taft considered the McNary-Haugen farm-subsidy bill so odious that he summarily dismissed it as "wrong in economic principle, and with a wasteful outlay that can do no good to anybody."[52] Starting out as a wheat-and-corn measure, it was passed, the Chief Justice charged, by "bribing the cotton people and the tobacco people in the South, these crops having been put in as beneficiaries." The President agreed, adding for good measure that it was also unconstitutional.[53] This veto message, one of the few vituperative public documents Coolidge ever wrote, Taft glorified as a "sockdolager."[54]

During the early 1920's, talk of disarmament filled the air. Voluntary reduction of British and American naval power gave Japan hegemony in the Pacific. The real threat, however, arose not from the relative diminution of our own military strength but from the military appropriations necessary to maintain it. These costs had to be reduced before they threatened to hamper budget balancing. Moreover, Taft assured Mellon, "there is not the slightest danger of war with Japan, or that if we went into war we would not be as well prepared for it as Japan without these heavy additional burdens."[55]

". . . I cannot refrain from urging you to urge him to take the most positive steps to veto all these bills," Taft admonished the Secretary.[56] Even Mellon seemed stunned by the Chief Justice's forthrightness. After sleeping on it, Mellon replied: "I appreciate fully that political times are perilous and that it is sometimes difficult to exercise calm and unbiased judgment. I have, however, confidence in the President's courage and political sense."[57] Properly rebuked, the Chief Justice confessed:

> As I look back, I think it was perhaps presumptuous in me to write such a letter to you, but I hope that you and the President will understand that the motive was good, however questionable the propriety.[58]

In 1924 the Chief had called on Mellon and the President to defeat those who sought public moneys from the Treasury. Now the tables were turned. Taft himself pressed for the immediate allocation of funds to purchase a site for the projected Supreme Court Building. The subject was close to the Chief Justice's heart. He wanted realization of his dreams during his own lifetime, not in his successor's. To accelerate the slowly grinding wheels of bureaucracy, he induced Mellon to include the necessary money in a pending Urgent Deficiency Bill.[59] Van Devanter, to whom he made the suggestion, was cool to it for reasons of propriety.[60] Taft, nevertheless, called on the Secretary, "to impress on him the necessity for getting our appropriation into the Urgent Deficiency Bill. . . . I don't know," the Chief Justice concluded, "but I think he will help."[61] Little more than two weeks later President Coolidge transmitted to the Speaker of the House a request for $1,700,000 to acquire a Supreme Court site.[62] Almost exactly two months after the conference, the first Deficiency Appropriation Act for Fiscal Year 1927 passed the Senate where the funds granted the Court were reduced to $1,500,000.[63] Taft's appeal to Mellon, though of dubious propriety, had culminated in a resounding success.

Other contacts with administration officials were more closely related to Supreme Court litigation—theoretically Taft's main function. In 1924 problems relating to oil were a major topic of conversation, and the Chief Justice was hardly less preoccupied with it than other prominent Washingtonians. Under Harding a Court-appointed receiver permitted the drilling and operation of oil wells in the river bed of the Red River. No one was certain who really owned this oil land or even where the interstate boundary lay. Since the Red River was navigable in the drilling area, the government contended the drillers were trespassing on Federal property. After a Boundary Commission had fixed the interstate boundary, Taft realized the validity of the government's argument.

Under the Act of March 4, 1923,[64] only the Secretary of the Interior could grant oil and gas leases for prospecting on Federal land. None had been issued—the oil was being stolen. The wheels turned fast during May 1924. "I am going down to see the President," Taft wrote his brother, "to see if I cannot help him to stop an attempt to steal some oil land away from the United States and avoid what might easily prove to be a scandal."[65] Taft's conference with the President was inconclusive. The executive branch needed more persuasion and the man to exert it was Attorney General Stone. "The Court," Taft told him, "feels a good deal of anxiety with reference to having the situation clearly understood by the President, Secretary of the Interior, and yourself as to the conditions that obtain in the oil wells to be turned over by the Receiver to the Secretary of the Interior."[66] Taft wanted fast action to stop the oil theft, and he suggested that Stone, together with Interior Secretary Hubert Work and Justice Van Devanter, who was on the case, confer with the Receiver and his counsel to agree on the details.[67] Meanwhile, the Chief Justice wrote memoranda designed to prod Van Devanter into writing an opinion directing the Receiver to surrender the wells.[68] Spurred by Taft, both members of the executive branch and Justice Van Devanter stepped up their efforts to resolve the minor conflicts. Finally, early in June 1924, Van Devanter came out with his decision calling upon the Receiver to turn his wells over to the Interior Department not later than June 30, 1924.[69]

Other interests took the Chief Justice to the War and State Departments. One was the selection of high ranking officials in the Philippine Islands. Once the governor general there, Taft retained an abiding interest in the Islands. During the Coolidge administration, Governor General Leonard Wood died. The Chief Justice, at the President's invitation, attended a meeting to discuss Wood's replacement—Henry L. Stimson.[70] In 1921, Secretary of War John W. Weeks solicited Taft's opinion on several candidates for Chief Justice of the Philippine Supreme Court.[71] Taft declared that he had "no hesitation in saying that the best man for Chief Justice out there . . . is Gregorio Araneta."[72] But Manuel Araullo, not Araneta, ascended to the Philippine bench.

Nevertheless, Taft kept trying. Governor General Henry L. Stimson vacated his Philippine post in 1929 to join Hoover's Cabinet. With the support of Taft, Hughes, and Root, the President-elect had selected Stimson to become Secretary of State.[73] His arrival in Washington was eagerly awaited; the Chief Justice had very definite ideas about Stimson's successor in the Philippines.[74] Eugene A. Gilmore had been Vice-Governor of the Islands for seven years, and

Taft wanted to see him in Malacanan Palace. Taft had previously pressed Gilmore on Stimson as "a very acceptable Judge of the Court of Customs Appeals.[75] . . . It may be," Taft wrote Stimson suggestively, "that I have a weakness for awarding those men who have cut loose from this country and broken up their relations here in order to serve the country in Manila and the Islands. I have a feeling that you share in that sentiment. . . ."[76] Stimson did concur in this policy, but apparently Hoover did not.[77] To everyone's surprise and to the dismay of many, the President offered the post to Coolidge's Secretary of War Dwight F. Davis.[78]

The Chief Justice dismissed this misguided policy as the kind of thing one could expect from Hoover. While Hoover was head of the Commerce Department, Taft seldom called on him. He was "not communicative, and . . . [had] a capacity for cutting off inquiry if he [did] not wish to be inquired of."[79] But the Chief Justice, at the outset, was not wholly blind to the Commerce Secretary's worth. In 1920 he told brother Horace that though Hoover had no chance of obtaining the Republican nomination, he "would be entirely willing to have him receive it. . . ."[80] After the Harding and Coolidge administrations, the Chief Justice looked more favorably than ever on Hoover's candidacy. "I think," he wrote Horace, "Hoover would make a good President—not a great one, because he lacks experience . . . , but he is a man of force and courage, and that means a great deal, and he has great power of organization."[81] That summer Hoover and Taft's ally Senator Charles Curtis became the Republican nominees.

Never especially intimate with Hoover, Taft took little part in the campaign. As it wore on, however, he learned from Van Devanter that the Republican Negro vote, a heritage of Lincoln and Reconstruction policies, was under heavy pressure from the Democrats.[82] Al Smith and local Democratic organizations were making strenuous efforts to organize Negroes in Ohio, Illinois, Indiana, and Kentucky.[83] "I was a good deal troubled about it," the Chief Justice told Horace, "so, as I had not seen Hoover during the campaign, I thought I would go and see him about it."[84]

At this meeting the Republican standard-bearer inveighed against the practice of Southern Negro politicians blackmailing every Republican administration into giving them Federal offices to sell.[85] "He is," recounted Taft, "intensely interested in his purpose to break up the solid south and to drive the negroes out of Republican politics and he thinks he can do so."[86] Hoover expressed confidence he could win the election even without the Negro vote. He did, temporarily breaking the Democratic grip on the Southern vote. Al Smith took the major share of urban votes, solidified Democratic strength in the cities, and paved the way for the 1932 sweep. This, however, was far in the future and far from Taft's mind. When Taft left the strategy conference with the Republican candidate, he was convinced that ". . . Hoover is one of the strongest men I have known in public life. He will be a great find."[87] After the election and further exposure to the new President, Taft had second thoughts. "My experience with Hoover makes me think that he is a good deal of a dreamer in respect to matters of which he knows nothing, like the judicial machinery of our government," the Chief Justice commented shortly before the inauguration.[88] When the President talked of judicial machinery, that was precisely what he meant—machinery. With a little tinkering, a few replacements, and some lubrication, the apparatus would operate just like any other turbine repaired by a competent engineer.

This narrow concept of the judicial establishment was thoroughly disillusioning. Hoover seemed to be making "a great crusade," Taft commented, "to stiffen everybody in the country . . . to a greater respect for the law and the machinery of law."[89] "I am afraid," the Chief Justice confessed wearily, "that Hoover thinks that he can with his eagerness to compass large results, ignore the smaller ones which are absolutely necessary upon which to build the progress that he anticipates."[90]

Two months later the much-heralded drive on crime was launched. In his inaugural address the new President blasted "disregard and disobedience of law," and called for "reform, reorganization, and strengthening of our whole judicial and enforcement system. . . ."[91]

In this crusade Hoover expected the Supreme Court to play a leading role. At a mid-March, 1929, luncheon with the Chief Justice,[92] the President deplored the difficulty of getting his proposed Commission on Law Observance and Enforcement off the drawing board. "He was . . . very much discouraged because he found so few men at the Bar that sized up with the kind of men whom he intended to put on the Commission."[93]

Though sympathetic, the Chief Justice stopped short of acquiescence in Hoover's desire to raid the Court for qualified personnel. Taft reacted icily to the President's suggestion that a Justice might temporarily withdraw to serve on the Commission. Any Justice who did this, Taft insisted, must retire from the bench. "The Court is a coordinate branch of the Government, and has to function. . . ."[94] A retirement, however, would not seriously affect the flow of decisions, and Taft told Hoover he would never stand in the way of any associate who wished to. He noted "there are two or three men on the Court, very valuable members, who could retire and accept positions on this Commission."[95] Foremost among them was Willis Van Devanter. While his loss to the Court would be great, Taft considered him "admirably equipped to revamp the criminal code of the United States and put it into proper condition."[96] Because of the illness of Van Devanter's wife, the Chief Justice thought there was a good chance he "might look forward with comfort to this way of getting off the Bench. . . ."[97] Unfortunately, Taft suspected that the President would "not value Van Devanter as much as he should."[98]

Brandeis was of retirement age; he was dispensable. "If," Taft suggested to Hoover, "he would take Van Devanter as Chairman and put Brandeis on with him, he would lay the basis for a Commission . . . that would do something."[99] Moreover, Brandeis's resignation would greatly facilitate judicial teamwork. This, however, was not likely to occur. The Associate Justice could not be induced to withdraw, Taft speculated, because of "his anxiety . . . to vindicate certain views as a dissenting member of the Court. . . ."[100]

To Taft's astonishment, the President favored neither Van Devanter nor Brandeis. He wanted former Attorney General Harlan Fiske Stone. The most recent appointee, Stone was nowhere near retirement age, nor was he prepared to retire, and, in Taft's mind, he "did not have the qualities."[101] Yet the President was "daft in respect to the qualities of our youngest member, Stone, because he has known him for a long time. . . ."[102] No amount of argument sufficed. Hoover was distinctly unimpressed by "the necessity of not bending the Court's requirements to his."[103] All during the ensuing weeks he kept hammering at the Chief Justice through Secretary of State Stimson and Attorney General Mitchell.[104] Meanwhile, he scoured the bench and bar for a man to head his commission—all in vain. No one of Stone's stature was available. Though the Court stood solidly behind Taft and Stone in their resolution not to be budged,[105] Hoover persisted. "It seems to me," the President wrote despairingly, "that this is so closely affiliated and so vital to the whole of the future of our judicial system that it would not comprise a precedent in your newly established custom." Taft's unyielding stand had jeopardized the success of a major undertaking. "I now realize," Hoover added, "that I should not have launched and pledged my administration to this venture."[106]

With the Court on his side, Taft refused to call the Justices back into conference to discuss Hoover's plea.[107] The Chief Justice had emerged victorious in the first round; the second was also his. By the middle of the next month, May 1929, he learned of the President's intention to appoint George W. Wickersham Chairman of the Crime Commission.[108] Two weeks before Hoover made it official, Taft applauded the selection of his old Attorney General. "I think," he said, "it is an admirable appointment and that it is far and away the best he could do."[109]

After this trying struggle with Hoover, the Chief Justice realized the insurmountable difficulty of dealing with him on a personal basis. Nor was this the sole reason for faltering rapport. The Chief Justice could talk forever on topics of which he had special knowledge, but Hoover, a nonlawyer, neither could nor would understand. The former Commerce Secretary had, moreover, acquired "his judgments by very curious methods and by resorting to professed Progressives. . . ."[110]

As the spring and summer of 1929 boomed along, Taft brooded over Hoover's "radical" tendencies. Progressives, old and new, clamored for government action. Their raucous voices, rising to a din, pierced the sensitive Chief Justice's ears. To Charles P. Taft II he confided:

> The situation of the Administration is one of quiet hope and just watching the vicious enemies who are praying for interference with business and with everything else. Their chief purpose is to do something that will hurt the rest of the country, especially that part of the country that does nothing but work hard, save money and carry on business.[111]

Formerly he had turned to the White House when political storms threatened. Never before had impending disaster been more obvious, nor had his power to affect its onrush ever been so weak. Once he had advised President Coolidge to follow a negative policy, and later he had influenced executive decisions through Secretary Mellon.

Now, a dying man, he poured out his recommendations to Colonel Isaac Ullman, a corset manufacturer and Republican boss of New Haven: "The only real hope we have is the 'Do Nothing' policy . . . for with the 'Do Nothing' policy the insurgents can literally do nothing. . . ."[112]

CHAPTER VII

PACKING THE COURT

PROBABLY NO MAN ever had as much influence on the choice of judicial personnel" as William Howard Taft. On the Circuit Court he demonstrated "unflagging interest in the selection of judges,"[1] strongly supporting those he favored and outspokenly opposing those he considered disqualified. As Secretary of War, his advice was freely given and often followed. From his first month in the White House he gave close attention to judicial personnel.

"The Judiciary has fallen into a very low state in this country," President Taft had told Military Aide Archie Butt early in his administration, "and I'll be damned if I put any man on the bench of whose character and ability there is the least doubt."[2] By 1910 the divisive Progressive issue within his own party had crystallized. As his political power waned, he cast about for ways of keeping his own principles firmly entrenched. Like outgoing President John Adams, who more than a century earlier anticipated Democratic-Republican dominance in which only the judiciary might remain in Federalist hands, Taft sought to determine the political persuasion of a majority of Supreme Court Justices. This was at least one thing, he affirmed, that "neither the insurgents nor the active statesman of Oyster Bay, nor any one else could prevent." Conservative principles, not party labels, were his criteria.

"Before the end of my term," the President told his brother, September 18, 1910, "I shall have the appointment of probably a majority of the Supreme Court . . . which in view of the present agitation, in respect to the Constitution, is very important."[3] Whatever the outcome of the 1912 presidential election, he could count on these judicial stalwarts to "preserve the fundamental structure of our government as our fathers gave it to us."[4] Strengthened judicial personnel was one accomplishment as President he could look back on with supreme satisfaction.

"Did you keep up with my appointments to the Federal bench during my term as President?" Taft once asked Josephus Daniels. Wilson's Secretary of the Navy assured him that his selections were greatly appreciated by Southern Democrats. "Yes," Taft commented wryly. "I am sure the Southern people like me. They would do anything except vote for me."[5]

The Chief Justiceship placed Taft in a position to enforce a political philosophy long in the making. This could be achieved, however, only with a Court made up of judges whose minds went along with his own. As Chief Executive he had used his appointing power with notable success, only to have his effort neutralized by President Wilson. "Seeking to break down the guarantees of the Constitution,"[6] Wilson appointed Louis D. Brandeis and John H. Clarke to the Supreme Court. Taft gravely surmised that in voting for Wilson intelligent men did not seem to realize "the catastrophe that will come to this country in having the Supreme Court reorganized by him."[7]

Determined to forestall what loomed before him as national disaster, he spoke out in the 1920 presidential campaign solely to underscore the bearing of the outcome on the ideological complexion of the Supreme Court. The man elected President could and perhaps would determine the future course of the law. No domestic issue in the election exceeded in importance "the maintenance of the Supreme Court as the bulwark to enforce the guaranty that no man shall be deprived of his property without due process of law. . . ."[8]

Taft's burgeoning conservatism stemmed as much from an

a priori theory of society and social change, through slow-moving, eminently safe processes of law, as from an unembarrassed indentification with the acquisitive ethic. Throughout his public career, particularly during the decade of his harassing political experience, and before he had realized his vision of the Apocalypse, the demagogues were making their way into the temple of jurisprudence. Both Congress and the Executive had retreated from their responsibilities. These forces and trends must be counteracted. Of the Clayton Act, he said:

It was passed for political purposes, to satisfy the demands of the leaders of the American Federation of Labor, with the hope of securing the votes of labor organizations. . . . What I object to is the cowardice of representatives who yield their own convictions as to how they ought to vote on such measures in fear of the organized power of unions. . . . What is needed to produce a sobering effect upon the truculent labor leaders, intoxicated with their sense of political power, is political courage on the part of those who seek to represent people in legislative and executive office.[9]

Congressional retreat from common sense was doubly culpable. It goaded laboring-class appetite for still more excessive demands; it played into the hands of Samuel Gompers and his ilk, who knew nothing of the good old Greek norms of moderation and "the golden mean."[10] Lawlessness was further encouraged by the "latitudinarian" jurisprudence of Brandeis and Clarke. Only a merciful God, by withholding from Wilson the chance to appoint more than three Justices (the third being the staunchly conservative James C. McReynolds), had prevented even greater injury to the Court.[11] Sometimes crucial judicial decisions were reached by the alarming 5-to-4 margin.[12]

The situation was urgent. After his White House years and the campaign of 1912, the former President sometimes suspected that he may have lost the chastity of a judicial statesman, while gaining the wisdom of a politician. "I was a judge so long ago," he had told the members of the American

Bar Association in 1916, "and have had so much demoralizing political experience since, I cannot claim the right to occupy the attitude of a judicial officer."[13] Nevertheless, he plunged into the 1920 presidential campaign, and following Senator Warren G. Harding's successful bid for the White House, he resumed his maneuvering for the Court's center chair with the unabashed naïveté of a child campaigning for his Christmas hobbyhorse. Singling out the vital issue, he wrote:

> [Woodrow Wilson] has made three appointments to the Supreme Court. He is understood to be greatly disappointed with the attitude of the first [McReynolds]. . . . The other two [Brandeis and Clarke] represent a new school of constitutional construction, which if allowed to prevail will greatly impair our fundamental law. Four of the incumbent Justices are beyond the retiring age of seventy, and the next President will probably be called upon to appoint their successors.[14]

Control over judicial personnel seemed as crucial now as during his own Presidency. The Supreme Court was not, the Chief Justice said, "in a strong position."[15] Republican victory opened "a possibility of great opportunity for Harding to make the Court staunch and strong."[16] Taft took the oath of office on July 11, 1921. Ten days later, he reported:

> The Attorney General assures me that he expects to talk with me all the time about the selection of judges, and I am very sure from what he says that he is determined to make his administration a memorable one, and one that will be looked upon with approval by the best people.[17]

The Chief Justice let President Harding know promptly that he would be available as presidential adviser. "I presume," he wrote C. D. Hilles suggestively, "I have a legitimate right to possess the President of such information as I think useful, if he desires to receive it."[18] It seemed especially appropriate—and useful—for the President to have his views on candidates coming from the Federal and state courts. "I think such correspondents as these," Taft explained to Harding, "will perhaps be franker with me than they would be with you, because of my intimate relations with them."[19] The President was in complete agreement—at least for a while. "Please be assured that I am very glad to have you convey to me the information which comes to you. I am anxious, of course, to make a thoroughly high-grade and satisfactory nomination."[20]

For a Chief Justice vitally concerned with efficiency and rapid dispatch of judicial business, the mere presence of sluggish colleagues was intolerable. Age alone rendered early replacements inevitable. Justices Day, seventy-three, Pitney, suffering from a nervous breakdown, and Clarke, bored with picayune judicial work and disenchanted with Brandeis, departed gracefully—all in 1922; Justice Joseph McKenna, seventy-nine, continued on until 1925, a cantankerous old man, as obdurate and senile as Judge Robert C. Grier had been fifty years before. Taft complained that McKenna "usually drags in the winter and begins to complain of the work."[21] The Chief Justice thought he should have retired several years before.[22] He was "not a useful member of the Court." McKenna resisted all pressure, believing that Holmes, two years his senior, should go first. Taft was entirely agreeable to Holmes's departure, not on the score of efficiency, but because of the desirability of eliminating a "noisy dissenter."

In the early fall of 1922 the outlook for Holmes's retirement appeared bright. As the October term opened, the Chief Justice noted that Holmes himself was beginning to realize "that his stay on the Bench ought not to be prolonged."[23] During the previous summer the Civil War veteran had undergone a prostate gland operation. "An operation at that age," Taft observed, "has in a great many instances that I have known proved to be merely a suspension of the trouble."[24] Back in judicial harness, however, Holmes exhibited his customary physical and mental vigor. The Chief Justice now had to revise his prognosis. Compared to Mc-

Kenna, Holmes was "vastly more useful" and capable of doing "a great deal more work."[25] Three years later the grand old man was in "fine condition, . . . enjoying the spring, . . . thirsting for more cases," and wishing to take them from other judges in order to help out. Prophetically, Taft remarked: "I told him he would probably live to bury us all."[26] Appointed by President Roosevelt in 1902, Holmes lived until 1935, five years after Taft's death.

During Harding's two years in the White House, the President made, besides Taft, three Supreme Court appointments: George Sutherland, Pierce Butler, and Edward T. Sanford. The Chief Justice's approval varied from enthusiastic support of Sutherland and Butler to acquiescence in the choice of Sanford. While appointments were pending, Taft bombarded President Harding with suggestions and recommendations. The Chief Justice finally found himself on the defensive. ". . . It isn't true," he told Edward Colston on February 1, 1923, "that judicial appointments are submitted to me. I can only make my recommendations known by affirmative and unsolicited action."[27] When newspapermen reported that Harding had surrendered the appointing power, Taft suspected that "the President had grown a little sensitive about constant reports that the matter is in a way delegated to me."[28] But the record contains no hint from Harding that Taft may have overstepped proper bounds. Though this happy state of affairs did not last, for the moment prospects were bright.

As the 1924 presidential elections approached, it seemed certain that friends of the Court would remain in control of the executive branch. Vice-President Calvin Coolidge, having succeeded to the Presidency after Harding's tragic death, headed the Republican ticket. His election, however, was by no means a foregone conclusion. Robert M. La Follette, campaigning under the Progressive banner of a third party, threatened loss of Western Republican votes. La Follette's election seemed highly improbable, but Republicans and Democrats alike were concerned lest the election be thrown into the House of Representatives. The over-all prospects became somewhat less gloomy after the nomination of John W. Davis, a Wall Street lawyer, as the Democratic presidential candidate. For Taft it was "a great comfort to know that if the Democrats succeed we shall have so sound a man, so conservative a man as Davis in the White House. He will never consent to injuring the weight or power of the Court and he would appoint high-class lawyers to the Court should he have the duty of appointing. . . ."[29] With Coolidge's triumphant election, the danger of diabolical Court packing receded.

To win Taft's certification, judicial aspirants had to meet certain requirements. Foremost among these was approved ideological orientation. Principle, not party, was his test. Even as President, Taft deemed it "impossible to be a strict party man and serve the whole country impartially."[30] "Our views are very much alike," he told newly appointed Justice Sutherland, "and it is important that they prevail."[31] Judges Benjamin N. Cardozo and Learned Hand were disqualified, not on grounds of party but because they might be inclined to "herd" with Holmes and Brandeis. Henry L. Stimson, though a Republican, was infected with "Frankfurtism" and might favor "breaking down the Constitution."[32] Membership on the lower Federal courts, though not an absolute qualification, was an advantage. Learning of Harding's opinion that certain candidates for Justice Pitney's place were overage, the former President mused: "It is too bad that when a man has worked for fifteen or twenty years, both on the District and Circuit Bench, and fitted himself to begin high-class work at once with us, he should be prevented from promotion just because the chance to appoint him comes after he has passed the mark of sixty."[33]

Edward T. Sanford, appointed in January 1923, was not the strongest man for the vacancy, but he had "one real advantage," and "a very important one"—his selection represented "recognition of the inferior Federal judiciary."[34] It was good policy to promote lower Federal court judges to the Supreme bench. The prestige of the entire judicial system was thereby advanced.

Above all, it was necessary to have colleagues, with views corresponding to his own, who would join in repelling assaults on the Constitution. "We prefer," he remarked to C. D. Hilles, former Chairman of the Republican National Committee, "to have a loyal member of the Court, and one who thinks more of the attitude of the Court than he does of his own particular record."[35] Constitutional conservatism of his own brand was the only safeguard against "radicals," "progressives," "bolshevists" and "socialists"—all, regardless of party, were equally subversive. The presence of mavericks like McReynolds, "too stiff-necked and too rambunctious," was equally unfortunate. Taft wanted solid conservatives, not fanatics or eccentrics. "I feel as if we ought not to have too many men on the Court who are as reactionary on the subject of the Constitution as McReynolds," he told Elihu Root, "and that we need men who are liberal but who still believe that the cornerstone of our civilization is in the proper maintenance of the guarantees of the Fourteenth Amendment and the Fifth Amendment."[36]

A year after Taft came to the Court, Justice Clarke, enamored of the League of Nations and convinced that judging was a relatively insignificant public service, abruptly retired. For Woodrow Wilson, now in retirement, the news of Clarke's sudden withdrawal was profoundly disquieting. Once again, as in 1916, Wilson saw eye to eye with Taft on at least one point: the ultimate decision on liberal courses of action lay with the Supreme Court. Wilson had tried, with a measure of success, to appoint Justices imbued with progressive principles; Taft was just as determined to hasten resignation or retirement of "destroyers of the Constitution," so as to replace them with Justices of "sound views." The effect of Justice Clarke's resignation on these conflicting ambitions is more complicated than usually supposed. Writing Justice Clarke on September 5, 1922, Wilson solicited an explanation of his seemingly sudden decision to quit the bench.

5th September 1922

MY DEAR FRIEND,

It has deeply grieved me to learn of your retirement from the Supreme Court. I have not the least inclination to criticize the action, because I know that you would have taken it from none but the highest motives. I am only sorry,—deeply sorry. Like thousands of other liberals throughout the country, I have been counting on the influence of you and Justice Brandeis to restrain the Court in some measure from the extreme reactionary course which it seems inclined to follow.

In my few dealings with Mr. Justice Sutherland [appointed Clarke's successor] I have seen no reason to suspect him of either principles or brains, and the substitution is most deplorable.

The most obvious and immediate danger to which we are exposed is that the courts will more and more outrage the common people's sense of justice and cause a revulsion against judicial authority which may seriously disturb the equilibrium of our institutions, and I can see nothing which can save us from this danger if the Supreme Court is to repudiate liberal courses of thought and action. . . .

Replying to the former President on September 9, 1922, Clarke wrote in longhand at great length:

. . . Unless you have much more intimate knowledge of the character of work which a Supreme Judge must do than I had before going to Washington you little realize the amount of grinding, uninteresting, bone labor there is in writing more than half the cases decided by the Supreme Court. Much more than ½ of the cases are of no considerable importance whether considered from the point of view of the principles or of the property involved in them, but, nevertheless, a conscientious judge writing them must master their details with the utmost care. My theory of writing opinions has always been that if clearly stated 9 cases out of 10 will decide themselves,—what the decision should be will emerge from the statement of the facts as certainly as the issues will. In this spirit I wrote always, and a recent re-reading of my more important opinions gives me a modest degree of confidence that they will stand fairly well the test of "the wise years."

I protested often, but in vain, that too many trifling cases were being written, that our strength should be conserved for better things, and that no amount of care could avoid hopeless confusion and conflict in the decisions. It resulted from all this and from court conditions which I cannot describe in writing that for 2 or 3 years the work kept growing more and more irksome to me. Still I suppose I would have continued, uncomfortable though I was, for a few more years had it not been for the death last year of my two sisters, the only near relations I had in the world. This so changed my outlook on life that the prospect of continuing the work became simply insupportable. . . .

Of one, and by no means the least distressing of the conditions I must write in answer to a suggestion in your note.

Judge Brandeis and I were agreeing less and less frequently in the decision of cases involving what we call, for want of a better designation, liberal principles. It is for you to judge which was falling away from the current standards. During the last year in the Hard Wood Anti-Trust Case,* which I wrote, B and Holmes dissented, B writing an opinion. It is one of the most important Anti-Trust cases ever decided by that Court for it involved for the first time there "the open competition plan" which was devised with all the cunning astute lawyers and conservative business men could command to defeat or circumvent the law. It seemed to me and to six others that it was a most flagrant case of law breaking. It may interest you to read the two opinions but in doing so please note that my quotations from the record show my statement of the facts to be scrupulously accurate.

In the last child labor case† I alone dissented. Unfortunately the case was considered and decided when one of my sisters was dying and I could not write a dissenting opinion. I am sure a dissent based on the decisions from the Oleomargarine‡ to the Narcotic Drug cases§ could have been made very convincing.

In a personal injury case involving the doctrine of attractive nuisance the Chief Justice and Justice Day joined in an opinion which I wrote dissenting from the rule that contributory negligence of a

* *American Column & Lumber Co.* v. *United States,* 257 U.S. 377 (1921).
† *Bailey* v. *Drexel Furniture Co.,* 259 U.S. 20 (1922).
‡ *McCray* v. *United States,* 195 U.S. 27 (1904).
§ *United States* v. *Doremus,* 249 U.S. 86 (1919).

trespassing child of tender years barred recovery in a case of flagrant poisoning of the water in a pool in an unfenced common in which two children perished when bathing.* The decision involved overruling two Supreme Court decisions† in order to substitute the mass rule. In a Mail Crane case‡ and in several safety appliance cases we differed.§ You doubtless noted how we differed with respect to the war legislation.

There is much more, but this will suffice to show that in leaving the Court I did not withdraw any support from Judge Brandeis. One or the other of us was shifting or had shifted his standards so that in critical or crucial cases we were seldom in agreement. Our personal relations, of course, continued entirely cordial.

McReynolds as you know is the most reactionary judge on the Court. There were many other things which had better not be set down in black and white which made the situation to me deplorable and harassing to such a degree that I thought myself not called on to sacrifice what of health and strength I may have left in a futile struggle against constantly increasing odds. Sometime I should like to tell you of it all. It was in some respects as disillusioning a chapter as Washington could afford—I am sure I need not say more than this to one who has suffered as you have in the recent past. . . .

Clarke's retirement had afforded President Harding opportunity to reward his braintruster, former Senator George Sutherland of Utah. "He will be one of our kind I think," Taft commented with satisfaction.[37] Noting La Follette's radical forays and the reckless attacks of labor on the Court, the Chief Justice was eager to discuss the situation with his new associate: "You now come into the Court with a general opinion as to the function of the Court similar to my own."[38]

Identity of outlook was absolutely essential. When Justice Day retired, John W. Davis, a prominent Democrat and Solicitor General in President Wilson's administration, was

---

* *United Zinc & Chemical Co.* v. *Britt*, 258 U.S. 268 (1922). Holmes delivered the opinion, in which Brandeis joined.

† *Railroad Co.* v. *Stout*, 17 Wall. 657; *Union Pacific R.R.* v. *McDonald*, 152 U.S. 262.

‡ *Lang* v. *New York Central R.R. Co.*, 255 U.S. 456 (1921).

§ *Southern Pacific Co.* v. *Berkshire Co.*, 254 U.S. 415 (1921).

among the possible appointees who measured up. The political balance on the bench had become heavily weighted on the Republican side and Taft considered appointment of a Democrat advantageous. Davis was "pre-eminently the man."[39] Writing Hilles, the Chief Justice observed: "Were [Harding] to appoint a Democrat and a Democrat of the sound views of Davis, it would please the country very much and would help the Court. . . ."[40]

The other possibility, Pierce Butler of Minnesota, was born in a log farmhouse, the sixth of eight children. Butler had risen to prominence in the best American tradition. A recognized expert in railroad rate litigation, he would do much to counter Brandeis. Moreover, he was a Roman Catholic, and his appointment would help to redress the religious imbalance. Next to Davis, Taft considered him the best qualified candidate.[41] After further soundings, the Chief Justice, realizing the extent of the President's partisan zeal, told Van Devanter: "I fear that Harding can not be induced to appoint a Democrat, though I think it would be a good thing both for the Court and politically."[42] Though strong pressure was brought to secure the Wall Street lawyer's acceptance, including the possibility of promotion to the Chief Justiceship if Taft retired, Davis refused to allow his name to be considered. He could not be persuaded to give up his lucrative law practice for a puny judicial salary of $15,000.

To secure Pierce Butler's appointment as a replacement for Justice Clarke, Taft did more than forward laudatory letters in Butler's behalf. He suggested ways of building up pressure. Unfamiliar with Washington politics, Butler needed an expert guide. "I think you are quite mistaken in supposing that letters do not do any good," the Chief Justice informed Butler. "Personal letters written directly to the President on the subject . . . by people whom the President is likely to know, like the Archbishop of your Diocese, and the head of the University of Minnesota, would be of the utmost value, and the sooner they are sent, the better."[43] Two weeks later he sent Butler detailed instructions, mentioning the names of Senators to whom letters should be sent. Senator Albert B. Cummins was "really the most important man on the Judiciary Committee." Senator Thomas Sterling of South Dakota and several others should be "properly primed." "I can attend to McKinley" (William B., of Illinois), the Chief Justice told Butler reassuringly.[44]

Butler needed all this support in scaling the confirmation hurdle. "The minute your name goes in, if it goes in, you ought to have all your friends . . . center their attention on the Senate, both Republicans and Democrats. . . . I think it is important that you should neglect nothing."[45] La Follette's motion to recommit to the Judiciary Committee fizzled; Butler's nomination was confirmed, 61 to 8.[46] Of his own part in this achievement, the Chief Justice commented modestly: "I recommended him as well as I could to the President, and I think perhaps that had some influence."[47] Others were less grudging. George W. Wickersham, Attorney General under President Taft, wrote: "I congratulate *you* on the President's selection of Pierce Butler for the existing vacancy in your Court."[48]

Butler's appointment was only the beginning. "I have a deep personal interest in the character of the men in that Court," the Chief Justice had written Butler, "because the sharing of the very heavy responsibility here makes the power of each man to pull his weight in the boat of the utmost importance to every other member of the crew."[49] Men like Butler on the Court meant victory for "the Constitution." "I observe that La Follette and Norris are about to attack Butler's nomination," Taft noted in a letter to President Harding. "It is part of the program they are deliberately setting out upon to attack you and the Court and the Constitution. . . . I hope you will feel that the best way to deal with them is to hit them between the eyes by the appointment of staunch friends of the Constitution who will do nothing to sap the pillars of our Government as they have weathered the storm of many assaults and vindicated the wisdom of our ancestors."[50]

Any candidate likely to prove unsympathetic with Taft's "sound" views had to be blocked at all cost. The "subversives" were strong and well organized. "In order to get a good man, and to prevent such influence from being formidable," Taft told Max Pam, "we had to start a barrage in favor of Pierce Butler, who is in every way worthy of our Court."[51] Exhaustive exploration of each candidate's qualifications was essential. Several "lightweights" had competed for Justice Day's place, including Solicitor General James M. Beck, Senator Knute Nelson of Minnesota, Senator Thomas J. Walsh of Montana, Nelson Phillips, former Chief Justice of Texas, and Judge Martin T. Manton of the Second Circuit. None were given serious consideration. "Jim Beck," Taft commented derisively, though wanting in "stamina to justify his appointment to the Bench, . . . will be nosing around." The Chief Justice also turned thumbs down on Manton, "a politician down to the ground, and a most undesirable and undignified appointment. . . ."[52] Phillips was "rather of an indolent mental tendency," one who "would not make more than a mediocre member of our Court."[53] This was all news to the President. "I must say," Harding wrote, "that the only unfavorable [opinions] concerning Judge Phillips have come through confidential expressions to you."[54] But Phillips did not receive the nomination.

Also included among possible appointees were certain "enemies of the Constitution," a radical coterie constantly trying to infiltrate the Court and bolster the Holmes-Brandeis faction. In 1922 Benjamin N. Cardozo, distinguished New York Court of Appeals judge, was mentioned as a possible successor to Justice Pitney. Of the New Yorker Taft wrote: "Cardozo is a Jew and a Democrat. I don't think he would always side with Brandeis, but he is what they call a progressive judge."[55] Judge Learned Hand was also in the running. As President, Taft had appointed him district court judge, and now considered him "of proper age, . . . an able judge and a hard worker. . . ."[56] Nevertheless, Hand's sole venture into politics as a Progressive in 1912 made him suspect. The Chief Justice recalled that "he turned out to be a wild Roosevelt man and a Progressive, and though on the bench, he went into the campaign."[57] Taft was certain that "if promoted to our bench, he would almost certainly herd with Brandeis and be a dissenter. I think it would be risking too much to appoint him."[58] Though a staunch Republican, Cuthbert W. Pound of the New York State Court of Appeals was likewise unacceptable. Recognized for his broad construction of legislative power, Pound had written the first judicial opinion in America upholding workmen's compensation.[59] "I see in a case we have he [Pound] dissented with Cardozo," Taft commented while Pound's name was under consideration. "I am afraid that if we get him into the Court, he may be a bit erratic, and that isn't the kind of man we want."[60] "He is," Taft remarked, "a kind of an off horse, and we need teamwork in our Court."[61]

Throughout Taft's tenure, the threat of "off-horse" ascendancy in the Supreme Court was reduced to the minimum. Close ties with members of the executive branch facilitated the appointment of loyal teammates in the entire Federal judiciary. He might, indeed, have looked back on the appointments made during his Chief Justiceship with almost the same satisfaction he experienced in reflecting on the six he named as President—"almost" because his influence was somewhat less than complete. Sutherland, whom he heartily endorsed, would have been named entirely apart from Taft's influence. He enthusiastically approved the selection of Pierce Butler, though he would have been as well, if not better, pleased with John W. Davis. Only one of Sanford's qualifications—judicial experience—particularly appealed to him. Taft's active intervention was more significant for the candidates whose appointments he discouraged

—among them Cardozo, Hand, and Pound—than for the success he enjoyed in winning acceptance of his favorites. One factor standing in the way of realization of model judicial personnel was money. With more than a trace of irritation, apropos of his failure to lure John W. Davis from Wall Street, he told New York lawyer Charles C. Burlingham, an enthusiastic supporter of "off-horse" candidates, that "it is not so easy to select a judge as you reformers think. . . . If you people in New York were not so eager for money and would be content to live on a reasonable salary . . . you might have some representatives on our bench, but you are all after the almighty dollar. Now put that in your pipe and smoke it."[62]

The weight of Taft's influence on appointments is difficult to assess. It is particularly uncertain as to Harlan Fiske Stone. When Judge McKenna was finally persuaded to retire, in 1925, Taft conferred with President Coolidge on his successor. Stone, then head of the Justice Department, was the man Coolidge wanted. The Attorney General appeared to meet all requirements, save one—judicial experience. "He is just about the right age," Taft observed, "he is a hard worker and a learned lawyer, . . . I like him. He is a straightforward, honest, kindly, judicially tempered man."[63] Yet Coolidge's Cabinet member aroused lurking suspicions: ". . . I am not so confident of his sturdy honesty and hewing to the line," the Chief Justice confided to his son Robert, "and I warned the President about it."[64] Despite these misgivings, Taft "knew his worth as attorney general" and told Coolidge "he was the strongest man that he could secure in New York that was entitled to the place."[65]

Though reluctant to permit Stone's withdrawal from the Justice Department, still recovering from the ministrations of A. Mitchell Palmer and Harry Daugherty, Coolidge appointed Stone. Taft believed that his influence had been strong, even decisive. With satisfaction he boasted: ". . . I rather forced the President into his appointment."[66] President Nicholas Murray Butler of Columbia University also claimed credit. Stone, a college mate of President Coolidge, and a prominent member of his Cabinet, was inclined to minimize both these external influences, believing that "responsibility for my appointment" did not "weigh very heavily on either of them."[67]

Stone's nomination fell under a barrage of criticism from Taft's enemies in the Senate—the insurgent Republicans. Suspicious of the administration's purpose to pack the Court with reactionaries, certain Senators used confirmation debates as an opportunity to air their grievances. In spite of the emotional outbursts of Heflin and Norris, Stone won an easy victory.

As Chief Justice, Taft continued his earlier practice of active participation in the choice of judicial personnel at all levels. It has truthfully been said that he "let no merely technical canon of propriety prevent him from using his influence in what he thought the right direction."[68] President Harding accorded the Chief Justice's views high priority. Through Attorney General Daugherty, in whose province Supreme Court appointments lay, Taft had easy access to the President. Daugherty assured Henry Taft "that he would not approve of anybody for appointment who was not approved by [the Chief Justice]."[69] "I think he also said that the President felt very much that way himself," brother Henry recalled, "but the trouble with the President is that he necessarily does not know the qualities that are essential in a Supreme Court judge."[70] Under President Harding, Chief Justice Taft exercised three rights: "the right to be consulted, the right to encourage, and the right to warn."[71] His actual influence was perhaps less than the flurry of activity might suggest. Under Presidents Coolidge and Hoover, the Chief Justice had only one opportunity to test his strength, enough to indicate that it had declined markedly.

Taft viewed his role as that of impartial adviser, "a kind of trustee or agent to present him the whole picture with respect to every candidate."[72] The Chief Justice could not understand "how I can avoid the impression that I am responsible for the defeat of any candidate who fails of appointment under the conditions. . . ."[73] His reports to the President were objective, he thought, "a full statement as to all the men, so far as I could find out, and . . . their qualifications or disqualifications."[74] Taft claimed he never pushed one candidate at the expense of another.[75] The Chief Justice was impartial in that he did not press the President to nominate any particular individual among several possessing satisfactory judicial and political attributes. John W. Davis and Pierce Butler were eminently qualified and acceptable. Hand and Cardozo could not even pass the qualifying round. By such reasoning Taft justified his role and defended his impartiality.

Taft did not succeed in getting his first choices accepted. His influence was chiefly negative. Suggested is an answer to the question repeatedly raised: Why should Learned Hand, who was to serve with distinction for more than half a century in the Federal judiciary, the man Cardozo identified as "the greatest living American jurist," have been passed over in favor of long-forgotten Edward T. Sanford?

Overpowering concern for judicial personnel was a logical outcome of Taft's political philosophy: belief in the moral basis of a good society, in the natural existence of classes, and in a differentiation of functions among the classes. Capping it all was a final element smacking of Plato—the Supreme Court was like the Nocturnal Council of *The Laws*. One of its functions was to revise the law as situations demanded; but the presumption lay with the greater wisdom of old prescriptions. Adjustment to the new must be undertaken cautiously, with due regard for existing rights, not in automatic response to whatever popular whim may be currently in numerical favor.

Constitutional law, properly conceived, represented a carefully thought-out pattern of regulation for the several classes in society. These could be variously regarded: from the aspect of numerical strength, from that of potential service to the community, or from the aspect of wealth. The function of law was to equalize these disparities so that, among other things, the nonpropertied class was not held in thralldom by its propertied counterparts. The opposite extreme dangerously portended a different theory, the Holmesian philosophy in particular, which saw law as essentially a reflection, almost a barometer, of public opinion. In Taft's eyes this was a danger hardly to be exaggerated. With the numerically dominant working classes now mobilized politically, half cowing the legislature and half encouraged by legislative irresponsibility, only a Court whose members held views in strict accord with his own could save the country from disaster.

Taft regarded 1920 as a year of Armageddon—the very word must have horrified him—quite apart from any personal interest as a party Republican and aspirant to the Chief Justiceship. The "moral uplift" which he had long prescribed for the nation had not been achieved; he was convinced that the increasing bitterness of factional controversy and the decreasing sense of responsibility within the executive and legislative branches made proper constitution of the judicial branch imperative. The threatening posture of organized labor implied an eventual leveling of the existing social and economic strata. By striking at the judiciary, labor hit directly at the buckle which held society together and at the shield which kept it "American." The Court's function is positive and creative. Properly packed, it could weigh and adjust class interests for the good of the whole. He apparently concurred with the views of Judge Martin J. Wade:

I do not agree with the man who believes that when a man goes on the Bench he sinks entirely into obscurity. I do not believe that he should lose interest in public affairs. When I was called to the Bench I did not leave anything behind me except my clients and my politics.

My duties of citizenship . . . have been enlarged instead of diminished.[76]

The Chief Justice made respectable what was heretofore tabooed. He opened the door to the Holy of Holies.[77] In 1920, Taft had identified Supreme Court personnel as the most pressing domestic issue. As Chief Justice, he merely confirmed the Supreme Court for what it was and always had been—a political institution.

CHAPTER VIII

THE LOWER FEDERAL COURTS

JUDGES OFTEN contend that they find the law, but Chief Justice Taft knew that they were quite capable of making some of their own. To ensure evolution of a body of law acceptable to him, he labored valiantly to man the Federal courts with honest and competent judges of "sound views"—those agreeing with his own. In this effort, he had a remarkable and unusual head start. As President, he had appointed almost 30 per cent of the Federal judges, many of them still on the bench.[1] As Chief Justice, he made staffing of the Federal bench a major preoccupation. A "sense of duty," he told his former White House press secretary Charles Hilles, "carried me into the matter."[2]

"What do you hear about candidates in addition to the one whom you recommend?" he anxiously inquired of an informant. "Tell me what Judge Tucker's age is, what his experience has been and what his politics are. . . ."[3] From Federal judges across the country Taft received firsthand reports on various judicial aspirants. Judge Rufus Foster, one of his own appointees, came up from Louisiana to explain the advantage of selecting a Democrat rather than a Republican for a vacant district court judgeship. Taft agreed "there is no competent Republican lawyer and we must appoint a Democrat."[4] But he was wary of becoming embroiled in these Southern appointments. He had scorched his fingers in a hot battle for a North Carolina judgeship and resolved to stay out of that state in the future. "They are so fierce in their candidacies there, it is such a political chase, that I did not wish to become involved further," he declared.[5]

In the appointive process, the Chief Justice has no formal powers. Furthermore, prior to Taft, the Court's titular head had rarely participated in such matters. Taft took a totally different view. Lower judges loyal to him—"team workers"—were necessary for carrying out Supreme Court decisions. After conferring with members of various bar associations and Federal judges, he freely transmitted recommendations to the Attorney General and the President.

Ostensibly the Senate only advises and consents. In reality senatorial preferences virtually determine the appointment of lower Federal court judges, whose jurisdictions coincide with their own. A Senator, balked by an unyielding Chief Executive, can retaliate, imperiling vital administration programs. After his years in the White House, former President Taft knew much about senatorial courtesy.[6] "Presidents come in determined to maintain a high standard of judges," he complained, "but Republican Senators exercise a vicious influence to lower it."[7]

Nothing had distressed him, as President, more than those "heartbreaking experiences . . . in which mediocre or unfit judicial appointments were compelled by the exigencies of politics, or by the requirements of senatorial courtesy. On no other subject did . . . his optimism . . . fail; . . . he was dissatisfied with the present and afraid of the future."[8] After 1921, despite unrelenting effort to remedy "the system," the Senate continued to dictate the selection of judicial incompetents. "Of course we can not have as large a body as the Federal judiciary without having some asses on it," he asserted, "and those who are chiefly responsible for the presence of such men are the Senators and Congressmen, who seek to foist on the judiciary a lot of the unfit candidates and who sometimes succeed."[9] Congress did not make such mistakes by accident either. "You would hardly believe," he told one correspondent, "some of the stories I could tell you about the smallness of members of that body [Senate] in this particular field of Judges. . . ."[10]

Only the most resolute President could withstand senatorial pressure. Executive will to resist appeared a dim prospect during Harding's incumbency. After eight years of Woodrow Wilson, Republican Senators endorsed a presidential candidate responsive to their wishes. Harding, one of their own, did not let them down. Immediately following his inauguration, the President publicly stated he "would look to the Republican Senator or Senators from the State to give final judgment as to the wisdom of appointments." Judges having been nominated by the Senators, Harding disclaimed any responsibility; but he would "hold Republican Senators to account for appointments made by him on their recommendation."[11]

The President's near abdication of executive responsibility destroyed any hope of countering senatorial demands. Foreseeing an unprecedented flood of pressure on Harding, the Chief Justice sprang into action.

"I hope I have established a very pleasant relation with the Attorney-General and with the President," he announced shortly after ascending to the Bench. "The Attorney-General assures me that he expects to talk with me all the time about the selection of judges, and I am very sure, from what he says, that he is determined to make his administration a memorable one. . . .[12]

As it turned out, Daugherty's administration of the Justice Department was unforgettable; its nefarious afterglow lingered a long, long time. Yet Taft had done what he could to make it a success.

Although he sometimes consulted directly with President Harding about the selection of Federal judges, he came to rely primarily on the Attorney General, who conferred with him "a good deal about judicial appointments."[13] In reality the Chief Justice exercised influence bordering on a power of veto. The Attorney General, he asserted, "rarely acts without invoking my assistance in getting at the truth."[14] Taft impressed on Daugherty the Senate's enormous capacity for evil. "It will cost a great deal of effort to resist the rapacious demands of Senators and Congressmen for particular favorites, who are not fitted, many of them, to be judges," the Chief Justice warned. "I urge that you and the President insist that these judges shall be selected not by agreement between political quantities but on their merits."[15]

The Attorney General cherished every word of Taft's advice, less perhaps because of its soundness than because of wide disparity in their strength of character. "He is only too willing to follow suggestions from me," Taft commented. "In other words, I think he wants to do right, and he wants to be told what is right."[16]

Unfortunately, others were also telling the easygoing Attorney General what was right. Meanwhile, a congressional probe conducted by Senator Thomas J. Walsh made things warm for members of the Interior Department and, by implication, for those in the Department of Justice as well. The Chief Justice's low opinion of Walsh inclined him to brush off the oil scandal as a plot of the Democrats and Progressives to discredit the G.O.P. As the guns turned on Daugherty, Taft lamented:

> In spite of all the attacks against Harry . . . he has stood up in the matter of judges and their appointment, which after all is the chief and most responsible thing he had to do, and he has secured, on the whole, against the vicious system of senatorial selection of candidates for political purposes, a good list of judges. But for him, Harding would have made a wreck of it, I fear.[17]

Harding's death marked the end of completely harmonious relations between the Chief Justice and the head of the Justice Department in the matter of judicial appointments. Daugherty remained in Coolidge's Cabinet until March

1924, when the President, under intense pressure, asked him to resign.

Daugherty was succeeded by Harlan Fiske Stone, former Dean of Columbia Law School. The new Attorney General was hardly installed before the Chief Justice set out for his office on Vermont Avenue. Much to his relief, Stone, whom he liked personally, contemplated no radical departures from procedures followed by his unsavory predecessor. "I wanted to have it understood," the Chief Justice told his wife, "that I could write him confidential letters that should be kept on a private file." And Taft added: "He has the same secretary as Daugherty and a very valuable man he is." Nothing seemed really changed; the institutional machinery remained very much intact.[18]

The Chief Justice wasted little time in putting earlier procedures to a test. In late winter 1924, a crisis gripped the Sixth Circuit. Circuit court Judge Loyal E. Knappen had decided to retire and wrote Taft of his intention. Meanwhile, the Chief Justice had learned that Judge Flem D. Sampson, of the Kentucky Supreme Court, was set on succeeding Knappen. Repelled by Sampson's questionable judicial ethics, Taft pleaded with the retiring judge:

> The situation with respect to your successor has unexpectedly become so dangerous that I wonder whether you could bring yourself to delay your resignation for another year until the danger could be averted. . . .[19]

When Knappen turned a deaf ear, Taft pressed him no further. Instead, he requested only that he receive advance notice of the exact date of retirement "so that I can notify the President . . . to prepare himself against doing some things that he ought not to do."[20]

Shortly after Stone's confirmation, the Chief advised the Attorney General to postpone filling the vacancy created by Knappen's retirement until after the November presidential election.[21] Satisfied with Stone's reliability, he labored to expand the contents of Daugherty's old private file by transmitting letters he had received. These, he noted, only confirmed "the verdict that it would be a great misfortune to have the Chief Justice of Kentucky appointed to the Federal bench in the Sixth Circuit."[22] Thanks to this intervention, Sampson did not receive the nomination and Knappen's successor was not named until after the election.

That August a vacancy opened in the Second Circuit Court of Appeals, and Taft once again called upon the Attorney General. "Learned Hand, I think, would probably be the best man to take," the Chief Justice advised. In 1909, the former President had appointed Hand to a United States district judgeship. Recalling that Hand had been a candidate for the New York Court of Appeals on the Progressive ticket, Taft observed: "I was very indignant at him for this because it seems to me that a man who is on the bench should consider himself cloistered from politics." But he concluded: ". . . While I think he made an ass of himself at that time, I believe he . . . would be a very able member of that Court of Appeals."[23] Hand finally received Stone's warm endorsement and the appointment.

In December 1924 a situation in the Ninth Circuit aroused the Chief Justice's thoughtful concern. Eighty-year-old Judge Erskine M. Ross of the Circuit Court of Appeals was senile, partly paralyzed, and wrongheaded. "He does very little work," the Chief Justice complained, "and that work is usually in writing dissenting opinions. He is an obstruction to the bench and therefore ought to be put on the retired list." "You might," Taft told Stone, "bring it to the attention of the President."[24] As Stone himself was soon to be preoccupied with his own promotion to the High Court, this matter had to await action by his successor, John Garibaldi Sargent of Vermont. A full year elapsed before Judge Ross departed from the Western Circuit.

The more Taft dealt with Attorney General Stone, the more enthusiastic he waxed. The former law-school dean exhibited determination to seek out the best possible men for judgeships—an aim dear to the Chief Justice's heart. In December 1924, Charles Hilles, chairman of the Republican National Committee, complained about Stone's endorsement of the appointment of Democrats to judicial posts. Reflecting Taft's own convictions, Attorney General Stone had replied coolly:

> I am deeply desirous of securing the best possible man not only because it is a public duty imposed upon me, but because I believe that thereby the greatest service will be rendered to the country and to the President, and to our [political] organization.[25]

Feeling rebuffed, Hilles recounted his frustrating experience. No sympathy was forthcoming. Instead, the Chief Justice rushed to Stone's defense. "I don't think you do Stone justice," he lectured. "You ought to come and see him and talk with him. I find him very satisfactory. If you would get a strong man for District Judge, you would not have the slightest trouble in getting him through. . . ."[25a]

Stone favored the selection of his Special Assistant, Alfred A. Wheat, because, the Chief Justice contended, "our Court thinks he is so good a man. He has been before us a great deal, and he has been one of the few strong men they have had in the Department."[26] Hilles was squelched, but neither Taft nor Attorney General Stone could counter the constant pressure of Senators on the President.

> The vicious disposition of the Senators to use appointments to the Bench for their own political purposes is a thing that the President needs the utmost courage to resist, and somebody has to keep him advised. The present Attorney General is all right, . . . but the Senators are persistent and gore the President with their unpatriotic attacks.[27]

A bad situation under Stone was destined to become worse, almost hopeless. For the former Attorney General's successor, Coolidge turned to Charles B. Warren, a distinguished Detroit lawyer with large sugar interests, tainted by a scandal going back to 1910. The Progressives were up in arms. When the President stubbornly stood by his man, Taft cited it as evidence that Coolidge "didn't consult enough people . . ." and "often consults the wrong people." The Warren incident was a glaring example. Though "a very agreeable man, . . . a man of acute mind and executive ability," he lacked "the sturdy character of Stone. . . . Warren resorts to evasion and concealed methods."[28]

When the Senate refused to confirm Warren, Coolidge named a legal nonentity and fellow Vermonter, John Sargent. The doors Taft had sought to close against senatorial dictation now swung wide open. The Chief Justice downgraded Sargent as "stupid and slow and utterly lacking in methods which will secure good appointees for the important places that he has to fill upon recommendation to the President."[29] Under Attorney General Sargent, it became "very hard to get politics out of the selection of the judiciary. . . ."[30] Sargent "seems to wish to find . . . what the President would like and then he is in favor of it."[31] "The President," Taft observed, "looks askance at my nonpartisan feeling about judges." "My dear friend, the President," he commented on another occasion, "has not the right conception about the selection of judges. They [Coolidge and Hilles] lower the dignity of the Senate by selecting a man for purely political purposes without the slightest regard for his ability."[32]

By comparison, even the ill-fated Harding-Daugherty regime seemed meritorious. On matters of judicial personnel, Taft and Coolidge were miles apart. Under Harding, Taft could always be sure that the President and the Attorney General would "go to the extent at least of reading what I have to say, with a knowledge of my interest."[33] No longer able to work through an understanding and cooperative Attorney General, Taft appealed directly to the new President.

There was the remarkable case of Senator Selden Spencer, Republican of Missouri, seeking appointment of his former law partner, State Judge Vital Garesche, to a vacant judgeship in the Eastern District of Missouri.[34] Spencer, Taft thought, had "a corrupt or at least a biased interest in securing the appointment so that he can be appointed Receiver or counsel to Receivers of that Court."[35] Armed with newspaper clippings and letters from other Federal judges in Missouri protesting Garesche's appointment, the Chief Justice had appealed to President Harding. "Of course, you have more evidence on the subject than I have," the Chief Justice commented apologetically, "but I venture to think that some people tell me more frankly the situation than perhaps they do you, and I had thought it my duty to bring this matter to your attention."[36]

The President's untimely death precipitated the issue. According to Taft, Senator Spencer "got himself appointed on the committee to attend Harding's funeral in order that he might go out with President Coolidge on his car for the purpose of securing Coolidge's promise to appoint Garesche." But the Chief Justice was in hot pursuit. "By good luck," he declared, "I went on the same car, and before I left Washington was able to put the case to Coolidge in such a way that I think he is convinced."[37]

Both the Republican Senator and the former Republican President were thoroughly indignant over each other's unabashed effort to influence the taciturn President. "Spencer has been most forward in his nudging up close to Coolidge," Taft protested.[38] Gus Karger, after sounding out Spencer, reported that he "is of the stout opinion that you had no right to 'butt in' on the judgeship; and that President Harding, in spite of your protest, would have named Garesche."[39] Taft, however, remained "reasonably sure that Harding would not have appointed Garesche, and that Coolidge [would] not do so."[40]

The wily Chief Justice took no chances. The train from Marion, Ohio, no sooner pulled into Union Station than he was on his way to the New Willard Hotel to see President

Coolidge. There, Taft went to work on the new President, and not without effect. From his remarks Taft "inferred that the situation was not that which Spencer would like to have it understood to be. . . ."[41] Yet the Chief Justice was uneasy. "I don't know that Coolidge will follow my advice," he remarked gloomily.[42] But he was certain that if the President examined Garesche's record, he would "find some facts there that will shake a man who has Massachusetts or Vermont ideals of what a judge should be."[43] Taft's efforts succeeded; Garesche never became a Federal district judge. Instead, after much maneuvering, the post went to Missouri Circuit Court Judge Charles B. Davis, whose credentials seemed unimpeachable.

The Chief Justice had taught Silent Cal a lesson. "He told me," Taft wrote, ". . . that he did not expect to be embarrassed by the attitude of Senators on the subject of judgeships."[44] Tempering his elation was the knowledge that Coolidge proposed to play politics although "he was prepared to draw a rigid line on some subjects and ignore political considerations in matters like judicial appointments. We'll see how he will square to this standard."[45]

Determined to build up in Coolidge the will to ignore senatorial pressure, Taft persisted:

> I hope you will permit me to write you on questions of this sort, where I have any means of information, because of my intense interest in securing a good judiciary, and my earnest desire to help you in your manifold labors where I think I can be of assistance in a field like this one.[46]

Taft's hopes were soon dashed. Early in the following year, he recommended the promotion of the judge for the Northern District of Illinois, George A. Carpenter, to the Seventh Circuit Court of Appeals. This court was weak; "Carpenter's appointment would strengthen it."[47] Instead, Coolidge selected Albert B. Anderson.

By 1925, Taft's star at the White House fell perceptibly.

"The President has not consulted me so much about the judges as he did," he wrote.[48] "I think my constant interest and my attitude of opposition to Senators have tired the appointing power."[49] Coolidge was "a singularly unsatisfactory person with whom to deal in respect to judges. He will remember the recommendations of the Senators, because there is a political bond there, but I doubt if he has in mind anything that I tell him, unless I make it almost a personal matter."[50] Taft fondly recalled "Dear old Harry Daugherty—much as they damned him, he did most excellent work in standing off Senators."[51] Stone, too, brought back happy memories. He "was anxious to know what I knew. . . . "[52] As Coolidge's term drew to an end, Taft felt ignored. "They pay no attention to me at the White House," he complained.[53]

He recognized that his personal influence had dwindled to almost nothing and that other strategy had to be devised. When an important vacancy opened on the Second Circuit Court of Appeals, he organized an oblique assault. His strong endorsement of Augustus Hand was not enough. Charles Evans Hughes was asked to "write a personal letter to President Coolidge, urging him to appoint Gus Hand. . . ."[54] The former Secretary of State immediately complied.[55] Stone, under orders from the Chief Justice, went to see the President.[56] Learning that Hughes had joined the campaign, Taft proclaimed: ". . . we are firing big guns at him."[57] All this to obtain "the kind of a safe judge that is needed on the bench."[58]

Less than a month after this exchange of letters, Coolidge named the eminently qualified Augustus Hand to succeed the distinguished Judge Charles M. Hough. Ecstatic over the result, the Chief Justice wrote Learned Hand: ". . . in our criticism of the selection of judges we must bear in mind that we have succeeded in getting some good ones from Calvin after a while."[59] But his elation was short-lived. Two months later Taft again issued complaints. "It seems now," he moaned, "that we have got to rejoice if we don't have a bad appointment. We can't aspire to good ones."[60] In light of his success, Taft seemed overly pessimistic.

The 1928 election of pseudo-Republican Herbert Hoover to the Presidency evoked mixed feelings. The campaign struggle itself, pitting ". . . all the vicious in the city against the conservative, patriotic, God-fearing people of the country,"[61] had been disheartening. But the Chief Justice was not entirely without hope. After four years of President Coolidge's fellow Vermonter John Garibaldi Sargent in the Justice Department, the Chief Justice could at least look forward to seeing an outstanding legal mind heading that department. Still proud of his own selection of George W. Wickersham as Attorney General, the former President exclaimed: "All the administrations back to mine have been short of a good Attorney General."[62] Stone shone like a gem, but provided only short respite. Both Daugherty before him and Sargent after him proved unequal to formulating a clear-cut policy. Vigorous law enforcement and orderly procedures marked neither of these administrations. The pending appointment was crucial.

In the choice of an Attorney General, Hoover would "do that which will either make or wreck his administration."[63] Moreover, the Chief Justice knew the one man who could make a success of the Justice Department—Pierce Butler's former law partner, William D. Mitchell of Minnesota. Mitchell was a Democrat but, like Pierce Butler, "not enough of a Democrat to hurt."[64] When James Beck retired as Solicitor General in 1925, Taft had strongly endorsed Mitchell as Beck's successor. Mitchell, he had told Attorney General Sargent, would "introduce a reform into that department under you that will make greatly for your comfort and that of the Court."[65] Sargent followed this advice. After Mitchell began to argue for the government, the Supreme Court "could decide cases correctly just on his briefs without looking at anything else. . . ."[66] "He is so accurate, so fair, so strong," Taft remarked enthusiastically. "He is a man of marked executive capacity, and . . . a man with practically no politics."[67]

The Chief Justice lost no time in bringing Mitchell's qualifications to the attention of the President-elect. Hoover remained noncommittal, and Taft feared "he was not disposed to take with the confidence that I think he ought, my recommendations."[68] Nevertheless, two months later, Attorney General Mitchell was hard at work rejuvenating the tattered Justice Department, modernizing the Federal Bureau of Investigation, reorganizing, consolidating, and expanding agencies charged with Prohibition enforcement.

In Mitchell, the Chief Justice found a crusader for a competent Federal judiciary. "Let us hope," he had declared on the eve of Hoover's inauguration, "that the next administration will be convinced that the selection of good judges is one of the most important functions that the Executive has."[69] Later that same year the new Attorney General echoed this sentiment: ". . . the President of the United States has no single function of more vital importance than the nomination and appointment of judges of the Federal courts."[70]

The Chief Justice apparently took little or no part in selecting the initial group of eleven judicial nominees submitted for Senate confirmation. Yet they all met the Chief Justice's standards of "integrity, character, experience, and knowledge of the law, together with wisdom and sound judgment."[71] "The President has made some very good judicial appointments," Taft remarked. "That is because he has had a first-class Attorney General."[72]

Advice from the Supreme Court once more was welcome at the Justice Department. In July 1929 the Chief Justice discovered that Judge Charles Sumner Lobingier, a man who had once attempted to bring a lawsuit against him, was campaigning for a place on the Philippine Supreme Court. Taft lost no time in writing Mitchell: ". . . there are many reasons, including a matter of temperament, . . . and his history, to which I refer you in the War Department, which make it very clear that he ought not to be appointed."[73] Rapport between Attorney General Mitchell and the Chief Justice approached perfection. On October 22, 1929, Mitchell inquired deferentially: "Are there any United States district judges in that circuit [Ninth] that you think have good records entitling them to promotion? I have heard some favorable comment of Judge [William P.] James of Los Angeles." From Taft came the prompt reply:

> I rather think that Judge James of Los Angeles is far and away the best material they have for Circuit Judge on the Coast. They have another difficulty on the west coast—in Washington. Judge [Edward Everett] Cushman used to be a pretty fair Judge, but he has become so timid and so much excited over things that he really seems to lack sanity. If we could get rid of him it would be a great thing. . . .[74]

It was not, however, all clear sailing. As in the past, the Senate forced Hoover and his Attorney General to compromise. When the President again appointed "two or three utterly incompetent Judges," Taft was distraught.[75] ". . . Hoover has yielded to the demands of two Senators in Kansas," he exclaimed. "I am very much disappointed at the Attorney General, upon whom I counted with a great deal of confidence, but he has been overcome by the political situation, and it isn't too much to say that it is a disgraceful surrender."[76] The President himself confessed failure. "With this club," Hoover complained, "the judicial appointments below the Supreme Court had become practically a perquisite of the Senators."[77]

Taft's concern for lower Federal court personnel was but another aspect of his abiding determination to unite and organize the judiciary of the country, not excluding state courts of last resort, into a harmonious system. "I am the head of the judicial branch of government," he proclaimed, and from that vantage point he attempted to "come into touch with the Federal judges of the country so that we may feel more allegiance to a team and do more team work."[78] Congress "had created a hierarchy of courts, not of judges."[79] In various ways, Chief Justice Taft sought to remedy this condition, but, thanks to the narrow limits within which he was forced to operate, only limited success rewarded his effort. Even after much of his legislation had become law, his power continued to be largely informal. Seeking to prod an Oregon district judge into disposing of a patent case pending four years in his court, Taft commented helplessly: "Of course I write this letter with no assumption that I may exercise direct authority over you in the discharge of your duties, but as head of the Federal judiciary I feel I do have to appeal to you, in its interest and in the interest of the public whom it is created to serve, to end this indefinite situation."[80] As his regime neared the end, and with more than a trace of understatement, he commented: "The fate of a Chief Justice in attempting to make District and Circuit Court Judges do what they are not disposed to do is a difficult one."[81]

CHAPTER IX

AT THE HELM

THE OFFICE OF Chief Justice carries scant inherent powers. The Chief Justice manages the docket, presents the cases in conference, and guides the discussion. When in the majority, he assigns the writing of opinions. Whatever influence he exerts in the exercise of these prerogatives rests less on formal authority than on elusive personal characteristics. Charles Evans Hughes, who had served as Associate Justice from 1910 to 1916 and later had been able to observe Taft's role in the Court over a period of seven years, considered the Chief Justice "the most important judicial officer in the world." His actual power, Hughes wrote in 1928, depended upon "the strength of his character and the demonstration of his ability in the intimate relations of the judges." The office affords "special opportunity for leadership."[1]

Certain Chief Justices, notably Harlan Fiske Stone, have held the office in low esteem. Disparaging its duties as janitorial, as "never enlarging the occupant's individual capacity for judicial work," he complained that the office "absorbs time and energies I should like to devote to what I consider more important things."[2] Not so William Howard Taft. At the time of his appointment, it was confidently predicted that certain personal qualifications alone would make him an effective leader. "Mr. Taft has such tact and good humor," the New York *Tribune* editorialized, "and has so unconquerable a spirit of fair play that he is greatly beloved of his fellow citizens." With Taft as moderator it seemed probable that the asperities formerly jarring the "celestial chamber . . . will be softened and not quite so often in the future will the Court divide 5 and 4."[3] Drawing on nearly every conceivable instrument and technique of command, Taft strove earnestly to fulfill this prediction.

ADMINISTRATIVE DETAIL

"Perhaps the main question as to a C.J.," Holmes remarked as Taft's first term began, "is his way of disposing of executive details." The new Chief Justice seemed likely "to take them easily and get through them without friction."[4] The minutiae Stone considered boring and unimportant Taft tackled with great relish. Tasks large and small confronted him. At the outset he had to wrestle with the seemingly trivial job of making William Stansbury acting Clerk of the Court. No statute authorized the appointment. Uncertain of his power, Taft requested advice from his colleagues. Holmes said he did not know enough to advise; Day said only he was for Stansbury.[5] McKenna bluntly told the Chief Justice what his office entailed. Other members of the Court expected him "to attend to the executive business of the Court and not bother them." Taft should realize "the Chief Justiceship was an office distinct from that of the associates in executive control. . . . All . . . the associates recognized . . . that in judicial decisions all were equal, but in management [he] must act and they would all stand by if ever question was made."[6] Reassured, Taft began reorganizing his staff in line with his own personal needs. He was determined to make his loyal secretary, W. W. Mischler, chief assistant, but his predecessor's former law clerk had appropriated the title "Secretary to the Chief Justice." "Now that is not his function," Taft insisted; "by law, it is 'Law Clerk.' . . . Mischler is my Secretary and I intend to appoint him and he will use the title."[7] The necessary legislative changes were made and "Misch" joined the Court's clerical force as Taft's private secretary.

No detail calculated to enhance the Court's independence and prestige was overlooked. Taft urged Congress to increase the compensation of the Clerk. In a lengthy letter to Representative Andrew J. Volstead he argued: ". . . the Clerk's office is not supported in any way by appropriation, but . . . by what comes in by services rendered, from litigants and others having to do with the office." Though stressing the Clerk's expanding responsibilities, Taft's primary motive was to enable the Court to "have large control in respect to the Clerk's office and especially of that part of his expenditure which is made in the confidential printing of opinions of the judges for circulation among them for correction and amendment and approval before delivery." With adequate salary the Court would be able to obtain clerks "who are proof against not infrequent corrupting efforts to secure advance information for sinister purpose."[8]

Taft came to the bench determined to make promptness "a model for the courts of the country." "As many men strive for riches," the *Christian Science Monitor* noted, "Mr. Taft strove for a clear docket."[9] Justice Holmes, continually setting records in disposing of cases, was enthusiastic about the Chief's "way of conducting business."[10] Though conferences for five or six hours at a stretch seemed "a pretty long pull," the eighty-two-year-old Justice hailed Taft's "disinclination to put cases over."[11]

In questions likely to call out attack, Chief Justice White had been a "great procrastinator." Determined to remedy this situation, the new Chief Justice boldly took up the highly controversial Coronado case, holding that labor unions, though unincorporated, are suable in the Federal courts.[12] The case had been argued October 15, 1920, and restored to the docket for reargument January 3, 1922. Taft's opinion for a unanimous Court came down June 5, 1922. "I determined to have the thing decided and gotten out of the way," he told brother Horace.[13]

Never did Taft work harder to speed up the Court's business than at the start of each term. Certain colleagues complained. "It has been a mistake to press things so hard,"

Holmes cautioned. "It wouldn't matter if we disposed of only twenty certioraries a week as far as I can see." Even the young and vigorous Stone felt the Chief Justice's pressure to clear the docket. The struggle to "keep up" entailed strain. "But," the Chief Justice warned, "we are not resigning on that account and we have got to face the music and I don't know anyone better able to do it than you are."[14]

To accelerate the Court's business, Taft suggested the recess be shortened. "We had seventeen weeks last year. I would like to cut them down to twelve. I think we might sit a week or two later in June."[15] To Taft's dismay his colleagues, some "lazy," others "old," demurred. They enjoyed these long recesses.[16]

A combination of factors sometimes frustrated the Chief Justice's attempt to keep everyone abreast. Van Devanter's wife was ill, delaying preparation of his opinions. The slowest member anyway, he produced practically nothing. McReynolds, the Court's problem child, was "always trying to escape work," unfailingly citing Sutherland's breakdown as an excuse for reducing the number of hearings. Holmes's advanced years always made it "easy to argue on that ground that we ought to cut down on the hearings."[17] As the term drew to a close, the Chief Justice was often faced with "a cabal in the Court to try to influence me to reduce work."[18] In 1928 his attempt to prevent his colleagues from decreasing the number of weeks allotted to hearings seemed hopeless. "I am afraid I could not carry a majority of them for the full time allowed."[19]

Yet, Taft's success was remarkable. At the end of the 1922 term the Court "broke all records in the number of cases disposed of by almost 100."[20] Formerly the period between the filing of a suit and the hearing of it had been approximately fifteen months. Now it was reduced to a little less than a year. Success only spurred greater determination "to keep up to the mark."[21] Two years before he stepped down from the center chair, Taft hailed the outcome as "far and away the best showing the Court has made since before the Civil War"; and, he added, "the present conditions are not comparable to those of that time."[22]

Taft sought to speed up disposition of cases not only by appeals to his colleagues, but also by revising the Court's rules. He was incensed by criminals who looked to the Supreme Court as a refuge for delay. "We have determined to have no delays in criminal cases due to our Court," he wrote. "We find that it has been too often the case that a defendant convicted in a state court would get into our Court by some hook or crook of constitutional suggestion, and then that the case would be forgotten and not pressed to our attention by the state officers." Lawyers appearing before Chief Justice White's Court had been unable to tell when a particular case would come up. Under pressure from Taft, the Court "adopted the rule of putting these cases out for hearing just as soon as they are ready."[23] Estimating the amount of business that could be done in a week, he notified the bar of the cases to be taken up. Lawyers would not be kept "hanging around the Court to await the possibility of a run on the docket."[24]

Chief Justice Taft was a zealous economizer. Early in his tenure he cracked down on counsel who were slow to make an additional deposit to cover estimated costs in cases subject to dismissal. The Court rules required that this sum be paid within ninety days from the date of docketing. Chief Justice White never strictly enforced the requirement, because he "was opposed to drastic treatment of such cases."[25] Taft was more rigid. He also led a successful effort to cut the cost of printing the records. Solicitor General James M. Beck complained that the Justice Department had been compelled to pass a number of cases because the Court Clerk had insufficient funds to print the government records.[26] Instead of petitioning Congress for more appropriations, Taft reduced printing costs by "eliminating the unnecessary repetitions and a good deal of formal matter . . . not essential to an understanding of the record."[27] Printing fees were cut from fifteen to ten cents. Three years later Taft, discovering that the Court had made a $12,000 profit, advocated reducing printing costs another 20 per cent—to eight cents. "I am itching," he told Brandeis, "to reduce expenses to the litigants in our Court."[28]

Justice Brandeis, whose longhand draft opinions went directly to the printer and passed through numerous revisions, misconstrued the reasoning behind the economy drive. Aware that his own peculiar methods swelled printing costs, the dissenter assured the Chief Justice of his willingness to pay for corrected proofs running to "more than the traffic will bear. . . . It would not, in the least, embarrass me to pay," Brandeis insisted. "But it would embarrass me to feel that I should curtail corrections."[29] Taft assured his colleague that he need not be "troubled at all at the cost of your cancellations and changes in your opinions. I have been talking the matter over with Van Devanter, and I agree that of all things in our Court the most important thing is to get our opinions right. . . ." In words particularly applicable to Brandeis, he continued: ". . . for some of us, especially those of us who go into subjects with some elaboration, it is necessary that we should have our opinions set up before we are able fully to determine the proper form to give them. . . . I think we would make a great mistake if we allowed the fear of expense to interfere with the necessary procedure in making our opinions what we wish them to be."[30]

In the interest of efficiency the Chief Justice organized his associates into committees. Brandeis's skill in financial matters recommended him for the Committee on Accounts. Accounts reviewed in an organized way would inform the auditors that their work was "subject to our examination and . . . really examined. . . . We can sleep better if these are matters of regular routine."[31] Willis Van Devanter, "more familiar with our rules than anyone on our bench,"[32] headed the Committee on Rules. Many problems arose out of the

Act of February 13, 1925, limiting the Court's obligatory jurisdiction. Van Devanter, McReynolds, and Taft altered the rules to meet the new situations. They also tried to "straighten out a good many inconsistencies and absurdities that have been handed down since the beginning of the Court."[33] Van Devanter carried the heaviest burden. He "drafted the last set of rules himself," Taft commented gratefully in 1927, "and he has had much to do with the legislation that has enabled the Court to reduce the arrears and to catch up with its docket."[34]

The Chief Justice's appointment of committees aroused little opposition. His power, however, was not absolute; it was subject to the approval of his colleagues. In December 1927 the United States circuit judge in Grand Rapids, Michigan, requested the Supreme Court to take up the question of fees for the clerks of the Circuit Court of Appeals. Taft replied that he would try to persuade the Court to appoint a committee "so that you can keep that member stirred up. My impression is that the best man to appoint for this is Stone, because he does things."[35] A majority of the Justices decided this was none of their business. Late in December, Taft informed Judge Arthur C. Denison that "application should be made to the Judiciary Committee of the Senate."[36]

TEAMWORK

Taft brought to the Court a clear image of the Chief Justiceship—the office and its powers. Motivating his tenure was a passion for "teamwork"; it alone would give "weight and solidarity" to judicial decisions. "Massing the Court" was a consuming ambition. To this end, he persuaded by example, frowned on dissents, exploited personal courtesy and charm, maximized the assignment and reassignment powers, relied on the expertise of his associates.

Much depended "on the personal equation."[37] Following Senate confirmation, Taft received a note of congratulations from the Court pessimist, James McReynolds. "There is a hard road ahead of us, but under your wise leadership I like to hope that all will be well."[38] Meetings were more pleasant, thanks not only to the lubricating effects of Taft's personality but also to "the disappearance of men with the habit of some of our older generation, that regarded a difference of opinion as a cockfight and often left a good deal to be desired in point of manners."[39] After the first conference it was apparent that judicial business would be "turned off with less feeling of friction and more rapidly . . . than with his predecessor."[40] "We are very happy with the present Chief," Holmes commented. "He is good-humored, laughs readily, not quite rapidly enough, but keeping things moving pleasantly."[41] On the bench since 1902, Holmes reported in 1925 that "never before . . . have we gotten along with so little jangling and dissension."[42] Taft echoed Holmes's friendliness. "In many ways," the Chief Justice found him "the life of the Court: . . . it is a great comfort to have such a well of pure common law undefiled immediately next [to] one so that one can drink and be sure one is getting the pure article."[43] At long last Taft was in his element. "The truth is," the Chief Justice wrote in 1925, "that in my present life I don't remember that I ever was President."[44]

Taft had long harbored a grudge against Brandeis for his participation in the Ballinger case of 1910. To forestall possible discord, Taft sent a cordial note touching a matter close to the Chief Justice's heart, but not likely to stir disagreement. "I am glad to hear that you are interested in readjusting the machinery of the Federal courts to better the dispatch of business," the letter began.

The mere increase of courts or judges will not suffice. We must have machinery of a quasi-executive character to mass our Judicial force where the congestion is, or is likely to be. We must have teamwork and judges must be under some sort of disciplinary obligation to go where they are most needed. In this way, we shall get more effective work out of each judge and he will be made conscious of observation by someone in authority of the work he is doing. . . .

It seems to me that through a committee of the Chief Justice and the Senior Circuit Judges, a survey of the state of business in federal courts could be made each year and plans adopted to send district judges from one district to another in the same circuit and from one circuit to another, so as to take up slack and utilize it where needed. . . .[45]

Such friendly appeals, brother Horace predicted, would enable the Chief Justice to "take them into camp." "I expect to see you and Brandeis hobnobbing together with the utmost good will. . . . The truth is," Horace reflected, "that, while Brandeis has been on the *New Republic* side, so to call it, in some cases, he has not put radical stump speeches into his opinions or done anything else to make him seem dangerous."[46] The hatchet had apparently been buried. Bubbling with enthusiasm, Taft reported that "Brandeis and I are on most excellent terms and have some sympathetic views in reference to a change in the relations of the Court to the Clerk as to financial matters. He can not be any more cordial to me, than I am to him, so that honors are easy."[47] Reciprocating the Chief Justice's good will, Brandeis reported that things were going "happily in the conference room with Taft. The Judges go home less tired emotionally and less weary physically than in White's day. When we differ we agree to differ without any ill feeling. It's all very friendly."[48]

Brandeis's sophistication contributed greatly to harmony. He recognized that "the great difficulty of all group action . . . is when and what concessions to make."[49] Where fundamentals were not at stake, he would make tactical concessions. During the first term Brandeis submitted an opinion in a labor case which "very much pleased" the Chief Justice, except for "the last 4 or 5 sentences in respect to the growth of the Constitution. I object to those words," Taft informed the man whose confirmation he had strongly opposed in 1916, "because they are certain to be used to support views that I could not subscribe to. . . . Now it is possible—I have felt that way myself sometimes—that these particular sentences constitute the feature of the opinion you most like, and that you don't care to eliminate them. If not, I can write a short concurring opinion, avoiding responsibility for those words."[50] Brandeis wrote back immediately: "I believe strongly in the views expressed in the last five sentences; but I agree with you that they are not necessary and I am perfectly willing to omit them." Concurring in the Chief Justice's drive for unanimity, he added: "I hope you will be able to induce some of our brethren to join us."[51]

"I can't always dissent," Brandeis observed. "I sometimes endorse an opinion with which I do not agree. I acquiesce."[52] An example of cooperative acquiescence is *Board of Trade of City of Chicago* v. *Olsen.*[53] "You will recall," Brandeis wrote, "that I voted the other way and the opinion has not removed my difficulties. Indeed I differ widely from McReynolds concerning the functions and practice of the Trade Court—as you know from the Gratz case.[54] But I have differed from the Court recently on three expressed dissents and concluded that in this case, I had better 'shut up.' "[55]

By the beginning of Taft's second term, Justice Clarke believed that Brandeis, fulfilling brother Horace's prediction, had been taken "into camp." One of the reasons he gave Wilson for resigning was that he and Brandeis "were agreeing less and less frequently in the decision of cases involving . . . liberal principles." Remaining on the Court meant "a futile struggle against increasing odds." Clarke mentioned several cases, and there are several others he might have cited.* What Clarke may or may not have known was that

* *Milwaukee Pub. Co.* v. *Burleson,* 255 U. S. 407 (1921). Clarke delivered the opinion of the Court; Holmes and Brandeis dissented. *Frey & Son* v. *Cudahy Packing Co.,* 256 U.S. 208 (1921). Justice McReynolds, joined by Brandeis, delivered the opinion of the Court; Justice Pitney, joined by Day

continued on page 202

Brandeis, in yielding to Taft, may have been playing a waiting game. Moved no doubt by strategic considerations, Taft also made concessions. It seems highly unlikely, as his letter to Wilson suggests, that Clarke would have been willing to sacrifice principle on the altar of strategy, whether the run be long or short. After listing certain cases in which he and Brandeis had disagreed, Clarke concluded: "There is much more, but this will suffice to show that in leaving the Court I did not withdraw any support from Judge Brandeis. One or the other of us was shifting or had shifted his standards so that in critical or crucial cases we were seldom in agreement." In Clarke's eyes, the Chief Justice's ambition to "mass the Court" was extraordinarily successful. Some of Brandeis's carefully prepared unpublished opinions are a tribute to Taft.[55a]

Taft persuaded by example as well as by precept. During the early part of his tenure especially, he displayed rare open-mindedness. On one occasion the Chief Justice requested Brandeis to prepare a memorandum on a complicated utility valuation case.[56] During the month devoted to it, some members became impatient. With Taft's active support, the matter was held up until Brandeis was ready. Then a whole day was set aside for discussion. "And," as Brandeis described it, "it was a thorough discussion. Some didn't grasp the facts and hadn't thoroughly mastered the memo, but it was a new method in the consideration of issues."[57]

"I am not an obstinate man," the Chief Justice told Holmes.[58] The Coronado case had dramatically underscored the point. By a narrow vote the White Court had decided that the union was liable under the Sherman Act. Brandeis dissented and prepared an opinion. After Taft became Chief Justice, the case was restored to the docket and

---

continued from page 201
and Clarke, dissented. *American Steel Foundries* v. *Tri-City Central Trades Council,* 257 U.S. 184 (1921). Chief Justice Taft delivered the opinion of the Court; Brandeis concurred in the substance of the opinion; Clarke dissented.

reargued. In conference the new Chief Justice presented the view that the union, though unincorporated, was suable, that evidence indicated intent to restrain interstate commerce.[59] Brandeis made it known that he would dissent, having already written the opinion. Meanwhile, Taft encountered difficulty in writing an opinion. Cautiously, Brandeis ventured: "I hesitate to [make] the few following suggestions. Please feel entirely free to discard any or all of them."[60] Taft replied the next day: ". . . thank you for the suggestions you make, all of which I shall adopt."[61]

Brandeis's suggestions changed not only Taft's views but also those of other members of the Court. At the conclusion of the 1921 term the Chief Justice delivered a unanimous opinion holding that the unions were not liable.[62] "They will take it from Taft but wouldn't take it from me," Brandeis remarked wryly. "If it is good enough for Taft, it is good enough for us, they say—and a natural sentiment."[63]

An even more striking example of the Chief Justice's open-mindedness is *Sonneborn Brothers* v. *Cureton.*[64] Brandeis, joined by Clarke and Pitney, had dissented from a cursory opinion by Justice McReynolds. After reargument, Taft reassigned the opinion to himself. Again there were exchanges with Brandeis, leading to a unanimous opinion delivered by the Chief Justice. Brandeis was proud of his accomplishment. "That's my opinion," he commented. "Taft wrote it on the basis of a memo in which I analyzed all the cases."[65]

"We haven't had many dissents and we have been pretty nearly solid in all cases,"[66] the Chief Justice boasted in 1925. Unanimity was achieved in the Coronado case,[67] and in Sonneborn,[68] near unanimity in the Child Labor Tax case,[69] all fraught with potential cleavages. With Taft in the center chair, it seemed that the bitter divisions which had characterized the White Court had been forever banished. Even in dissents, the Chief Justice would sometimes set an example of sweet reasonableness. "I have your dissenting opinion in Nos. 96, 213 and 231," he wrote Brandeis, November 19, 1926, "and I think you may add that I concur with you in the dissent. I was at first not inclined to express my differing view, but as you have done so, I shall go with you."*[70]

The Chief Justice's willingness to make concessions influenced the entire Court. In the Chicago Drainage case[71] Justice Butler had sought to modify Taft's broad construction of Congress's power to regulate commerce. Coming around to Butler's view meant "a real sacrifice of personal preference. . . . I was much opposed to striking out of the opinion . . . the constitutional arguments," he told Butler,

> because I think there is no doubt of their soundness, and that any other result would shake the principles that have obtained since Marshall's day in respect to the absolute control by Congress of interstate commerce. . . . I have come to agree with you and Van that it will perhaps steady matters not to dismiss the other view when doubt on the question created in this argument might weaken the action of the Court by inviting Congressional interference in order to relieve Chicago of the burden which she ought to assume and meet. But it is the duty of us all to control our personal preferences to the main object of the Court, which is to do effective justice. . . .[72]

An unwavering adherent of Taft's teamwork policy, Butler felt that dissents were seldom justified. "They often do harm. For myself I say lead us not into temptation."[73] "You can always be sure there will be no 'kicking' or hesitation or mental reservation on my part," Butler assured the Chief Justice. "To me it is genuine pleasure to help—if I can at all—to lessen your load and to make the road we are traveling easy and pleasant."[74]

For a while, Harlan Stone shared the Chief Justice's passion for harmony. "You know I am a team player and I should not have kicked over the traces if you had not accepted any of my views. . . . I have only been trying to be

* The cases were *Risty* v. *Chicago, Minneapolis, & St. Paul Ry. Co.*, 270 U.S. 378 (1925); *Reading Co.* v. *Koons*, 271 U.S. 58 (1925); *Chicago, Rock Island and Pacific Ry. Co.* v. *Murphy*, 271 U.S. 642 (1925).

helpful in this way which I believe we should all be, in carrying on the difficult work of this Court."[75] Four years later, when Stone "kicked over the traces" and deserted the team, Taft was distressed. "I have not been greatly impressed," he commented sadly, "with Stone's judgment of men or things."[76]

Happy working relations were not accidental. Taft went to great pains to establish *esprit de corps*. Seemingly trivial personal considerations—the sending of salmon to Justice Van Devanter,[77] the customary ride he gave Holmes and Brandeis after the Saturday conference,[78] the Christmas card that always went out to Justice McKenna—all such personal attention to highly dissimilar human beings contributed immeasurably to judicial teamwork. "I cannot tell you how your tender note of sympathy touches my heart and comforts me," Justice Clarke wrote in response to a letter of condolence when his sister died.[79] Genuine warmth pervades the letter sent Justice Sutherland in 1927 while the Judge was recovering from a breakdown: "We all love you, George, and we would all regard it as the greatest loss to the country to have you become discouraged over your work, and we realize of what great importance it is to the country that you should be restored to your working capacity."[80] When Justice Holmes's ninety-year-old wife died, Taft immediately made arrangements for the funeral at Arlington Cemetery. Holmes was eternally grateful. "How can one help loving a man with such a kind heart?" he wrote.[81]

Taft's capacity for bearing more than his fair share of the Court's load re-enforced the magnetism of his personality. Reviewing certioraris is the Chief Justice's primary responsibility. Though they were eventually read by all the members, Taft had to prepare a memorandum on each certiorari, stating the grounds for and against granting it.[82] This function could not be delegated. Nor could he spare himself in taking cases which generated little enthusiasm. "As Chief Justice," Stone recalled, Taft "was extremely generous in the assignment of cases, often keeping for himself some of the least desirable ones in order to treat his brethren fairly."[83] Patent cases ranked high among those to be shunned—"just like a dead pull," Taft described them.[84] Patent cases were unappealing not only because the subject matter was technical but also because of the voluminous records. Once he had plunged in, he usually found patent litigation to his liking.* But much spadework was necessary before he could grasp the issues and master the vocabulary.[85] In one case the record was so lengthy that Taft had to spend three days reading it.[86] In another it took an entire week to write an opinion and even then he was not "entirely satisfied with it."[87]

Justice Clarke shared patent-case assignments.[88] His resignation left only McKenna with a liking for them. By 1924, however, McKenna could not "dispose of any case with a big record and complicated facts or questions of law." "That," said Taft, "throws the matter on me."[89] The Chief Justice's hope that Justice Sanford could be trained to take over was disappointed.[90] Five years after Sanford's appointment Taft found himself loaded with a patent case so complicated that his colleagues had taken the extraordinary step of not voting, leaving its disposition wholly to the Chief Justice's discretion. "We very rarely do such a thing as this in our Court," he explained, "but the character of the case is such, with the length of the record, that it is difficult to do otherwise. It is a very common thing in most Supreme Courts to refer a case to one Judge and let him work it out. We never, or certainly very rarely, do that."[91]

Because of his expertise in tax and rate litigation, Brandeis, as opinion writer, was a special source of gratification. Taft turned to him with confidence. In the October, 1922 term, Brandeis wrestled long and hard with a number of

---

* On the Sixth Circuit, Taft's patent opinions had been "generally accepted as guides along the right road" (Judge Arthur C. Denison, 285 U.S. (1931) XIII).

North Carolina Railroad Tax cases.[92] "I have tried to be gentle with you on account of them," Taft wrote.[93] He had little choice, since no one else could be expected to do a competent job. "Admirable, compact, forcible, and clear," Taft said of the completed opinion. "It relieves me greatly to get rid of such a case so satisfactorily."[94]

In May 1923 the Chief Justice was searching for a way to prevent *Hill* v. *Wallace* from becoming "an uncomfortable precedent." At one point the Court voted 5 to 4 against sustaining the Future Trading Act as a regulation of interstate commerce. Later, by vote of 5 to 3, Justice Brandeis not voting, its validity was upheld. Brandeis suggested that the tax imposed under the act was "in effect a penalty, because prohibitive and intended to stop. . . ." Accepting the suggestion, Taft wrote: "I shall try and add something to the opinion of that sort so as to relieve us from embarrassment in the future."[95] An "uncomfortable precedent" was finally avoided by invoking the Child Labor Tax case, which, as Taft said, "completely covers this case." The details of administration and the penalties imposed for violations made it impossible "to escape the conviction . . . that it was enacted for the purpose of regulating the conduct of boards of trade through supervision of the Secretary of Agriculture and use of an administrative tribunal consisting of that Secretary, the Secretary of Commerce, and the Attorney General."[96] Justice Brandeis agreed that the Future Trading Act was unconstitutional for the reasons assigned, but doubted whether the plaintiffs were in a position to require the Court to pass on the constitutional issue.

Justice McReynolds claimed expert knowledge in admiralty law—"the boss in Admiralty," Holmes called him, adding that "he has carried through a series of decisions that I don't believe in at all."[97] Taft recognized that McReynolds had "a great deal of experience in admiralty law," but shared Holmes's skepticism. "I don't know how deep it is. Perhaps he is more familiar with the constitutional features of that branch of our jurisdiction than he is with the everyday details and questions arising."[98] Despite Taft's misgivings, he tended to assign cases of this genre to McReynolds.

Taft usually assigned land claim cases and Indian litigation to the former Chief Justice of Wyoming, Willis Van Devanter.[99] Justice Sutherland of Utah, well grounded in the complicated and technical law involving boundary lines, water rights, and irrigation projects, usually received the lion's share in these fields, especially if they came from the Far West.[100]

Ability to gauge the capacities of his colleagues contributed greatly to Taft's success in the assignment of opinions. Apart from his "radical" views, Holmes was a source of much satisfaction. The old man was really "a great feature" of the Court.[101] In the assignment of opinions, however, Holmes's age made heavy demands on Taft's customary tact. Once the Chief Justice telephoned to ask whether "a case that he proposed to assign . . . would be too troublesome." Considerably annoyed, Holmes commented: ". . . if he spared me in that way I ought to leave."[102] When Mrs. Holmes died, Taft assigned Holmes a larger number of cases, hoping that the extra load would help take his mind off her passing. Lighter assignments did, in fact, go to Holmes, but Brandeis assured him that the "C.J." did not give him easy ones in consideration of his age.[103] "Of course I don't give him the cases that have very heavy records and that require a great deal of work in reading them," Taft explained, "but I give him important cases and try to give him cases that he likes."[104] The rapidity with which the eighty-five-year-old judge turned out opinions caused continual wonder. "The only thing that tries him," the Chief Justice observed, "is not to be able to announce the opinion assigned to him on one Saturday night on a week from the following Monday."[105]

Assignments to Holmes were simple compared with the difficulties encountered with some others. McKenna was "so unsatisfactory in his opinions that [Taft had] to select the simplest . . . in order that he may not work damage to the Court."[106] Sutherland was a "very strong man," but he had to drive himself unmercifully to get his opinions out,[107] thus preventing Taft from giving him any considerable number. In 1924 he felt constrained from pressing Pierce Butler and Edward Sanford until they became accustomed to "quick disposition" of their assigned cases.[108]

Van Devanter presented a unique problem. Though the "strongest man on the Court" and indispensable in conference, the Associate Justice was "opinion-shy." He was, moreover, a perfectionist, "never content to let an opinion go until he has polished it and worked on it until it is a gem. But he is only able to get out a few opinions during the year on that account."[109] The Chief Justice took every possible step to relieve him.[110] Once when Van Devanter, near collapse due to his backlog of cases, posed "a nerve straining situation," the Chief Justice told brother Horace: ". . . we have all got to unite to help him out."[111] The extra load usually fell on Taft himself. During the eight full terms of the Taft regime, Van Devanter wrote a total of only ninety-one opinions for the Court compared with Taft's two hundred and forty-nine.*

Physical breakdowns often required the Chief Justice to reassign opinions, a task calling for the utmost tact. Sanford, though often lagging behind, created no trouble. Van Devanter, on the other hand, became "very sensitive, cross and unreasonable."[112]

> He does not write [Taft explained] and yet he hates to have any comment made or action taken in respect to the matter. I turned over two of his cases to Brandeis but B. though[t] Van would cherish resentment against him. So I had to take Van's cases myself and turn over some of mine to Brandeis. I told Brandeis that the experiences of a Chief Justice were those of an impresario with his company of artists.[113]

* The count varies slightly, depending on how the record is compiled.

Van Devanter was also upset by the reassignment of *Fiske v. Kansas*[114] to Sanford. The shift seemed reasonable, since Sanford was at work on a number of opinions in other syndicalism cases. It would have been an easy matter to take over the Kansas case.[115] Yet Van Devanter voiced strong protest, insisting that Sanford had shown "some weakness on the subject." Reassignment should be delayed, he thought, until Sanford had written opinions in similar cases already assigned him.[116]

Taft himself was well aware of those among "his company of artists" who might show "some weakness." Reassignment did not correspond to a game of chance, nor did it always mean a second opportunity to tighten the bonds of judicial friendship. Although necessitated by uncontrollable factors, reassignment afforded Taft another opportunity to promote what he deemed the Court's best interests. In the summer of 1926 Taft concluded that it was beyond his strength to consider the long, heavy Chemical Foundation case.[117] He selected Pierce Butler to take it. "Pierce is young and strong," the Chief Justice explained, "able and willing, and I thought I would trespass on him." But there was a more compelling reason. "He is the only one to whom I can properly give it. He was appointed by Harding and not by Wilson, and I rather think we ought to have somebody other than an appointee of Wilson to consider and decide the case."[118] Safe and sound Justice Butler, not the less dependable Brandeis, got the reassignment. In another instance Taft reassigned two cases from Van Devanter to Holmes, who had originally voted with the majority in both cases.[119] Much to the Chief Justice's surprise, Holmes returned both cases, stating that he could not write the opinions. "In other words," Taft told Butler, "I think he is going to vote the other way. As a consequence, I shall have to assign it to a more solid person, and you are it."[120]

When the need for reassignments arose, Taft often found he had a narrow choice of potential assignees. In the spring of 1929 he was casting about for work horses to take on extra cases. To his chagrin he discovered that Brandeis was busy filing a great dissenting opinion in an interstate commerce case,[121] running forty-five pages, compared with the majority opinion of only eight. Patience tried, the Chief Justice noted that this had delayed "getting rid of 5 cases that he had assigned to him, but now that he has got rid of this, I hope he may get through . . . so that he can leave a clean list."[122] At least one goal—a clear docket, for which Taft vigorously employed his assignment power—would be reached.

Near the end the Chief Justice was forced to relieve himself of burdens he knew were his. Shortly before he resigned, he turned over to Sanford a patent case. "I thought I ought to take it myself; but the truth is that I have been sick for nearly a month and I haven't been able to do any work."[123]

Illness was not the only cause for reshuffling. If the judge to whom an opinion had been initially assigned failed to enlist the largest possible support, Taft reserved the right to reassign it. In 1924 McReynolds had been assigned an important case under the Transportation Act of 1920.[124] Brandeis could not endorse McReynolds's opinion because it would "bother us in the future."[125] Although Van Devanter persuaded McReynolds to change it, the revisions still did not satisfy Brandeis. Thereupon, "the Chief took over . . . and put out what is now the Court's opinion."[126] Holmes found Taft's revised opinion "so powerfully put" that he decided to change his vote and join the majority.[127] The Chief Justice was elated. Brandeis "came over, saying that he too would shut his mouth."[128] "I suppressed my dissent," Brandeis commented, "because after all, it's merely a question of statutory construction and the worst things were removed by the Chief."[129] McReynolds was furious. Threatening to retire, he vowed he would file his old opinion. The only effect was a burst of laughter from Van Devanter.[130] Within two days the irascible Justice capitulated.[131] Taft could barely restrain his sense of triumph. "By writing it anew," he gloated, "I brought Brandeis and Holmes over."[132]

Taft used his assignment power to promote unanimous or near-unanimous opinions. Obsessed by fear of dissents, he especially hated "an exactly divided Court" merely affirming the judgment below.[133] "The chief duty of a court of last resort," he wrote, "is not to dispose of the case but to elaborate the principles, the importance of which justify the bringing of the case here at all, to make the discussion of those principles and the conclusion reached useful to the country and to the Bar in clarifying doubtful questions of constitutional law and fundamental law."[134] To achieve this, the Chief Justice must round up a convincing majority. In his early years Taft was successful. Holmes and Brandeis's concurrence in the American Steel Foundries case[135] prompted Max Pam to write: "I think it marks the beginning of one of the greatest achievements to be had in the Court under your leadership, and that is to win, and if possible continue, unanimity in the Court."[136] The subsequent defection of Holmes, Brandeis, and Stone marred the bright prospects envisioned in 1921. With rare exceptions, a solid core held "steady in the boat." Van Devanter and Butler were joined by that "real good fellow,"[137] George Sutherland. For a while Taft could turn to Mahlon Pitney for advice.[138] Justice McKenna, though "never . . . a very strong Judge,"[139] was "a good fellow and a good man, a man of high principles, somewhat narrow in view."[140] With the help of these Associates, Taft sought to achieve efficiency, unanimity, and harmonious relations.

OBSTACLES TO TEAMWORK

Taft did not always succeed in his drive to "mass the Court." Impaired health of some of his Associates and his own declining physical strength constantly threw monkey wrenches in his path. Personal idiosyncrasies also contributed to the growing disharmony, the break finally taking the form of bitter dissents. During Taft's last years at the helm these came fast and furious.

The physical deterioration of several colleagues continually plagued the Taft Court. In 1922 Holmes was suffering from asthma and the Chief Justice suspected it was of a "cardiac character."[141] Pitney, with a breakdown, and Day, suffering from the grippe, were "weak members of the Court to whom [Taft could] not assign cases."[142] The Court's senior member, Joseph McKenna, posed the most delicate problem. Appointed by President McKinley, he was seventy-eight years old and failing. "In case after case he will write an opinion," Taft commented, "and bring it into conference, and it will meet objection because he has missed a point in one case, or, as in one instance, he wrote an opinion deciding the case one way when there had been a unanimous vote the other, including his own."[143] In 1924 the senile judge completely missed the main point in the case assigned him. "It seems to me, with deference," Taft wrote, "that you have not stated the real point of the case as agreed upon in Conference."[144] Assisted by a statement from the Chief Justice covering the central issue, McKenna tried again. "It seems to me, with deference," the despairing Chief repeated, "that you still miss the point in your opinion upon which the Conference determined that this case should turn."[145]

As Senior Associate Justice, McKenna ran the Court during the Chief Justice's absence. In May 1923 Taft was ill and missed a conference. "I had all my cases prepared in typewriting," he explained to former Justice Clarke, "and sent them to brother McKenna to use, but he preferred not to read them at all, and the Conference did not amount to much, so that we had to do most of it over again the next week."[146] At the end of the term Taft was at his wit's end, complaining to his daughter: "He [McKenna] is an Irishman . . . and makes up his mind now on the impressionistic principle. He is a Cubist on the bench, and Cubists are not safe on the bench."[147]

Cubist McKenna had yet to perform the *coup de grâce*, circulating an opinion which left the Chief Justice in doubt as to its identity. McKenna's "language is as fog," the baffled Chief commented. "He does not know what he means himself. Certainly no one else does. I try to give him the easiest cases but nothing is too easy for him."[148]

McKenna interpreted polite criticisms as thinly veiled attempts to force him off the bench. "He is exceedingly sensitive," the Chief Justice noted, "and loses his temper and at times creates little scenes in the Conference."[149] In the final conference, June 1924, "McKenna, just in order to show that there was life left in him, printed a dissenting opinion in which he differed from the entire Court and made a lot of remarks that seemed to me to be quite inapt and almost ridiculous."

The situation was critical, for, as Taft said, "McKenna's vote may change the judgment of the Court on important issues, and it is too bad to have a man like that decide when he is not able to grasp the point, or give a wise and deliberate consideration of it."[150] "I don't know exactly what we are going to do."[151] A partial solution was found November 10, 1924, when, after a meeting at Taft's house, it was agreed not to decide cases in which McKenna's vote was crucial.

The long-run cure was to persuade McKenna to resign, but this was much easier said than done. McKenna's firm conviction that "when a man retires, he disappears and nobody cares for him," made him balk.[152] By the end of 1923 Taft's patience had worn thin. "If he [McKenna] doesn't show some intention of withdrawing," Taft wrote brother Horace early in the 1923 term, "we may before the end of the year have to adopt some united action in bringing to bear influence upon him. Of course that will fall on me as the spokesman, and is not a pleasant duty to look forward to, because I shall never be forgiven."[153] In the spring of 1924 the Chief Justice made an unsuccessful attempt to persuade McKenna to retire. Holmes refused to give his assent, disliking, Taft explained, "to agree tho' he agrees it ought to be done." Older than McKenna, Holmes might have suspected that once his junior colleague retired, the next move might well be aimed at him. Taft thought Brandeis refused "because . . . he would like to have a Democratic President appoint."[154]

Taft pushed on. He and Van Devanter consulted McKenna's physician, who confirmed the judge's incompetence. The Associates finally authorized the Chief Justice to confer with the ailing Justice. Despite Taft's extremely tactful approach, McKenna refused to cooperate, but he finally agreed that the Court's opinion must control. Taft "told him how deeply regretful all the members of the Court were, how deeply they loved him, how chivalrous they found him, how tender of the feelings of others he always was, and how peculiarly trying it was, therefore, to act in the present instance from a personal standpoint."[155] Painful duty disposed of, a farewell ceremony was arranged at the final Court session, and, as Taft said, "it was really quite impressive."[156]

Another major obstacle to judicial teamwork was James C. McReynolds. Taft had never held the former Attorney General in high regard. Describing President Wilson's appointee as "too stiff-necked and too rambunctious," he predicted McReynolds would be "a weak man on the bench."[157] As a colleague, the Chief Justice complained that "McReynolds tries my patience."[158] He was, Taft said, "the greatest censor of the Court" and the most irresponsible.[159] "In the absence of McReynolds," the Chief Justice wrote in the spring of 1924, "everything went smoothly."

McReynolds was difficult, not because of his views, which usually did not differ basically from Taft's, but because of personal shortcomings. Though an "able man," he was "selfish to the last degree, . . . fuller of prejudice than any man I have ever known, . . . one who delights in making others uncomfortable. He has no sense of duty. He is a continual grouch; and . . . really seems to have less of a loyal spirit to the Court than anybody."[160]

McReynolds's barbs, usually aimed at Brandeis and Clarke, occasionally hit the Chief Justice. "I do not like your opinion in #206,"[161] McReynolds commented bluntly. "I think . . . you can put the case in a much more condensed and lucid way. The opinion is hard for me to follow and is almost sure to produce confusion and add to our difficulty." "Of course," he added reassuringly, "I have no purpose to make even a mild row in public."[162] McReynolds could not always be counted on to hold his fire. Of his performance in the Carroll case, Taft reported: "McReynolds delivered himself without reference to his written opinion" in a grandstand play to the galleries. Turning to the new member of the Court, Harlan Stone, Holmes remarked "that there were some people who could be most unmannerly in their dissenting opinions."[163]

Strongly addicted to vacations, McReynolds took off more time "than any of the rest of us." In 1929 he cavalierly asked the Chief to announce the opinions assigned him, explaining that "an imperious voice has called me out of town. I don't think my sudden illness will prove fatal, but strange things some time happen around Thanksgiving."[164] Duck hunting season had opened and the judge was off to Maryland's Eastern "sho' " to fire away. In 1925 the "imperious voice" had called so suddenly that he had no opportunity to notify the Chief Justice of his departure. Taft was infuriated; he had wanted to deliver two important decisions, and McReynolds had made off before handing in a dissent in one of them, thereby holding up the Chief's opinion.[165] "He came back with few ducks," Taft reported tartly, and "the weather was icy."[166]

For McReynolds the Court's *bête noire* was fellow Democrat Justice Brandeis. In 1922 Taft proposed that members of the Court accompany him to Philadelphia on a ceremonial occasion. "As you know," McReynolds responded, "I am not always to be found when there is a Hebrew abroad. Therefore my 'inability' to attend must not surprise you."[167] McReynolds even refused to sit next to Brandeis for the Court photograph. "The difficulty is with me and me alone," McReynolds wrote the Chief Justice in 1924. ". . . I have absolutely refused to go through the bore of picture-taking again until there is a change in the Court and maybe not then."[168] The Chief Justice had to capitulate; no photograph was taken in 1924.[169]

McReynolds's hates included Justice John H. Clarke. The Chief Justice suggested this explanation: "McReynolds has a masterful, domineering, inconsiderate and bitter nature. He had to do with Clarke's selection as district judge and felt, therefore, that Clarke, when he came into the Court, should follow him. And when Clarke, yielding to his natural bent, went often with Brandeis, McReynolds almost cut him."[170] Clarke once asked Taft to urge McReynolds to modify some of his harsh language, explaining: "I never deign—or dare—to make suggestions to McReynolds as to his opinions." Listing his proposed changes, Clarke concluded: "There are others but these are so glaring that they are respectfully submitted to the Head of the House."[171] McReynolds's meanness emerged in all its dinginess when he refused to sign the joint letter sent Justice Clarke on his resignation. The Chief Justice, thoroughly annoyed, commented: "This is a fair sample of McReynolds's personal character and the difficulty of getting along with him."[172] Taft let McReynolds's silence proclaim its spiteful message.

Taft's own opinion of Justice Clarke was not unqualified. "Clarke had certain predilections that injured much of his usefulness on the Bench. There were certain cases which came to him which he decided in advance. Even Holmes spoke to me of this."[173] ". . . He really acted in the Court as if each case was something to vote on as he would vote on it in the Senate or House, rather than to decide as a judge."[174]

Despite misgivings about his philosophy, Taft still considered Clarke a "good fellow."[175]

Brandeis presented a somewhat different problem. Surface friendliness and a remarkable degree of give and take on both sides obscured Taft's deep-seated distrust. When Brandeis strayed, the Chief Justice tended to erupt, in later years with extreme vehemence. Brandeis's appointment to the Court had been for the ex-President "one of the deepest wounds that I have had as an American and a lover of the Constitution and a believer in progressive conservatism."[176] Taft retained an abiding suspicion. In 1924 there were widespread rumors that the Justice might be named Robert La Follette's running mate on the Progressive ticket. "I know enough about Brandeis," Taft commented to Max Pam, "to know that that [the Vice-Presidency] is the last position which he would accept, but his sympathies may be with La Follette, though I should not think he would go so far as La Follette with reference to the abolition of the power of the Court."[177]

Taft's suspicions deepened when Brandeis refused to join in pressing Congress for enactment of a bill enabling the Court to limit its jurisdiction and thereby ease the pressure of increasingly heavy dockets. By the late fall of 1924, a clear majority of the judges had expressed their support. But Brandeis had "grave doubts whether the simple expedient of expanding our discretionary jurisdiction is the most effective or the safest method of securing the needed relief."[178] Though he did not approve the bill, Brandeis agreed that the Chief Justice had a mandate from the Court. "I am willing," Brandeis wrote, "that you should say that the Court approves the bill—without stating whether or not individual members approve it. For, in relation to proposed legislation directly affecting the Court, the Chief Justice, when supported by a clear majority, should be permitted to speak for it as a unit; and the difference of view among its members should not be made a matter of public discussion."[179]

But this was not what the Chief Justice wanted. He sent a copy of Brandeis's reply to loyal teammate Willis Van Devanter with the indignant comment: "Because Walsh [Senator Thomas J. Walsh of Montana] is opposed to it, as he told me, because he [Brandeis] talked with Walsh, and because he always wishes to appear on the off side and a champion of the offsiders, he declines to help us."[180] By mid-December 1924, the outlook for the bill had brightened and Taft was less inclined to arraign the dissenter. "He tries hard to be a good fellow," Taft commented magnanimously, "but he misses it every little while."[181]

Brandeis missed it again when the Chief Justice sought support for making the bankruptcy procedures in New York more efficient. A majority of the district and circuit judges in New York approved, but not Brandeis. "I am sorry to say," the Chief Justice wrote, "that, what so often occurs in dealing with our reformer Brandeis, he always finds some reason for interfering with the course necessary to accomplish real reform. Brandeis contents himself with saying that what we ought to do is to reform the whole educational system in law." Lashing out at Brandeis's motives, Taft concluded: "The truth is that when we make rules that interfere with the young Russian Jews [who composed the bulk of the bankruptcy petitioners] . . . we find him a real obstructionist."[182] Taft thought, apparently, that Brandeis's action after 1925 was in violation of Canon 19 of the code of judicial ethics drawn up by a committee headed by the Chief Justice:

> It is of high importance that judges constituting a court of last resort should use effort and self-restraint to promote solidarity of conclusion and the consequent influence of judicial decision. A judge should not yield to pride of opinion or value more highly his individual reputation than that of the court to which he should be loyal. Except in case of conscientious difference of opinion on fundamental principle, dissenting opinions should be discouraged in courts of last resort.

Having returned to the "liberal principles" Clarke thought his colleague had abandoned in 1922, Brandeis incurred the Chief Justice's vehement ill will.

Taft feared that Brandeis's diabolical influence engulfed Justice Holmes. He was "so completely under the control of Brother Brandeis that it gives to Brandeis two votes instead of one." Holmes has "more interest in, and gives more attention to, his dissents than he does to the opinions for the Court, which are very short, and not very helpful."[183] The Chief Justice suspected Holmes's advanced years made "him a little more subordinate and yielding to Brandeis, who is his constant companion, than he would have been in his prime."[184] A "very poor constitutional lawyer," lacking "the experience of affairs in government that would keep him straight on constitutional questions,"[185] Holmes's "unsound" constitutional views were due in great part "to the influence which Brandeis has had on him."[186] If the Court had followed Holmes, "I don't think we would have had much of a Constitution to deal with."[187]

Evidence of Brandeis's influence is scattered through the Holmes-Laski correspondence: "unless I let Brandeis egg me on to write a dissent in advance"; on that day came down an opinion that stirred the innards of Brandeis and me and he spurred me to write a dissent"; "when I can get calm I am catspawed by Brandeis to do another dissent on burning themes"; "Brandeis . . . reminded me of a case argued last term in which he said I should have to write a dissent"; "but meantime a dissent that the ever active Brandeis put upon my conscience waits untouched."[187a]

The troubles stirred up by Taft's recalcitrant colleagues were accentuated by the Chief Justice's own physical disabilities. After his heart attack in April 1924, Taft's impaired physical vigor forced him to curtail his working hours. The result was "a good deal of difficulty in keeping up." As Chief Justice, he felt compelled to be "a little ahead of all the rest."

> I am conscious [he wrote his son Robert] that I am not doing the thorough work I used to do in the first three years, but it seems impossible for me to examine as minutely as I should the records in each case. The others have an advantage of me in that they are able to examine certain cases closely and then let the others go, because they are not subject to cross-examination on any case; and they can merely vote, so that I find myself constantly exposed to the humiliation of not discovering things in cases, especially in matters of jurisdiction which are very intricate and most exasperating.[188]

The Chief Justice's lack of sure command at the conference table forced him to turn increasingly to Willis Van Devanter. The Montana Justice exercised "a good deal more influence than any other member of the Court, just because the members of the Court know his qualities. . . . His experience, his judicial statesmanship, his sense of proportion and his intimate familiarity with the precedents established by the Court" made Van Devanter a tower of strength.[189] On him fell the primary responsibility for "keeping the Court straight and consistent with itself." Declared the grateful Chief Justice: "His power of statement and his exactness and his immense memory for our cases make him an antagonist in the Conference who generally wins against opposition."[190] He was "the mainstay of the Court"—"my Chancellor," Taft called him. Even if Van Devanter wrote no opinions at all, "we could hardly get along without him," the Chief Justice declared.[191]

The honorific title "lord chancellor"[192] seemed apt for Van Devanter, not only for the assistance he rendered in the conference but also for the effective chain of command the Chief Justice was able to establish through him. Time and again Van Devanter played reconnaissance scout: "Justice Brandeis just telephoned asking for a talk this afternoon about the Keokuk Bridge tax case[193] and of course I told him to come along," Van Devanter wrote the Chief Justice. With this conference in the offing, "there may be a good prospect of putting the matter on its right foot."[194]

Taft's memorandum opinions regularly went out to Van Devanter. Sending his opinion in the historic Truax case,[195] Taft wrote: "I have not sent this to the whole Court because I want to have the benefit of your suggestions and corrections before doing so." Taft told Van Devanter to "cut and slash," because "I found on looking into the case that it seemed necessary to take up the due process feature rather more than I had anticipated."[196]

Forthright criticism from Van Devanter was not unusual. After reading Taft's opinion in *Wolff Packing Company* v. *Court of Industrial Relations*,[197] Van Devanter wrote: "Candidly, I think the opinion does not get off well or do what it is intended to do. It halts a tendency for the moment, but does not conduct us into or build a sound road for the future." Van Devanter, feeling the Court was incapable of handling the case "at the end of what has been rather a perplexing term," cautioned the Chief Justice: the case "presents a real opportunity, and the muddled state of pronouncements in its near vicinity emphasizes the need of a thoroughly considered and carefully prepared opinion. I almost feel like suggesting that you carry the case over. Would it not be well for you to take also the judgment of one or more among McReynolds, Sutherland and Butler?"[198] As in the Wolff Packing case, such effort sometimes resulted in unanimity.

After 1927, Van Devanter's health failed, and his effectiveness as conference leader declined. This loss, combined with Taft's own failing health, made the Chief Justice increasingly despondent. A little more than a year before he died, Taft complained: "The work of the Court is not so much in writing opinions as in getting ready for Conferences [which] grows heavier and heavier. I feel tired over it and suffer from a lack of quickness of comprehension, which has not heretofore troubled me much. The truth is that my mind does not work as well as it did, and I scatter."[199] "Still I must worry along until I get to the end of my ten years, content to aid in the deliberations when there is a difference of opinion."[200] "There was," Justice Stone recalled, "much more inclination to rush things through, especially if he thought he had the support of certain members of the Court."[201]

When the Chief fell short of the goal, as he frequently did in his latter years, he placed the blame on a hard core of "knockers." "Three of the nine," he complained, "are pretty radical, and occasionally they get some of the other brethren, which is disquieting."[202] In 1922 dissenters were merely "disquieting"; by 1928 they had moved beyond the pale of both rationality and patriotism. "The three dissenters act on the principle that a decision of the whole Court by a majority is not a decision at all, and therefore they are not bound by the authority of the decision, which if followed out would leave the dissenters to be the only constitutional lawbreakers in the country."[203] To the very end Taft could usually round up a safe majority on his side, leaving the minority in the posture of irreconcilables. "I would not think of opposing the views of my brethren," he commented somewhat self-righteously in 1927, "if there was a majority against my own."[204] True to his word, Taft rarely dissented,* and he suppressed at least two hundred dissenting votes during his Chief Justiceship.† Explaining his position to Justice Clarke, he observed: "I don't approve of dissents generally, for I think in many cases where I differ from the majority, it is more important to stand by the Court and give its judgment weight than merely to record my individual

* Hughes (285 U.S. [1931], xxxiv) fixes the number at 17, in only three of which did Taft write a dissenting opinion. A record of high output and a minimum of dissent had been established in the Sixth Circuit, where in eight years he wrote 200 opinions of the Court, 4 separate opinions, and only 1 dissenting opinion. See *Federal Reporter,* Vols. 51–101.

† David J. Danelski, "The Influence of the Chief Justice in the Decisional Process of the Supreme Court," Unpublished paper, September 1963, p. 20, n. 122.

dissent where it is better to have the law certain than to have it settled either way."

Evenly divided situations sometimes required calculated manipulations. In the West Virginia gas case,[205] for example, Justice Day, who voted with Taft and Van Devanter in the majority, was about to retire. Realizing the case would have to be reargued, if not decided before the resignation took effect, the Chief Justice wrote Van Devanter: "We ought to decide the West Virginia gas case before he [Day] goes off, because we need his vote. . . ."[206] In the Prohibition cases, the Chief Justice invariably encountered trouble. "It would seem," Taft remarked, "as if more feeling could be engendered over the Prohibition Act than almost any other subject that we have in the Court unless it is the technical questions of jurisdiction."[207] Once opposed to Prohibition, Taft as Chief Justice favored strict enforcement. Detesting the unavoidable dissension these cases aroused, he complained: "There are certain members of our Court who I dislike to say are becoming a bit raw in their opposition to the Volstead Act. There is something about the issue that seems to engender bitterness."[208]

In the October term of 1924, the prospect of unanimity in Prohibition cases was almost nil. Of the difficulties presented, often resulting in close margins, sometimes five to four, Taft wrote: It is "a good deal easier to write an opinion when the Court is all with you than where the distinctions are narrow, the record is badly made and some rather new principle is to be established against a vigorous opposition."[209] Taft hoped to bring Justice Butler over by use of gentle persuasion. "I note what you say about Brother Butler," he wrote Van Devanter, "and shall try to steer [him] away from the suggestion that we are introducing any new law and new principle of constitutional construction, but are only adapting old principles and applying them to new conditions created by the change in national policy which the 18th Amendment requires."[210] Less than a week later Justice Brandeis, usually with the drys, abandoned the majority. He had gone up to Harvard where, according to the disgusted Chief Justice, he "must have communed with Frankfurter and that crowd, and he came back with a notice to me that he was going to change his vote."[211] Although Holmes, Van Devanter, Brandeis, and Sanford were usually "still steady in the boat,"[212] the Chief Justice's "dear friends" Pierce Butler and George Sutherland tended to oppose him in Prohibition cases. Stone, a connoisseur of fine wines, presented a puzzle. Said Taft: "Stone wobbles a good deal on the subject, and I don't quite see where he stands, and I am not quite sure that he does."[213]

An entirely different situation arose in the historic Myers case[214]—a "monument," Taft called it. Failure to win unanimity for the sweeping dictum that the President's power to remove officials appointed by him is plenary stirred bitter feelings. After the conference, Taft issued an invitation to those "whose votes can be counted on" for a Sunday afternoon meeting at his house.[215] The Chief Justice invited Van Devanter, Sutherland, Butler, Sanford, and the new judge, Stone. "I don't know how the other three [Brandeis, Holmes, McReynolds] will stand," he explained to Sanford, "but I want to get it [the opinion] into shape so that it will be ready for their careful consideration."[216] At this preliminary meeting, six judges agreed on the conclusion. A majority assured, Taft thought it "well not to make any concession but to take the position that we have already taken."[217]

For Taft, the Myers case was a test of loyalty to the American system of government. A majority stood firmly with the Chief Justice,[218] though Stone seemed "a little bit fuzzy and captious in respect to form of statement, and [betrayed] in some degree a little of the legal school master."[219] Taft's attack on Brandeis bordered on the irrational:

> Brandeis puts himself where he naturally belongs. He is in favor evidently of the group system. He is opposed to a strong Executive. He loves the veto of the group upon effective legislation or effective administration. He loves the kicker, and is therefore in sympathy with the power of the Senate to prevent the Executive from removing obnoxious persons, because he always sympathizes with the obnoxious person. His ideals do not include effective and uniform administration unless he is the head. That of course is the attitude of the socialist till he and his fellow socialists of small number acquire absolute power, and then he believes in a unit administration with a vengeance.[220]

After receiving the dissenting opinions of Brandeis and McReynolds, the Chief relented: "I am old enough to know that the best way to get along with people is to restrain your impatience and consider that, doubtless, you have your own peculiarities that try other people."[221] Aware that the Chief Justice abhorred long opinions, especially long dissents, Brandeis offered to pay the cost of printing his dissent out of his own pocket. "I think we can have too much economy in the matter of perfecting opinions [for publication]," Taft replied. "The appropriation for that purpose is large and ought to be."[222] Still he felt resentment. "I thought mine was pretty long," he wrote brother Horace, "but his is 41 pages, with an enormous number of fine-print notes, and with citations without number."[223] "Brandeis can not avoid writing an opinion in a way in which he wishes to spread himself, as if he were writing an article for the Harvard Law Review. When that is not in his mind, he writes a very concise and a very satisfactory opinion, but his dissents are of a different character."[224]

Even the lapse of nearly a year failed to allay the bitterness aroused by these strange bedfellows in dissent. "McReynolds and Brandeis belong to a class of people that have no loyalty to the court and sacrifice almost everything to the gratification of their own publicity and wish to stir up dissatisfaction with the decision of the Court, if they don't happen to agree with it."[225] Taft's castigation of McReynolds exceeded that against Brandeis: "The more agitation against [the Court] growing out of any opinion of his, the better he likes it, because it exalts in a way that tickles in him the spirit of opposition. His exhibition in the Court room was such as to disgust Holmes."[226]

The Chief Justice grew more and more impatient with differences. In *Olmstead* v. *United States*,[227] Brandeis, after agreeing to limit discussion, explored the ethics of wire-tapping. "Where we make a limitation we ought to stick to it," Taft said, "and I think anyone would have done so but the lawless member of our Court. Nevertheless, I think we might as well meet the issue as it is, and provide hereafter for making people shinny on their own side."[228] Even Butler refused to stay in line; but Holmes, Brandeis, and Stone, not Butler, infuriated the Chief Justice. "They went on general principles completely unsustained by the great mass of precedent."[229] Justice Holmes wrote "the nastiest opinion in dissent."[230] "Holmes has no respect for Marshall, he exaggerates the power of Congress."[231] That Holmes had abandoned ship at the crucial moment was even more galling. "The truth is," Taft charged, "Holmes voted the other way till Brandeis got after him and induced him to change on the ground that a state law in Washington forbade wiretapping."[232]

An ardent supporter of the thousands of law-enforcement officers responsible for the success of the National Prohibition Act, Taft saw the automobile as a new and powerful weapon in the hands of criminals. Agents of the underworld had seized upon new inventions, "and these idealist gentlemen urge a conclusion which facilitates the crime by their use and furnishes immunity from conviction by seeking to bring its use by government officers within the obstruction of the bill of rights and the 4th Amendment."[233] The Court must follow "the old-time common-law practice . . . that if evidence is pertinent it is admissible however obtained."[234]

Stressing civil liberties, Brandeis had written:

. . . In a government of laws, existence of the government will be imperilled if it fails to observe the law scrupulously. Our government is the potent, the omnipresent, teacher. For good or for ill, it teaches the whole people by its example. Crime is contagious. If the government becomes a lawbreaker, it breeds contempt for law; it invites every man to become a law unto himself; it invites anarchy. To declare that in the administration of the criminal law the end justifies the means—to declare that the government may commit crimes in order to secure the conviction of a private criminal—would bring terrible retribution. Against that pernicious doctrine this court should resolutely set its face.[235]

"It is rather trying," Taft complained, "to have to be held up as immoral by one who is full of tricks all the time. . . . But," the Chief Justice added, "he can become full of eloquent denunciation without great effort."[236] Worse, Brandeis could obtain allies; he had kidnaped Holmes right out from under Taft's nose and had corrupted Justice Stone. Of the latter, the Chief Justice observed bitterly: "Stone has become subservient to Holmes and Brandeis. I am very much disappointed in him; he hungers for the applause of the law-school professors and the admirers of Holmes."[237] Sharing Taft's wrath, Van Devanter predicted: "Every communist in the country and every sympathizer with communism naturally will be against the decision, and so will those who call themselves reformers but in truth are infected with communism."[238]

Excepting Butler, the dissenters in *Myers* and *Olmstead* were so hopeless that Taft could only roundly denounce them. In *Bedford Cut Stone Co.* v. *Journeymen Stone Cutters' Association of North America,*[239] the line-up was marginal. Two of the four who voted against Taft's majority in conference wavered. They must be brought into line lest Brandeis's labor views gain the ascendancy. Taft had never seen Brandeis "in such a state of rejoicing after getting Sanford and Stone apparently into his army and into his plan of weakening the Court by boring from within."[240] Effort must be exerted to "convince Sanford that he is very much out of plumb with respect to the Bedford Stone Company against the Stone Cutters' Union. . . . It seems to me," Taft explained, "that it is impossible to follow the reasoning in the Loewe v. Lawler, the Hitchman Coal case and the Duplex case, without reaching the conclusion that the use of such a combination to interfere with interstate trade and prevent interstate sales is an illegal restraint under the Anti-Trust law, and if we so hold we will be doing exactly what the Court has done since the questions have arisen, and that to take a different view is to side with Justice Brandeis, who has been against the Court on every decision of the Court on such issues."[241] Sanford was apparently unconvinced.

Stone might be more cooperative. "The continuity and weight of our opinions on important questions of law," Taft pleaded, "should not be broken any more than we can help by dissents. . . . There are some [presumably Holmes and Brandeis] who have deep convictions on the subject of the law governing relations between employer and employee. . . . It is to be expected that in their attitude of protest in the past they should find distinctions enabling them to continue their attitude in cases presenting what are substantially the same issues."[242]

In the campaign for Stone's vote,[243] McReynolds came to the Chief's support. Bombarded, Stone promised to "go over the whole matter afresh."[244] He seemed inclined to yield: "I, of course, appreciate the importance of avoiding dissents which do not seem necessary. . . . My vote should not be taken to have the finality which perhaps it appears to have."[245] Thus encouraged, the Chief Justice persisted. "I don't think we ought to let up in seeking to have them take the proper view," he had told Sutherland. "I am inclined to think that it is better not to have the case rushed through but to give time enough to let us discuss with these people carefully what the issues are—in other words, to let the matter grow cold and take it up again."[246] Two months later, the case still under consideration, the Chief Justice advised Sutherland, the majority's spokesman: "I don't think you quite meet the second phase of Stone's difficulties. . . . I am anxious to meet what will trouble Stone, and I think, too, will trouble Sanford."[247]

Though Sanford and Stone concurred, Taft was far from satisfied. "We have an important labor opinion to deliver which Sutherland wrote, and in which Brandeis has written one of his meanest opinions," Taft commented in mid-April, 1927. "Holmes sides with him, and while Sanford and Stone concur in our opinion, they do it grudgingly, Stone with a kind of kickback that will make nobody happy."[248]

By 1927 Stone was definitely on the wrong team. In the same month the Bedford case came down, he told the Chief Justice of certain difficulties encountered in writing a memorandum opinion in *Fidelity National Bank and Trust Company of Kansas City* v. *Swope*.[249] An article in the *Yale Law Journal* by Professor Edwin M. Borchard indicated the desirability of reopening the issue in *Liberty Warehouse* v. *Grannis*.[250] Without Stone's knowledge, Borchard himself had sent the Court an apparently indiscreet letter urging such action. Suspecting a dark conspiracy, Taft told the former Columbia Law School dean how "Borchard has roused the indignation of the members of the Court at his method of attempting to induce the Court to reconsider or rehear the issue in which he is so much interested."[251] Belatedly aware of this unwitting coincidence, Stone tried to convince the Chief Justice that his suggestion "was entirely on my own initiative and for the reasons stated. It was not inspired by Borchard's letter, as I did not receive it until the day after I had sent my letter to you." Exhibiting independence Taft may not have suspected, Stone concluded: "I am more concerned with the thoroughness and scientific quality of our decisions and opinions than I am with the lack of propriety of others for whom we are not responsible."[252]

As his sense of balance and fair play declined, Taft became ever more rigid in his determination to have everyone endorse the opinion on his side. This effort had been frustrated, first by Clarke and McReynolds; later by Brandeis, Holmes, and Stone. Nevertheless, the Chief still hoped for harmony. On returning from his last summer vacation, he echoed the tolerance and optimism of early years: "They are all in a good frame of mind, and I hope that we shall not be very much disturbed by differences of opinion."[253] By this time, however, the gulf was too wide to be spanned by a bridge built of tact, good humor, and the strategic application of pressure.

In December 1929 the Chief Justice was fatally stricken. Preoccupation with executive details, coupled with unwillingness to spare himself, contributed to his physical breakdown. From 1921 to 1930 the Court delivered fifteen hundred and ninety-six opinions. Of these Taft wrote two hundred and fifty-three for the Court, or one sixth of the total.[254] Whenever his Associates became incapacitated, he felt obligated to assign himself a heavier load. In the fall of 1922 the Court was "shot to pieces." Justice Day, on the eve of retirement, had "been doing no work," Van Devanter had trouble with his eyes, and McReynolds suffered from the gout. Pitney was "ill at home," never to return; Clarke, depreciating the Court's work, wanted to quit.[255] "Somebody has to do the work," as the Chief Justice said, so he assigned to himself two or three opinions more than to his colleagues.[256] From 1921 to 1928 he wrote an average of 30.25 opinions per term, while his colleagues averaged only 20.25.[257]

In 1924 he was forced to halt this hard-driving pace. "The truth is that I have attempted to do too much, and I have got to be more moderate," he promised.[258] This meant he was "not going to bother about the cases of others of the judges who have not kept up with their allotments." His resolution was more than justified: "I shall have written, I think, quite my share of the cases and if others don't keep up, I am not just now in a situation to join in relieving them."[259] Yet even on this reduced schedule, Taft in 1924 wrote only fifteen opinions fewer than he had the previous year, four more than any other judge.[260] The next year he complained: "It doesn't seem to me that I write as rapidly as I used to."[261] But he could still say that "up to this time I have pulled my weight in the boat of the Court."[262] He did so, in part, by assigning himself difficult cases. In early January he had chosen to take "a very heavy case" which he thought "appropriate that I should handle, although it contains an enormous record."[263] Later that same year he again made a serious effort to reduce his work load. He found the other judges "most considerate."[26] At the "earnest insistence of Mr. Justice Holmes," he was persuaded to "cut down the distribution of certiorari from 50 to 30 a week."[265] Holmes had long advocated a less hectic pace, but it was not until the Chief Justice himself felt it necessary to limit his activities that other members of the Court could expect relief.

CHIEF EXECUTIVE AS CHIEF JUSTICE

For Taft a kind of futility had encumbered the position of President.[266] The work was onerous and frustrating; on the Court it was relatively easy, congenial, and rewarding. Things proceeded by "systematic routine, and at the end of the day you have the satisfaction of knowing that something tangible has been accomplished."[267] Taft savored judicial leadership; for the most part he was free from the endless wrangles inseparable from the Presidency.

The highest executive office, requiring swift *ex parte* decisions, had been isolating and exhausting. On the bench, "you have the assistance of your colleagues, who share in the responsibility of the conclusions, the benefit of oral argument by counsel and of briefs submitted on both sides of the controversy."[268] Work and responsibility were divided. The weighing of evidence, the fusion of reason and authority, the deliberative character of the judicial function were extremely satisfying. Steady and regular by nature, Taft strove to make the judicial process more so. It allowed "control of your time for careful study" and enabled one to "order life, if you do not overdo the social part." It is "consistent with long life, hard as the work is."[269] Holmes believed that Taft had been "all the better Chief Justice for having been President."[270]

In a speech prepared shortly after the death of Chief Justice White, Taft expounded the requirements of the highest judicial office. "The Chief Justice is the head of the Court, and while his vote counts but one in the nine, he is, if he be a man of strong and persuasive personality, abiding convictions, recognized learning and statesmanlike foresight, expected to promote teamwork by the Court, so as to give weight and solidarity to its opinions." A great Chief Justice, referring to both Marshall and White, "was winning in his way, strong in his responsibility for the Court, earnest in his desire to avoid divisions, and highly skilled in reconciling difficulties in the minds of his brethren."[271]

As President, Taft possessed extensive power. But since he did not know, as T.R. said, the "joys of leadership," the experience had been frustrating.[272] "The Presidency," he said, "is the office that attracts in the sense of power one is supposed to exercise, and there are those who greatly enjoy its constant exercise."[273] Taft was not among them. As Chief Justice, he wielded the kind of authority he thoroughly enjoyed. To realize it in full measure required definite goals and qualifications. Success demanded "leadership in the Conferences, in the statement of the cases, and especially with respect to applications for certiorari."[274] It meant ability, through sheer force of personality, to "mass" the Court. "John Jay did not think much of the power of the Court," Taft recalled, "and so declined to exercise it; but times have changed."[275] Justice Clarke's voluntary relinquishment of judicial power was puzzling. "You are 65 and leaving the bench," the Chief Justice commented. "I am 65 and have just begun. Perhaps it would have been better for me never to have come on to the Court, but I could not resist an itching for the only public service I love. Few men have laid down power as you are doing."[276]

Taft had brought to the Court a truly magisterial conception of the office and powers of the Chief Justice. Under him the incumbent was more than merely *primus inter pares.* Certain control was exercised not only over his colleagues but also over the entire third branch of government. Thanks to his effort, the formal powers of the Chief Justiceship were augmented. Nor was this all. No technical canon of judicial propriety prevented him from using his wide-ranging informal powers in what he considered the right direction.[277] Enamored of "the executive principle," the need for "teamwork," a policy of "no dissent unless absolutely necessary," he set out to maximize the limited powers of the Chief Justice in a way that contrasts sharply with his failure to exercise the actual powers of the Chief Executive. Although he had viewed presidential power narrowly, as being circumscribed by specific grants in the Constitution, he saw the Chief Justiceship in terms analogous to John Locke's "prerogative" theory of executive power. The President, Taft had written in 1916, has "no undefined residuum of power which he can exercise because it seems to him to be in the public interest."[278] As Chief Justice, he tried to endow the office with executive prerogatives he had abjured as President.

Taft did not sit with the Court after January 6, 1930. His resignation on February 3 evoked from his colleagues a heart-warming appraisal, stressing the qualities that had made his years at the helm significant.

We call you Chief Justice still, for we can not quickly give up the title by which we have known you for all these later years and which you have made so dear to us. We can not let you leave us without trying to tell you how dear you have made it. You came to us from achievements in other fields, and with the prestige of the illustrious place that you lately had held, and you showed in a new form your voluminous capacity for work and for getting work done, your humor that smoothed the rough places, your golden heart that has brought you love from every side, and, most of all, from your brethren whose tasks you have made happy and light. . . .[279]

CHAPTER X

CONSTITUTIONAL CREED

SHORTLY AFTER Taft's appointment, an unsigned editorial in *The New Republic* seriously questioned his qualifications.[1] Lamenting the overwhelming approval of the former President's ascension to the Chief Justiceship, the editorial declared that the "very Progressivism which President Taft provoked" should "uncompromisingly have resented Chief Justice Taft." Liberal opposition should not have been "a mere partisan expression, but the manifestation of a sound political instinct." Forces, conscious or unconscious, which make a man conservative or liberal in the White House are "fundamentally the same forces which determine his decisions on the Supreme Court."[2]

Various reasons were advanced to explain the favorable attitude toward the new Chief Justice. Foremost was Taft's personality: "He was a bad President, but a good sport." His customary geniality aroused "a pervasively lazy good nature towards him." Thanks to "an unconscious law of compensation," there was an unfounded assumption as to his judicial fitness. His very incompetence as President led to the monstrous inference that he must be "great as a judge." Taft had gradually been built into "a myth of judicial greatness." Admittedly, he had been "a good judge," but surely, *The New Republic* speculated, "informed professional opinion would not think of him in the same class with such judges as . . . , [Benjamin N.] Cardozo or Learned Hand." For twenty years, moreover, Taft's judicial ability had gone unused. As professor of law at Yale, he had contributed "practically nothing to legal thought."

Besides Taft's personality, more profound causes accounted for the "almost universal acclaim." Unaware that the judiciary was and always had been "the field of statesmanship," the public still failed to grasp "the real significance of the Supreme Court in the political life of the nation." Taking a realistic stance, *The New Republic* affirmed that judges were not "merely passive interpreters of ready-made law; they adjust conflicting interests, and by so doing enforce, consciously or unconsciously, varying conceptions of public policy." The ground swell of popular approval merely reflected "the present temporary triumph of reaction."

Labor is cowed, liberalism is confused, and the country's thinking generally is done in the storm cellar. The New Republic does not begrudge Mr. Taft this outpour of good will. But the Chief Justiceship of the Supreme Court is not a subject for mere good nature. . . . Cases involving the social control allowed the states under the fourteenth amendment, or the exercise of federal power for police purposes, such as the Child Labor law, will soon again call forth a clash of differing conceptions of policy and of the proper scope of the Court's ultimate veto power. . . .

Written but not signed by Felix Frankfurter, the editorial, on the whole, was a realistic appraisal. Completely overlooked was the long and persistent campaign Taft had waged for judicial reorganization and reform. There was no hint that his drive might be stepped up from the vantage point of the judiciary.

The thrust of the editorial throughout was the conviction that Taft's craving for the Chief Justiceship was stimulated by his recognition of the Court as the molder of social and economic policy.

On the vital public issues of the day, *The New Republic* had no doubt where the new Chief Justice would stand. The magazine feared the worst. Taft's first major opinion, in *Truax* v. *Corrigan*,[3] did not come as a surprise. A landmark case, it inspired "more animadversion" than any other decision in the 1921–22 term.[4] Writing for the majority, Taft severely restricted a significant area of what *The New Republic* called "the social control allowed the states under the fourteenth amendment."

The case involved the constitutionality of an Arizona statute, barring state courts from issuing injunctions in labor cases except under special circumstances. Restaurant owners in Bisbee, Arizona, had resorted to the injunctive remedy against a boycott and picketing of their place of business by ex-employees. The Arizona court's denial of equitable relief evoked from the plaintiffs in error the contention that the statute, as interpreted by the state supreme court, deprived them of property without due process of law and denied equal protection of the laws contrary to the Fourteenth Amendment. By a slim, five-to-four margin, the Supreme Court sustained this view.

The facts raised an issue with which the Chief Justice had been closely identified since his early years of judging in Ohio and in the Sixth Circuit. A strong exponent of the injunctive process in labor disputes, he seized this opportunity to pit the Fourteenth Amendment against state legislation favorable to labor. Taft began by defining plaintiffs' business as a property right; free access to it was an "incident to such right." If defendants used illegal means to prevent customers from patronizing plaintiffs' business, the due-process clause might protect plaintiffs' property, despite the Arizona statute legalizing the activities employed. The conclusion followed irresistibly:

> A law which operates to make lawful such a wrong as is described in plaintiffs' complaint deprives the owner of the business and the premises of his property without due process, and can not be held valid under the Fourteenth Amendment.[5]

Defendants had argued that the property right was not absolute, that "while the right to conduct a lawful business is property," no person had "a vested right" against state regulation in the public interest of the conditions surrounding that business. "It is true," the Chief Justice admitted, "that no one has a vested right in any particular rule of the common law." It was "also true" that:

the legislative power of a State can only be exerted in subordination to the fundamental principles of right and justice which the guaranty of due process in the Fourteenth Amendment is intended to preserve, and that a purely arbitrary or capricious exercise of that power whereby a wrongful and highly injurious invasion of property rights, as here, is practically sanctioned and the owner stripped of all real remedy, is wholly at variance with those principles.[6]

Taft was careful to confine his ruling to the particular means the defendants employed. "The real question here is, were the means used illegal?"[7] States could and did differ on the legality of "peaceful" means, but this was not "the mere case of a peaceful secondary boycott." The illegality of the methods used was "without doubt and fundamental." The "libelous and abusive attacks on the plaintiffs' reputation, like attacks on their employees and customers, threats of such attacks on would-be customers, picketing and patrolling of the entrance to their place of business, and the consequent obstruction of free access thereto—all with the purpose of depriving the plaintiffs of their business"—were means no statute could constitutionally legalize. There is a minimum of protection to which property is entitled and of which it may not be deprived without infringing "due process."

To give operation to a statute whereby serious losses inflicted by such unlawful means are in effect made remediless, is, we think, to disregard fundamental rights of liberty and property and to deprive the person suffering the loss of due process of law.[8]

Taft's opinion had assumed that the Arizona court's construction of the statute in question operated to grant the defendants immunity from both civil and criminal action. Suppose, however, the highest court of Arizona meant to withhold from plaintiffs only the equitable relief of injunction. Would this construction imply a denial of the equal protection of the laws?

Taft's reply was no less equivocal than his answer to the due-process issue: "If this is not a denial of the equal protection of the laws, then it is hard to conceive what would be." Here was "a direct invasion" of property rights, "unlawful when committed by any one, and remediable because of its otherwise irreparable character by equitable process"—*except* "when committed by ex-employees of the injured person."[9] The Chief Justice deplored the rationale behind such legislation. "Classification like the one with which we are here dealing," he explained, "is said to be the development of the philosophic thought of the world and is opening the door to legalized experiment." The Court must protect property rights from the shattering impact of legalized experiments. "When fundamental rights are thus attempted to be taken away," Taft warned, "we may well subject such experiment to attentive judgment. . . . The Constitution was intended, its very purpose was, to *prevent* experimentation with the fundamental rights of the individual."[10]

The state law must fall; it violated the Fourteenth Amendment. State legislatures could not constitutionally sanction the "illegal means" of organized labor, for this would infringe property rights protected by the due-process clause; nor could they simply deny aggrieved plaintiffs an equitable remedy since this would run counter to the equal-protection clause. Here, perhaps, was an example of "that faction we have to hit every little while, because they are continually violating the law and depending on threats and violence to accomplish their purpose."[11] Such also were the predilections that made Taft highly suspect in liberal quarters. *The Nation*, protesting his appointment, had observed, "It was not a Taft, but a Brandeis, or a Holmes, that the hour called for."[12] In his first significant opinion the Chief

Justice crossed swords with the Justices *The Nation* and *The New Republic* would have preferred in his place.

For Holmes, Taft's opinion exemplified the "dangers of delusive exactness" in applying the Fourteenth Amendment. By calling a business "property," Holmes argued, "you make it seem like land" and thereby invite the conclusion that "a statute cannot substantially cut down the advantages of ownership existing before the statute was passed." To Taft's assertion that the Constitution was intended as a perpetual bar to legislative experimentation, Holmes countered: "Legislation may begin where an evil begins. If, as many intelligent people believe, there is more danger that the injunction will be abused in labor cases than elsewhere I can feel no doubt of the power of the legislature to deny it in such cases." The Great Dissenter minced no words in denouncing the Chief Justice's constitutional jurisprudence:

> . . . There is nothing that I more deprecate than the use of the Fourteenth Amendment beyond the absolute compulsion of its words to prevent the making of social experiments that an important part of the community desires, in the insulated chambers afforded by the several States, even though the experiments may seem futile or even noxious to me and to those whose judgment I most respect.[13]

Brandeis's dissenting shafts riddled Taft's reasoning. Property rights were not beyond legislative reach; "for cause," they "may be interfered with and even be destroyed." To Brandeis the case involved competing rights; the rules governing the contest between property rights and other rights "necessarily change from time to time." Conditions change; "the rules evolved, being merely experiments in government, must be discarded when they prove to be failures."[14] Admonishing the Court not "to close the door to experiment within the law,"[15] Brandeis reviewed with approval the bases of much popular opposition to the use of the injunction in labor disputes. It had been urged, he noted, that "the real motive in seeking the injunction was not ordinarily to prevent property from being injured nor to protect the owner in its use, but to endow property with active, militant power which would make it dominant over men. In other words, that, under the guise of protecting property rights, the employer was seeking sovereign power."

The approaches of the Chief Justice and Brandeis were in sharp contrast. Attributing ignoble motives to the former President's favorite device for "settling" labor disputes, Brandeis concluded that "the law of property was not appropriate for dealing with the forces beneath social unrest."[16] The "rights of property and the liberty of the individual must be remolded, from time to time, to meet the changing needs of society."[17]

Taft's first major opinion seemed to confirm his critics' worst fears. Taking a predictable position, the Chief Justice had strongly endorsed private property rights at the expense of social experimentation. Even Holmes, to whom legislative innovations were sometimes noxious, insisted that the Court defer to legislative judgment on the widom of public policy.

Implicit in this landmark decision was a cleavage not easily fitted into the usual liberal-conservative dichotomy. The real breach concerned the Court's role: what was the proper scope of judicial review? In the Truax case, the Chief Justice's position seemed clear. His next major opinion in *Stafford* v. *Wallace*,[18] however, not only upheld broad Federal power under the commerce clause, but announced that Congress had a wide area of discretion, effectively free from judicial second-guessing.

At issue was the Packers and Stockyards Act of 1921, which sought to regulate the business of the packers done in interstate commerce. The object was to secure free and untrammeled flow of livestock from the ranges and farms of the West and the Southwest through the various stockyards and ultimately in the form of meat products to consumers throughout the country. The "chief evil" Congress sought to regulate was the monopoly of the packers, "enabling them unduly and arbitrarily to lower prices to the shipper who sells, and unduly and arbitrarily to increase the price to the consumer who buys."[19]

Taft's opinion evinced marked sensitivity to the factual situation. The stockyards were obviously "not a place of rest or final destination." Indeed, they were but "a throat through which the current flows, and the transactions which occur therein are only incident to this current from the West to the East, and from one State to another." Clearly the stockyards and the sales there made were "necessary factors in the middle of this current of commerce." Congress, therefore, had treated the various stockyards as "great national public utilities," subject to national regulation.[20]

The only question, Taft declared, was "whether the business done in the stockyards between the receipt of the livestock in the yards and the shipment of them therefrom is a part of interstate commerce, or is so associated with it as to bring it within the power of national regulation." The controlling precedent was *Swift* v. *United States*,[21] in which Justice Holmes had left the Court "little but the obvious application of the principles there declared."[22] "Commerce among the States," Holmes had written, "is not a technical legal conception, but a practical one, drawn from the course of business."[23] In language suggesting that of an enlightened Progressive, Taft held that application of the commerce clause in *Swift* was "the result of the natural development of interstate commerce under modern conditions."

> It was the inevitable recognition of the great central fact that such streams of commerce from one part of the country to another which are ever flowing are in their very essence the commerce among the States and with foreign nations which historically it was one of the chief purposes of the Constitution to bring under national protection and control. This court [in *Swift*] declined to defeat this purpose in respect of such a stream and take it out of complete national regulation by a nice and technical inquiry into the non-interstate character of some of its necessary incidents and facilities when considered alone

and without reference to their association with the movement of which they were an essential but subordinate part.[24]

Endorsing the nationalist jurisprudence of Chief Justice Marshall, Taft wrote: "Whatever amounts to more or less constant practice, and threatens to obstruct or unduly to burden the freedom of interstate commerce, is within the regulatory power of Congress under the commerce clause, and it is primarily for Congress to consider and decide the fact of danger and meet it. . . . This court," the Chief Justice declared emphatically, "will certainly not substitute its judgment for that of Congress in such a matter unless the relation of the subject to interstate commerce and its effect upon it are clearly nonexistent."[25]

Taft's broad conception of national commerce power, along with his deference to legislative judgment, soon found reaffirmation. In *Board of Trade* v. *Olsen,*[26] sustaining the Act of September 21, 1922, forbidding trading in grain futures except under the supervision of the Secretary of Agriculture, he relied heavily on both *Stafford* and *Swift.* Just as the Chief Justice found it impossible to distinguish the facts in *Stafford* from those in *Swift,* so *Olsen* was indistinguishable from the two leading precedents. The "current of commerce" concept controlled. *Swift,* in which the notion was first adumbrated, was "a milestone in the interpretation of the commerce clause of the Constitution."

. . . It refused to permit local incidents of great interstate movement, which taken alone were intrastate, to characterize the movement as such. The *Swift Case* merely fitted the commerce clause to the real and practical essence of modern business growth. . . .[27]

Though Taft's views of national power under the commerce clause are reminiscent of John Marshall, his ideas on the Federal taxing power would have made the Great Nationalist turn over in his grave. *Bailey* v. *Drexel*[28] provides the context for one of Taft's most cogent statements on federalism and judicial review. Taft's majority opinion, Clarke dissenting in silence, represented judicial nullification of congressional efforts to regulate child labor for the second time in four years. Thwarted in 1918 by the Court's 5-to-4 decision[29] outlawing the first Federal child labor act passed under the commerce power, Congress tried again the next year. In 1922 the nearly unanimous Court declared unconstitutional the special tax levied by the Act of February 24, 1919, on incomes of concerns employing children. The act was not intended to raise revenue, the Court ruled, but to regulate the employment of children, a subject reserved exclusively to the states.

Taft's opinion was a striking example of conscious judicial involvement in the policy implications of legislation. The Chief Justice conceded that if the tax had been an excise on a commodity or other thing of value, the Court "might not be permitted . . . to infer solely from its heavy burden that the act intends a prohibition instead of a tax. . . . But," he insisted, "this act is more."[30] Certain features clearly indicated its purpose to regulate child labor.

> . . . a court must be blind not to see that the so-called tax is imposed to stop the employment of children within the age limits prescribed. Its prohibitory and regulatory effect and purpose are palpable. All others can see and understand this. How can we properly shut our minds to it?[31]

Critics of the decision pointed out that it was never the business of the Court to delve into legislative motive. Arguing for plaintiff in error, Solicitor General Beck had insisted that Congress's motive was "immaterial." The Court was "powerless to say judicially that the motive of Congress in levying the tax . . . was not to impose a tax, but to regulate child labor."

> Moreover, if, in levying the tax upon manufacturers that employ child labor, Congress did so with a recognition that such a tax might result in no revenue at all, and virtually prohibit the employment of child

labor, such purpose, while it may be *politically anti-constitutional*, in the sense that it may indirectly and incidentally regulate a matter otherwise within the discretion of the States, yet it is not *juridically unconstitutional*, because it is an exercise of an undoubted power to impose a tax; and the motives and objectives of the tax are within that broad field of political discretion into which the judiciary is powerless to enter. To use Madison's phrase, it is an "extra-judicial" question and as such beyond the power of the court.[32]

Taft unequivocally rejected Beck's suggestion that the Court was "powerless" to preserve the federal system against indirect, "anti-constitutional" attacks on it by a presumptuous Congress.* "It is the high duty and function of this court," the Chief Justice retorted, ". . . to decline to recognize or enforce seeming laws of Congress, dealing with subjects not entrusted to Congress but left or committed by the supreme law of the land to the control of the States."[33] Conjuring up a parade of imaginary horribles, his eye on consequences at odds with preconceived values instead of on constitutional power, Taft hypothesized:

. . . Grant the validity of this law, and all that Congress would need to do, hereafter, in seeking to take over to its control any one of the great number of subjects of public interest, jurisdiction of which the States have never parted with, and which are reserved to them by the Tenth Amendment, would be to enact a detailed measure of complete regulation of the subject and enforce it by a so-called tax upon departures from it. To give such magic to the word "tax" would be to

* Beck's argument seemed ingenious, yet the Solicitor General's heart was not completely in it. Writing Taft, May 16, 1922, he confessed:

"You may be surprised to know that, although I presented the government's contention in the child labor cases as strongly as I was able, yet none who heard you deliver the opinion welcomed the decision more than I. Had the Court adhered tenaciously to the views of the late Chief Justice White in McCray v. United States, our form of government would have sustained a serious injury. Your opinion will, I predict, be quoted for many years to come and is a notable landmark in our jurisprudence."

The next day Taft replied:

"I had an impression that your soul was not wrapped up in the child labor cases, although you certainly made as strong a case as could be made out of the previous authority."

break down all constitutional limitation of the power of Congress and completely wipe out the sovereignty of the States.[34]

The Chief Justice had adopted the approach suggested by counsel for defendant in error:

. . . After all is said and done, there remains the question of *practical effect*, and there must be a point, the location of which depends to some extent on the qualities and characteristics of *statesmanship* of the members of the court, where the court must say, "Thus far and no farther."[35]

Having announced his decision, Taft had no difficulty finding a viable precedent. "The case before us cannot be distinguished from that of *Hammer* v. *Dagenhart*. . . ." The analogy was "clear." Just as Congress violated the commerce power by using it as a guise to regulate "state concerns," so the "so-called tax" was "a penalty to coerce people of a State to act as Congress wishes them to act in respect of a matter completely the business of the state government under the Federal Constitution."[36]

The Chief Justice had one last barrier to hurdle: how to dispose of the leading case of *McCray* v. *United States*.[37] An earlier Court had upheld a Federal tax on yellow oleomargarine, forty times the rate of a levy on white oleomargarine, evidently imposed to coerce manufacturers to distinguish their substitute product from butter. "The decisions of this Court from the beginning," Chief Justice White had written, "lend no support whatever to the assumption that the judiciary may restrain the exercise of lawful power on the assumption that a wrongful purpose or motive has caused the power to be exerted."[38] Straining for a distinction, Taft pointed out that the tax in *McCray* lacked "the detailed specifications of a regulation of a state concern and business with a heavy exaction to promote the efficacy of such regulation."[39] Such features, he insisted, were present on the face of the statute in *Bailey*.

Taft's opinion had effectively driven a second spike into

congressional efforts to regulate child labor. Moreover, in *Bailey* the Chief Justice had usurped power "to overturn for alleged unconstitutional *purpose* acts of Congress otherwise valid."

> For the first time in the history of judicial review legislative motive is made a test of legislative action, and any effort by Congress to bring within its control matters normally falling to the states alone raises the question of valid motive.[40]

Lending support to Taft's opinion in *Bailey*, a decision otherwise greeted with scorn by respected students of the Court, was the silent accord of Justices Brandeis and Holmes, forceful dissenters in *Hammer* v. *Dagenhart*. As recently as 1953, Justice Frankfurter, drawing on the still influential *Bailey* decision to buttress a dissenting opinion, stressed the significance of the Great Dissenters' concurrence.[41] Overlooked is the fact that Brandeis and Holmes "sometimes suppressed dissents for tactical reasons." Brandeis's unpublished opinion in *Atherton Mills* v. *Johnston*[42] supports the inference that he believed the tax in *Bailey* to be constitutional.[43]

Justice Clarke dissented alone; he would have written an opinion had not one of his sisters been dying at the time the case came down. "I am sure," Clarke wrote former President Wilson on September 9, 1922, "a dissent based on the decisions from the Oleomargarine[44] to the Narcotic Drug cases[45] could have been made very convincing." In Clarke's eyes, Brandeis's vote for the majority was but another example, and a striking one, of his "falling away from . . . liberal principles."

The reasons Holmes and Brandeis joined the Chief Justice in *Bailey* are speculative. Not so in *Adkins* v. *Children's Hospital*.[46] Here their agreement was on matters of substance. The majority, Brandeis not participating and Taft and Holmes writing separate dissenting opinions, overturned the section of the Minimum Wage Act of 1918 establishing standards of minimum wages for women in all occupations in the District of Columbia. Sutherland struck down, as a violation of the due-process clause of the Fifth Amendment, this alleged invasion of vested property rights. "There is, of course," he admitted, "no such thing as absolute freedom of contract." It was subject to "a great variety of restraints. But," the Justice added,

> freedom of contract is, nevertheless, the general rule and restraint the exception; and the exercise of legislative authority to abridge it can be justified only by the existence of exceptional circumstances. . . .[47]

In a forthright opinion, the Chief Justice attacked his colleague's use of distinctions "formal rather than real." Pointing to the "evils of the sweating system and of the long hours and low wages which are characteristic of it," "well-known" conditions which the legislation was designed to remedy, Taft emphasized that certain classes of employees were in no position to exercise freedom of contract. They were "not on a full level of equality of choice with their employer," were "prone to accept pretty much anything that is offered," and consequently were "peculiarly subject to the overreaching of the harsh and greedy employer."[48]

Taft conceded that the value of hours-and-wage legislation was an open question, subject to dispute. "But it is not the function of this Court," he insisted, applying the rule of judicial restraint which he had previously been accused of violating, "to hold congressional acts invalid simply because they are passed to carry out economic views which the Court believes to be unwise or unsound."[49] Whether legislative regulation was a useful remedy for the evils of sweatshops was a political question, meet for the legislature, not the judiciary.

Pressing his argument, the Chief Justice proceeded to dissect Sutherland's opinion. That the Fifth and Fourteenth Amendments did not bar legislative limitation of hours of employment "on the score of the health of the employee" had become "firmly established"—a "well-formulated rule." *Lochner* v. *New York*[50] had admittedly shaken this doctrine, first established in *Holden* v. *Hardy*.[51] But then came a series of cases, beginning with *Muller* v. *Oregon*[52] and concluding with the recently decided *Bunting* v. *Oregon*,[53] a decision clearly incompatible with *Lochner*. In view of *Bunting*, covering "the whole field of industrial employment," Taft had "supposed that the Lochner Case was thus overruled *sub silentio*."[54] Yet Sutherland's opinion rested on the discredited Lochner case!

Since the majority opinion did not overrule *Bunting*, Taft could only assume that "the conclusion in this case rests on the distinction between a minimum of wages and a maximum of hours in the limiting of liberty to contract." He rejected the distinction, both elements being equally important in an employment contract. "One is the multiplier and the other is the multiplicand." Furthermore, the evidence showed that long hours of labor and low wages of pay were "equally harmful" to the employee's health. "Congress took this view," and the principle of judicial restraint suggested that "we can not say that it was not warranted in so doing."[55] *Muller* v. *Oregon*, upholding a state law establishing maximum hours for women, controlled the case.[56] Sutherland's fine-spun distinction between wages and hours simply would not wash; it was a distinction without a difference.

For all these reasons, the Chief Justice would have upheld the Federal Minimum Wage Act. He would, moreover, have concurred silently in Holmes's separate dissent, but for "some general observations" he could not endorse.[57] Apparently Taft objected to Holmes's irreverent treatment of "the dogma, Liberty of Contract," a concept engrafted onto the Fourteenth Amendment, Holmes suggested, and now onto the Fifth by spurious judicial construction.[58] This was going too far. Despite his concessions to legislative regulation, Taft's dedication to the preservation of property rights included liberty of contract.

That Taft's dissent in *Adkins* may have been an aberration, more indicative of his devotion to the image of stability and continuity fostered by adherence to precedent than modification of his conservatism, finds some support in his opinion for a unanimous Court in *Wolff Packing Company* v. *Court of Industrial Relations,*[59] decided shortly after *Adkins*. The Wolff case, in which the Court voided Kansas' plan of compulsory arbitration of wage disputes as a deprivation of property and liberty of contract without due process, differed only slightly from *Adkins*. True, state, not federal regulation was involved here. Moreover, the wage arbitration did not apply exclusively to women, and Taft in *Adkins* had expressly withheld opinion on the constitutionality of minimum wage legislation for adult men.[60] Still, the principle was the same. Indeed, at the outset of his opinion in *Wolff*, Taft cited with approval Sutherland's opinion in *Adkins*. In language almost identical with Sutherland's, the Chief Justice said:

> While there is no such thing as absolute freedom of contract and it is subject to a variety of restraints, they must not be arbitrary or unreasonable. Freedom is the general rule, and restraint the exception. The legislative authority to abridge can be justified only by exceptional circumstances. *Adkins* v. *Children's Hospital*. . . .[61]

It followed that state legislation impinging liberty of contract would be presumed unconstitutional, thrusting upon the state the burden to show "exceptional circumstances."

Responding to the contention that *Munn* v. *Illinois*[62] supported the state's power to determine a business affected with a public interest and then to regulate it, Taft classified into three categories "businesses clothed with a public interest justifying some public regulation." The businesses Kansas sought to regulate, those engaged in the production of food, clothing, and fuel, did not fall into either of the first two categories, covering industries carried on under a public grant and certain occupations regarded as "exceptional." The third category included businesses which had "become," through changed circumstances, clothed with a public interest.[63] A legislative declaration on this matter was "not conclusive."

> . . . The circumstances of its [a business] alleged change from the status of a private business and its freedom from regulation into one in which the public have come to have an interest are always a subject of judicial inquiry.[64]

To win judicial approval, there must be "a peculiarly close relation" between the public and the business sought to be regulated and "an affirmative obligation" on the part of the business to be "reasonable in dealing with the public."[65] Taft added still another requirement:

> In nearly all the businesses included under the third head above, the thing which gave the public interest was the indispensable nature of the service and the exorbitant charges and arbitrary control to which the public might be subjected without regulation.[66]

Taft found no justification for the Kansas law. He admitted that the rule for defining a business affected with a public interest was not clear-cut; it depended on the nature of the particular business. Nevertheless, the Court had the duty to apply the rule. "It is not a matter of legislative discretion solely." To uphold the act would effect "a revolution in the relation of government to general business."[67]

The state had argued, however, that the exercise of compulsory arbitration under the act rested upon the existence of a temporary emergency, as in *Wilson* v. *New*,[68] where the Court upheld congressional wage-fixing to settle a nationwide dispute between railroad companies and their train operatives. The cases were distinguishable, Taft replied: "the great temporary public exigencies recognized by all and declared by Congress, were very different from that upon which the control under this act is asserted." The "chief and conclusive distinction" turned on the nature of the businesses regulated. In *Wilson* a common carrier, having accepted a railroad franchise, was not free to withdraw that service from the public; in *Wolff* the businesses concerned never assumed an obligation of continued service.[69]

So the Kansas law fell; even Holmes and Brandeis went along. Warmly approving Taft's opinion, Brandeis thought it would "clarify thought and bury the ashes of a sometime [compulsory-arbitration] boom." He was particularly pleased with the Chief Justice's treatment of the Wilson case, agreeing it was no precedent for upholding the Kansas act. "In *Wilson* v. *New*," Brandeis wrote Taft, "there was 'clear and present danger' and the 'curse was on its bigness.' "[70]

Despite judicial solidarity in *Wolff*, the breach within the Court was beginning to widen. By 1926 the gulf could no longer be hidden. That year witnessed one of the most significant decisions in American constitutional history—the 6-to-3 ruling in *Myers* v. *United States*,[71] upholding the President's authority to remove a postmaster without the consent of the Senate. "I never wrote an opinion that I felt to be so important in its effect," Taft said after the decision came down.[72] The previous year he had upheld the President's power to pardon a criminal contemnor. Writing for a unanimous Court in Ex parte *Grossman*,[73] the former President, obviously influenced by his White House experience, had rejected the contention that sustaining such executive authority would necessarily weaken the power and dignity of the judiciary.[74] He now seized the opportunity further to aggrandize the President's power, but not without aggravating the deep split in his own Court.

Taft might have adopted the so-called "middle ground" proposed by Solicitor General Beck in his brief for the government. This position would have permitted Congress to "guide and direct the discretion of the President by such statutory qualifications as are properly inherent in the nature of an office, but without disturbing the power of removal as the Constitution vested it" in the President.[75] The Chief Justice might have restricted his holding to the facts at bar—to purely executive officers. Instead, he chose to exalt the President's office and power by extending to him unlimited power to remove any executive officer, in high-level or "inferior" posts.[76]

Nor was this merely a reflection of his White House experience. Speaking as Solicitor General more than three decades earlier, his broad concept of the removal power had been clearly adumbrated. The Assistant Secretary of the Treasury had asked for an opinion on the power to remove an assistant appraiser in the Customs Service, whose fidelity was suspect. Said Solicitor General Taft:

> I cannot state that Mr. Clark [the appraiser] should be removed on a specific charge. It is impossible to properly conduct a department and limit the power of removal to cases where specific charges can be proven of inefficiency, negligence, or want of fidelity. All I can say is that if I were Secretary of the Treasury, in charge of the duty of administering that great department, I should not wish to have as one of my subordinates a man who allows himself to manifest so much sympathy, and render so much substantial aid to persons whose interests are entirely opposed to those of the Government.[77]

Taft's opinion in the Myers case aroused sharp dissents from Holmes, McReynolds, and Brandeis. Brandeis railed at the Chief Justice's application of the "executive principle." To Taft's insistence that the President have absolute removal power to assure "that unity and coordination in executive administration essential to effective action,"[78] Brandeis reminded the majority that the doctrine of separation of powers was adopted "not to promote efficiency, but to preclude the exercise of arbitrary power." "The purpose was, not to avoid friction, but, by means of the inevitable friction incident to the distribution of governmental powers among three departments, to save the people from autocracy."[79]

Taft did not live to see the dramatic sequel to the Myers case. In 1935, President Roosevelt, finding that Federal Trade Commissioner Humphrey's mind did not "go along together" with his own, summarily removed him. The President's action had been based squarely on implications drawn from the *Myers* decision,[80] yet the four Justices still on the Court who voted with Taft joined in a unanimous decision repudiating Roosevelt's action. Certain expressions in Taft's opinion did "tend to sustain the Government's contention, but these," the Court said in *Humphrey's Executor* v. *United States,*[81] "are beyond the point involved and, therefore, do not come within the rule of *stare decisis.*" "The narrow point actually decided," Sutherland observed, "was only that the President had power to remove a postmaster of the first class, without the consent of the Senate as required by act of Congress." The Court did not make an about-face; it did not adopt the views of the dissenters in *Myers.* It simply shifted the emphasis of the *Myers* decision from the "simple logic" of Article II of the Constitution—that the removal power is inherently "executive"—to the theory that a postmaster "is merely one of the units in the executive department and hence inherently subject to the exclusive and illimitable power of removal by the Chief Executive, whose subordinate and aide he is."[82]

As the Chief Justice's tenure drew to a close, dissents came more frequently and more vehemently. Holmes and Brandeis had dissented from Taft's first major opinion in the Truax case; they objected to his last major opinion in *Olmstead* v. *United States.*[83] This time they were joined by Justice Stone, a recent convert to the dissenting wing, and by the Chief Justice's usually strong supporter, Justice Butler. The case raised the question, whether the use of evidence against a criminal defendant, obtained by tapping the wires of his private telephone, constituted violation of the search-and-seizure clause of the Fourth Amendment and of the self-incrimination clause of the Fifth Amendment.

Writing for a divided Court, Taft responded in the negative. His stance was understandable and predictable. Long a staunch opponent of criminal evasion of justice in general and of the lawlessness resulting from national Prohibition in particular, his crusade for stricter enforcement of the criminal law reached its zenith in *Olmstead.* Defendant Olmstead's $200,000-a-month bootlegging ring represented precisely the lawlessness Taft had long deplored. No sympathy could be expected from him.[84] Accordingly, he refused to treat wiretapping as an unreasonable search and seizure. The language of the Fourth Amendment clearly demonstrated that the search must be of "material things—the person, the house, his papers or his effects." In the case at bar there was no trespass, no entry:

> . . . The Amendment does not forbid what was done here. There was no searching. There was no seizure. The evidence was secured by the use of the sense of hearing and that only. There was no entry of the houses or offices of the defendants.[85]

Congress, Taft suggested, could protect the secrecy of telephone communications by making them inadmissible as evidence in Federal criminal trials. "But the courts," he insisted, "may not adopt such a policy by attributing an enlarged and unusual meaning to the Fourth Amendment." "The reasonable view," he explained,

> is that one who installs in his house a telephone instrument with connecting wires intends to project his voice to those quite outside, and that the wires beyond his house and messages while passing over them are not within the protection of the Fourth Amendment. . . .[86]

The second issue—the admissibility of wiretap evidence, a subject the Court had originally agreed not to consider—received little attention from the Chief Justice. The Fourth Amendment having not been violated, the Fifth could not be invoked on behalf of defendants. Nor could Taft "subscribe to the suggestion that the courts have a discretion to exclude evidence, the admission of which is not unconstitutional, because unethically [or illegally] secured."[87] He relied on the old common-law rule that admissibility of evidence is unaffected by the illegality of the means by which it was obtained and argued that precedent was lacking to sustain a refusal to admit evidence procured by unethical means.[88] Thus, neither the Washington statute making wiretapping a misdemeanor nor the propriety of the Federal government's methods were relevant to the admissibility of the evidence.

Holmes's brief dissent went to the heart of the matter. Without committing himself on whether defendant's rights under the Fourth and Fifth Amendments were violated, Holmes pinpointed the conflicting principles involved:

> . . . It is desirable that criminals should be detected, and to that end that all available evidence should be used. It is also desirable that the Government should not itself foster and pay for other crimes, when they are the means by which the evidence is to be obtained. . . .

Between these principles the Court had to choose, and Holmes thought "it a less evil that some criminals should escape than that the Government should play an ignoble part."[89] This was precisely the "sentimental" attitude against which Taft had long inveighed.

Butler's dissent rejected the majority's literal approach to the Fourth Amendment. Ignoring the principles upon which the Amendment was founded, Taft's opinion recognized only the "direct operation or literal meaning of the words." Yet, the underlying principles of the Amendment implied "safeguards against all evils that are like and equivalent to those embraced within the ordinary meaning of its words."[90] Taft had forgotten that "it is a *constitution* we are expounding."[91] In effect, Butler likened the Chief Justice to the proverbial country judge who, faced with a criminal defendant accused of stealing a white horse, reluctantly discharged him since the judge could find references only to the theft of black horses in his law books. Worse still, Taft's peculiar jurisprudence resulted in conviction.[92]

Brandeis's famous dissent, in which Stone concurred, went even beyond Butler's. Rebelling against Taft's strait-jacket construction of the Constitution, Brandeis gave the Chief Justice a sharp lecture on constitutional interpretation. "Clauses guaranteeing to the individual protection against specific abuses of power," he insisted, "must have a . . . capacity of adaptation to a changing world."[93] As the Court had once said, "a principle to be vital must be capable of wider application than the mischief which gave it birth"—a requirement "peculiarly true of constitutions."[94] The mischiefs which gave rise to the Fourth Amendment had become more advanced through the progress of science:

> . . . Subtler and more far-reaching means of invading privacy have become available to the Government. Discovery and invention have made it possible for the Government, by means far more effective than stretching upon the rack, to obtain disclosure in court of what is whispered in the closet.[95]

Time and again, Brandeis recalled, the Court had refused to place an "unduly literal construction" upon the Fourth Amendment.[96] Must the Court now close its eyes to the advances of civilization? Must it impart to the words of the Fourth Amendment no more than a literal meaning? "Can it be that the Constitution affords no protection against such invasions of individual security?"[97] The framers of the Constitution would have been appalled.

> . . . They conferred, as against the Government, the right to be let alone—the most comprehensive of rights and the right most valued by civilized men. To protect that right, every unjustifiable intrusion by the Government upon the privacy of the individual, whatever the means employed, must be deemed a violation of the Fourth Amendment. And the use, as evidence in a criminal proceeding, of facts ascertained by such intrusion must be deemed a violation of the Fifth. . . . And it is . . . immaterial that the intrusion was in aid of law enforcement. Experience should teach us to be most on our guard to protect liberty when the Government's purposes are beneficent. Men born to freedom are naturally alert to repel invasion of their liberty by

evil-minded rulers. The greatest dangers to liberty lurk in insidious encroachments by men of zeal, well-meaning but without understanding.[98]

When *Olmstead* was greeted, as anticipated, with hostile criticism, Taft stood stubbornly by his guns. Against Brandeis's "claques in the law school contingent," the Chief Justice challenged: "If they think we are going to be frightened in our effort to stand by the law and give the public a chance to punish criminals, they are mistaken, even though we are condemned for lack of high ideals."[99] The Fourth Amendment, too often used as a loophole against criminal prosecution, had been firmed up by Taft and his majority, despite the "idealist" dissenters who urged "a conclusion which facilitates crime."[100] "I hope that ultimately it will be seen," Taft wrote Justice Sutherland, "that we in the majority were right."[101]

From *Truax* to *Olmstead*—both decisions weakened by the scathing dissents of Holmes and Brandeis—Taft had attempted to make his mark on our constitutional jurisprudence. Driven for years to achieve the kind of distinction that had eluded him during his unwanted, unhappy term as President, the Chief Justice, nearing the end of his service on the nation's highest tribunal, could now take stock. Had *The New Republic* been correct in predicting that *Chief Justice* Taft, no better than "competent" as a judge, would be the same enemy of progressivism that *President* Taft had been? Was Thomas W. Shelton's forecast, likening Taft to John Marshall, nearer the mark? In short, how assess Taft's contribution to American constitutional law?

Taft himself respected no man more than Marshall. One day, going by the west entrance of the Capitol, President Taft paused in front of the bronze statue of Chief Justice Marshall. "Would you rather have been him than President?" a friend asked. "Of course," Taft answered. "I would rather have been Marshall than any other American unless it had been Washington, and I am inclined to think that I would rather have been Marshall than Washington. He made this country. . . . Marshall is certainly the greatest jurist America has ever produced and Hamilton our greatest constructive statesman. There you have my opinion of our greatest men."[102]

Taft sometimes emulated—or appeared to emulate—his idol. For Taft the power of Congress under the commerce clause "is . . . exactly what it would be in a government without states."[103] Nor is this the only parallel with "the great Chief Justice." Taft's opinion in *Stafford* seemed to place him squarely in the Marshall tradition. In *Gibbons* v. *Ogden*, Marshall, upholding the Federal commerce power, had emphasized the primacy of political over judicial checks on Congress:

> . . . The wisdom and the discretion of Congress, their identity with the people, and the influence which their constituents possess at elections, are, in this, as in many other instances, . . . the sole restraints on which they have relied, to secure them from its abuse. They are the restraints on which the people must often rely solely, in all representative governments.[104]

In a similar vein, Taft deferred to congressional judgment in *Stafford*. The Court, he said, would "certainly not substitute its judgment for that of Congress" unless the subject Congress attempted to regulate bore "clearly" no relation whatever to interstate commerce.

Likewise in *Bailey*, Taft purported to follow Marshall. He quoted the dictum in *McCulloch* v. *Maryland* to support judicial probing into legislative motive. "Should Congress, in the execution of its powers," Marshall had written,

> adopt measures which are prohibited by the constitution; or should Congress, under the pretext of executing its powers, pass laws for the accomplishment of objects not entrusted to the government; it would become the painful duty of this tribunal, should a case requiring such a decision come before it, to say that such an act was not the law of the land. . . .[105]

The rub here was that Taft neglected to insert the next sentence from Marshall's opinion:

> But where the law is not prohibited, and is really calculated to effect any of the objects entrusted to the government, to undertake here to enquire into the degree of its necessity, would be to pass the line which circumscribes the judicial department, and to tread on legislative ground. This court disclaims all pretensions to such a power.[106]

Nor did Taft bother to include ellipses indicating omission of Marshall's qualifier. In this way Taft used the Tenth Amendment as an independent limitation on national taxing power. Marshall, in interpreting national power, never referred to the Tenth Amendment as a restriction. Its purpose, he declared, was to quiet "the excessive jealousies which had been excited" during the debates on ratification of the Constitution.[107] It was but a truism, a constitutional tranquilizer, restating the content of the supremacy clause.

Chameleonlike, Taft adopted the judicial hands-off approach again in *Adkins*, chastising Sutherland's majority for invalidating a congressional act "simply because" it was "passed to carry out economic views which the Court believes to be unwise or unsound." Yet shortly thereafter, in *Wolff*, the Chief Justice himself violated the canons of judicial restraint, expressly relying on Sutherland's opinion in *Adkins!* Converting the old formula, "business affected with a public interest"—originally used to justify regulation—into a restrictive device, Taft presumed all regulatory legislation impinging on freedom of contract suspect on constitutional grounds, sustainable only in "exceptional" circumstances. A legislative determination that a business was affected with a public interest was "not conclusive"; it was "always a subject of judicial inquiry."

Taft raised Marshall to the zenith of American statesmanship. "He made this country," Taft said. Having established judicial review, Chief Justice Marshall utilized it to enlarge rather than restrict national power. Only one of many mechanisms devised by the framers to restrain the exercise of arbitrary authority, its scope was narrow. For Marshall the primary restraints on government were political. Taft sometimes converted the auxiliary control into a primary check. Under him the "Guardian Kings" became a bulwark against the "overwhelming mass of ill-digested legislation poured out by lawmakers." The heart of his Constitution was the Fifth and Fourteenth Amendments.

In the name of the people he tried to protect the people from themselves. Since the people had enthroned private property and liberty of contract in the Constitution, it became the Court's function to safeguard these fundamental rights against "legalized experiment." Purporting always to judge *under* the law, he declared: "I do not allow myself to be moved by anything except the law,"[108] Taft's reverence for "the law"—his law—probably did more to undermine popular respect for *the law* than he realized.*

In 1893, James Bradley Thayer had solemnly underscored the danger of substituting judicial supremacy for judicial review. Not always sensitive to this threat, Taft attempted to identify judicial gloss with the Constitution itself. The Supreme Court thus became "a sacred priesthood immune from profane criticism."[109] That is why he accorded high value to judicial stability—continuity from one case to the next, consistency with the most recent precedents. In *Stafford,* he went back to *Swift,* not to *Knight.* The unanimous decision in *Bailey* followed the three-year-old prece-

---

* Said Roscoe Pound:

Perhaps nothing has contributed so much to create and foster hostility to courts and law and constitutions as this conception of the courts as guardians of individual natural rights against the state and against society, of the law as a final and absolute body of doctrine declaring these individual natural rights, and of constitutions as declaratory of common-law principles, anterior to the state and of superior validity to enactments by the authority of the state, having for their purpose to guarantee and maintain the natural rights of individuals against the government and all its agencies. "The End of Law as Developed in Juristic Thought," 27 *Harvard Law Review,* 605, 626–27 (1914).

dent established by a narrowly divided Court in *Hammer* v. *Dagenhart*. In *Adkins*, he preferred to rely on *Bunting* rather than join the majority's resurrection of *Lochner*. In *Wolff*, Taft relied on the majority opinion in *Adkins* from which he had just dissented. Reliance on the most recent precedents eliminated the tiresome task of distinguishing intervening cases. It avoided bickering about departures from recently traveled paths, making it easier to build a majority. Older precedents could be ignored, forgotten—overruled *sub silentio*. His interests lay not merely in a persuasive adjudication of the particular case, but in the integrity of the entire system of jurisprudence of which the instant case was a part.* Taft achieved these ends by good fellowship, by an engaging sense of humor, and by contagious appeals to his colleagues' respect for the Court as an institution. The significant occa-

* Chief Justice Hughes likewise valued "stability" in judicial decisions, but an important difference should be noted. Hughes sometimes selected precedents from the distant past, despite intervening decisions that undermined or discredited them. In his *Schechter* opinion and *Carter Coal* concurrence, he went back to the Sugar Trust case of 1895, ignoring Holmes's intervening *Swift* opinion of 1905 and Taft's forward-looking *Stafford* ruling only a decade away. In the New York minimum-wage case, he blithely skipped over the implications of the Nebbia and Minnesota Moratorium cases to reinstate the reactionary *Adkins* precedent. Hughes's habit of invoking discredited rulings tended to make him appear a stronger defender of the *status quo* than Taft.

In his quest for continuity, Hughes was forced to fall back on formulas and mechanical devices. The result was a series of decisions drawing fine distinctions, glossing over seemingly irreconcilable differences. On occasion he resorted to bald statements that stirred profound incredulity. In upholding the Wagner Act, he insisted that *Schechter* and *Carter Coal* were not controlling, but his reasoning obscured rather than clarified the assertion.

Hughes's approach has been sharply criticized because each opinion raised questions as to why certain recent precedents had been ignored. By using standard techniques of constitutional interpretation, Taft managed to reach his ends without incurring self-inflicted wounds. Before the famous "switch in time," the Hughes Court was bleeding from a whole series of irreconcilable decisions. Moreover, when the judicial revolution occurred in *Jones-Laughlin*, Hughes reverted to Chief Justice Taft's realistic construction of "commerce" and of the commerce power in *Stafford*. At the same time he cited *E. C. Knight* and *Schechter* as controlling authorities! See 301 U.S. 1 at 35–37. "He [Hughes] could pose polar opposites," Thomas Reed Powell noted, "without confessing they were opposites. . . ." 67 *Political Science Quarterly* 161 (1952), 172.

sions on which Justice Brandeis withheld his fire is a measure of Taft's remarkable success in utilizing these very human weapons.

In *Adkins,* the Chief Justice seemed to stray from his conservative values. He may have felt it was far better to stick to controlling precedent rather than incur the risk of tarnishing the image of stability. In the long run, continuity of decision would better serve the interest of private property than obvious judicial flaunting of precedent. So the Chief Justice lodged one of his rare dissents, chastising the majority for rejecting *stare decisis.* The same rationale underlay his earlier preference that the abortive Income Tax decision of 1895 be reversed by amendment rather than by mere legislative enactment. For Congress to assume that the Court will reverse itself, and to enact legislation on such an assumption, would not strengthen popular confidence in the judiciary.

It might be thought that Taft loved "the law" more than he loved property. This overlooks the intimate relationship he saw between judicial protection of property and the pristine judicial image. The illusion of stability preserved popular respect for courts, making it easier to wield judicial power in defense of property. At bottom, Taft's love for the law was an expedient romance. "Taft worshiped the law," his biographer writes in a final appraisal. "No understanding of him is possible without appreciation of that fact. The fallacy in his philosophy lies, of course, in the fact that there is no such thing as 'the law.' . . . What Taft really did was to revere the law, as he understood it, himself, or as judges with whom he agreed had interpreted it."[110]

It seems never to have occurred to Taft that this presumably objective rule often coincided with subjective desire. An absolutist at heart, "the law" was his instrument of power. Taft revealed this tendency long before coming to the Court. In certain respects, the governorship of the Philippines seems to have been more satisfying than any other post he ever held. He was virtually "a dictator in the archipelago of the far Pacific."

> No Senate Progressives plagued him there. . . . No Democrats abused and attacked him. No Theodore Roosevelt turned against him. The politicos of the Philippines disagreed with his policies, of course, but in the last analysis Taft could impose his will. His voice was the law. He was, again, a judge.[111]

Taft had been loath to enter presidential politics. Nor were his misgivings unfounded. The White House complex—forcing bad actions and decisions, preventing or checking desirable ones—had been confusing, limiting, and frustrating. After his unhappy years as President, he continued to yearn for judicial office, preferably the Chief Justiceship, where he could enforce "the law" without fear or favor. From "the seat under the clock," his voice might again be law.* For a while it was; dissents were few; the Chief Justice regularly succeeded in "massing the Court." Soon the façade of solidity began to crumble. Finally, with the defection of the once loyal Stone to the Holmes-Brandeis bloc, Taft ironically became the prisoner of the same force—popular power—that had wreaked such havoc on his Presidency. Even the Court, conceived as an antidemocratic insti-

---

* Felix Frankfurter reports this significant exchange with Justice Brandeis after Taft became Chief Justice:

"Felix, do you still think that Taft was as bad a President as we thought he was?"

I [Frankfurter] said that I hadn't changed my mind on that subject; looking back on it I still thought that he was as bad a President as I thought he was contemporaneously. Then I said to him, "Why do you raise the question? Why are you ready to reconsider that judgment?"

Then he [Brandeis] said, "It's very difficult for me to understand why a man who is so good as Chief Justice, in his function of presiding officer, could have been so bad as President. How do you explain that?"

To which I replied, "The explanation is very simple. He loathed being President and being Chief Justice was all happiness for him. He fought against being President and yielded to the acceptance of that heritage because of the insistence of Mrs. Taft—very ambitious in that direction. It always had been the ambition of his life to be on the Supreme Court. Taft once said that the Supreme Court was his notion of what heaven must be like." *Felix Frankfurter Reminisces,* pp. 85–86.

tution, designed to check ill-tempered mass excesses, was not immune from the blight of sheer numbers. Votes counted there, just as surely as they did in Congress or in the voting booths; and each vote was equal. Formerly Taft had reckoned rather successfully with the politics of judicial decision-making; now dissents came in droves. "Holmes, Brandeis, and Stone, dissenting" became a commonplace. Worse still, the dissenters stood for popular government—the right of the people to rule. The Chief Justice envisaged the deluge, the popular uprising against which he had so vigorously and so effectively pitted a conservative Court. During his last few years at the judicial helm, as during his Presidency, Taft might well have yearned for the good old days in the Philippines, where he had carried on such a satisfying romance with "the law."

CHAPTER XI

PROPRIETIES

To UNNUMBERED Americans William Howard Taft appeared to be almost the stereotype of a Chief Justice—"a perfect fit."[1] He was physically impressive. Large of frame and good-natured, with more than a little bay window, he filled out the popular image of the venerable patriarch dispensing unadulterated justice. Taft was known as "the politest man alive." "I heard that recently he arose in a streetcar," Justice Brewer reported, "and gave his seat to three women."

In all aspects of the Court's work, Taft felt a keen sense of personal responsibility. In ways large and small, he sought to build it up in the public mind. A strong believer in the magic of judicial dress, especially the robe, he required lawyers without waistcoats to button up their coats and tuck in their four-in-hand ties.[2] One attorney came before the Justices clad in a Palm Beach suit. The perspiring Chief Justice summarily dismissed him before arguing his case. A country lawyer, appearing to be sworn in as a member of the Supreme Court bar, was so flustered that he forgot to leave his hat in the cloakroom. While still clutching it in his hand, awaiting his turn, he was curtly dismissed.[3]

Taft was meticulous about the conduct, no less than the dress, of attorneys at the bar of his Court. He complained of young lawyers who "get into court and seek to establish the correctness of the arguments they press . . . by contemptuous reference to the court or courts whose decision they seek to reverse."[4] Tracing this practice to its apparent source, he reminded law-school faculties that "the free language of the recitation room and the uncomplicated comment upon opinions in the class may mislead those just from that atmosphere into the use of this in court briefs."[5] Disparaging comment filed by opposing counsel was chastised for its "bad temper and recklessness."[6] Taft was apt to be abrupt with counsel who failed to argue the merits of the case and neglected to show any "reason for being there."[7] "What I want to know is . . . ," the Chief Justice would boom out, preliminary to a long list of embarrassing jurisdictional questions.[8]

In 1925 Senator Reed of Missouri, an old adversary, delivered "half an hour's agonized effort on the necessity for the maintenance of the freedom of the press . . . and almost wept."[9] Holmes, sitting next to the Chief Justice, muttered: "This is drool."[10] Reed, delivering "himself in true Senate style," had brought along a stenographer, hoping, the former President suspected, to get it all into the Hearst papers.[11] But the Chief Justice could be generous and charmingly good-natured. One flustered lawyer, addressing the Court as "Gentlemen," instead of the customary "Your Honors," stammered out an apology. Taft promptly put him at ease. The lawyer "need not apologize for calling them gentlemen, for that was what they all hoped they were."[12]

The behavior of colleagues was also a matter of concern. Opinions had to be written in a style befitting the highest tribunal in the nation. On one occasion,[13] Justice Holmes, objecting to the lengthy recital of a statute, remarked that these were unnecessary amplifications "to stop rat holes." Taft considered such language undignified. Amused by this disagreement on literary style, Holmes suggested that Court reports "were dull because we had the notion that judicial dignity required solemn fluffy speech."[14] Suspicious of the subversive influence of the law schools, the Chief Justice frowned on the citation of law review articles in judicial opinions. Near the end of his tenure, when intra-Court differences threatened to break out into the open, he urged his colleagues to phrase their dissents "so as to be dignified at least." He was worried lest the Court on opinion day "degenerate into a place to attract people as the Senate attracts people with Heflin speaking."[15]

Taft was sensitive, though less so than most of his predecessors, to the bearing of his own conduct on the public attitude toward his Court. Chief Justice White had refused to attend the annual Gridiron Dinner fearing that uncomplimentary remarks might undermine the Court's awe-inspiring impact.[16] White even refused to lend his support to a new Supreme Court building, believing that if the Court sat anywhere but in the Capitol the public would lose interest in it. Chief Justice Taft took exactly the opposite position. The suggestion that space be found in the Department of Justice, making it a sort of continental palace of justice, was utterly unacceptable to him. "The chief body at the head of the judiciary branch of the government," he insisted, "ought to have a building of its own," and "one under our control."[17]

Taft wanted not only to elevate the Court in the governmental hierarchy but also to heighten the Chief Justice's prestige. His concept of the office was breath-taking, revolutionary. To exalt his beloved Court, he not only added significantly to its inherent powers, but strained his traditional authority to the limit. Having augmented the Chief Justice's formal and informal powers, he was sensitive to any condition that might jeopardize the Court's dignity.

Wide discrepancies between salaries of the Justices and those of Cabinet members represented an unpardonable slight. High Court judges should receive at least $18,000 or $20,000 a year if for no other reason than "to dignify the office."[18] The Chief Justice should, he thought, receive the highest judicial salary in the country. Even at $20,000 his salary would be less by $5,000 than that of the Chief Judge of the New York Court of Appeals.[19]

More subtle slights undermined the Court's position, particularly that of the Chief Justice. Until 1925 all the Justices, including Taft, assumed that at state functions, they outranked Cabinet officers. "Matters of precedence with me are not matters of primary importance . . . ," the Chief wrote C. Bascom Slemp, adding, "I presume it is not denied that the Supreme Court of the United States comes first."[20] Shortly thereafter, the Chief expressed his wounded feeling to Secretary of State Hughes. At a recent embassy party, Justice McReynolds had been outranked by Cabinet members, offending his personal vanity and damaging the body of which he was a member.[21] In response to an inquiry, the State Department told the Chief Justice that Supreme Court Justices ranked ahead of all Cabinet officers except the Secretary of State, who, as ambassador at foreign embassy functions, necessarily took precedence.[22] McReynolds continued to press his complaint, finally eliciting assurances from Secretary of State Hughes himself that thereafter "the Chief Justice of the United States should have precedence over the Secretary of State."[*23]

When Congress appeared to trample on the Court's prerogatives, the Chief Justice reacted even more heatedly. Senator Charles Curtis of Kansas, the Gibraltar of Republicanism, received a sizzling letter when he hesitated in distributing a ticket for the 1925 inaugural ceremony to the wife of Taft's late associate, Mahlon Pitney. "I should like to know," Taft asked, "whether the Supreme Court is going to get any tickets. We are members of the Government and occupy a part of the Capitol."[24] "You can not keep me out at any rate," the Chief Justice challenged, "because I have got to swear in the President. I suppose they will give me a seat on the platform for that."[25] Two weeks later unmistakable evidence of congressional capitulation lay on the Chief Jus-

* A news item, October 1, 1961, announcing that the Speaker of the House had been accorded in the 1962 "Green Book" seating ahead of the Chief Justice, erroneously declared that the higher rank had been granted the Chief Justice in 1921 because he was also a former President.

tice's desk—three tickets to Calvin Coolidge's inauguration.[26] These seemingly trivial episodes reveal Taft's interest in intangibles, indicating the lengths to which he went in his effort to build up his Court.

Maintenance of the judiciary's position depended less on social protocol than on the daily conduct of the Justices, especially that of the Chief. As Chief Executive, Taft had held a highly restricted conception of the powers at his command. As Chief Justice, he took the opposite tack, investing his office with prerogatives for which there were few, if any, precedents. After four difficult years in the White House, he realized that "if you go pussyfooting . . . when you try to do something worthwhile, my experience convinces me that you will fail."[27]

The vague canons of propriety were useful chiefly as an excuse for preferred courses of action. To resolve a three-year contest between the Bethlehem Steel Company and 38,000 former employees, Acting Secretary of War Jonathan M. Wainwright requested an advisory opinion. A claim of $1,500,000 in back pay[28] was based on a 1918 National War Labor Board decision. Ex-President Taft had headed the Board, and Wainwright, whose department processed these cases, naturally wanted his advice. In 1918 the former President had taken no position on the issue. Nor would he do so now. "I ought not to disqualify myself by present expression of opinion, should the issue come before the Supreme Court. . . . For that reason, I am going to ask you to excuse me from discussing the subject at all."[*][29]

One of the most firmly established rules of propriety is that a judge must not fraternize with lawyers appearing before his Court. Perhaps there is none which Chief Justice Taft more easily honored in the breach. It seemed quite natural to exhibit cordiality toward lawyer friends whose integrity could not be impeached. One day Charles Evans Hughes

* Despite persistent rumors Taft supported the workers' claims; the War Department rejected them. *The New York Times,* Aug. 28, 1921.

had appeared at the Capitol to argue before the high bench. The Court had adjourned and the Justices were on their way to the robing room. Suddenly the Chief Justice, seeing Hughes, rushed up, clapped him on the shoulder and exclaimed jovially,

> "Hughes, my boy, I am delighted to see you."
>
> "Mr. Chief Justice," Hughes replied with frigid propriety, "I am honored to see you."
>
> Taft was puzzled and astonished. Asked by a friend why he had treated the Chief Justice so coldly, Hughes replied:
>
> "I did it intentionally, as I intend to win my cases on their merits and not through friendship with the judges."[30]

One suspects that the implications of Hughes's reaction would have been even more astonishing to Chief Justice Taft than the initial snub.

The propriety of participating in extrajudicial tasks was weighed more carefully. A strong supporter of the League of Nations and the World Court, he was "glad to help judicial settlement of international controversies."[31] An opportunity arose shortly after his appointment in 1921. That year the United States intervened to halt hostilities between Panama and Costa Rica over disputed boundaries. In 1914 Chief Justice White, acting under the 1910 Porras-Anderson Treaty, had arbitrated this controversy. His arbitral decision called on Panama to cede portions of its territory to Costa Rica.[32] Panama, however, neither recognized the award, nor joined in selecting a member of the Boundary Commission provided for in Article II of the Treaty. The Chief Justice of the United States was authorized to name two surveyors, but White had never done so. When the 1921 crisis arose, Costa Rica, anxious to make the award irrevocable, requested Taft to carry out the treaty's terms by appointing the engineers. Pondering the proprieties, Taft wondered "whether my succession to the office of Chief Justice makes me succeed White as arbitrator."[33] To resolve his doubts, he called on

Secretary of State Charles Evans Hughes. Together they decided that the prerogative of the appointment belonged to the Chief Justice and not to White personally. His misgivings quelled, Taft appointed two professors to make the survey.[34]

Extrajudicial tasks sometimes won his endorsement. When President Hoover selected Willis Van Devanter to arbitrate the "I'm Alone" case, Taft, having satisfied himself that Van's absence would be of short duration, warmly approved the choice.[35] Taft had concluded "that it was not of such an extended character that it could not be disposed of very promptly. . . ."[36] President Hoover's determination to appoint Justice Stone to head the Law Enforcement Commission was an altogether different matter. Service on the Commission would continue through the two or three years of its life. It might prove disabling in the performance of his judicial duties.[37] Taft favored the appointment of Brandeis or Van Devanter, both being entitled to retire. When the President finally turned to former Attorney General George Wickersham, the Chief Justice commented dourly: "My impression is that Hoover is so much under Progressive influence that it would be enough to be against George on account of his relation to me in the past, although I would think that George could put the thing through rather more promptly and effectively than any of them."[38]

Dinner invitations inundated the Chief Justice. Balancing judicial proprieties with the demands of social obligations was not easy. "We have had to go through rather a social campaign," he groaned at the end of the 1922 winter season.[39] In early 1922, Senator Norris, noting the Chief Justice's whirlwind social life, scathingly deplored it as a corrupting influence.[40] Stung to the quick, Taft commented: "You can see that even on the bench, one does not escape the yawping of some demagogues."[41] Norris had resorted to "a trivial and contemptible method of seeking to undermine one's influence and that of the Court."[42] Two days later, in declining a dinner invitation from the G. Stuart Pattersons, of Chestnut Hill, Pennsylvania, the Chief Justice explained: "I have had a warning from Senator Norris that I am likely to be corrupted by dinners, and of course I must preserve the eminence of the judiciary."[43]

The insurgent Senator's onslaught was only the beginning. A year later William Randolph Hearst splashed across his pages the report that Taft was receiving a $10,000 annuity from the Carnegie Corporation, the interest on $200,000 in mortgage bonds of the United States Steel Corporation. Taft, as ex-President, had become involved as a result of the generosity of steelmaster Andrew Carnegie. Carnegie's will provided an income of $10,000 during Taft's life and the same amount to Mrs. Taft should she survive him. With an estate, including insurance, worth about $300,000, he did not need the money, and he hesitated to accept it. But on the urgings of others, including Elihu Root, and under pressure from his wife, he had decided to take it. "Mrs. Taft wishes me to do it, and she is an interested party," Taft explained.[44] The press rallied strongly to the Chief Justice's support. Much gratified, he observed "that no other newspapers took any part in the attack, and those which have spoken have noted its injustice."[45]

The Hearst attack struck at the very fiber of his financial ethics. Refusing to risk the prestige of his Court which, "next to my wife and children, is the nearest thing to my heart in life,"[46] he assigned all benefits to Yale University. "I am profoundly concerned," he wrote President Angell, "that the usefulness and influence of the Court should not be lessened on this account. . . ."[47] Still pondering this troublesome annuity episode, he wrote:

A Chief Justice has to be more circumspect than Caesar's wife, and life is so varied for him that there are many pitfalls, due to many laws which he can easily violate. When, therefore, a case arose in which prejudiced men would rejoice to point the finger of scorn at my inconsistency and violation of the law, however innocent and in good faith, and could injure me in the estimate of men and women whose good opinion is worth having and, which is far more important, could injure the Court of which I am the head, I think it was very natural that I should worry.[48]

Participation in numerous voluntary organizations, many of them holdovers from years of private life, also raised the issue of propriety. These associations absorbed time and energy; more important, membership might prove awkward in litigation involving them.[49] Resigning from the National Civic Federation, he explained: " . . . it is not proper for a Chief Justice of the United States to be included in an organization dealing with controversial questions of a political or social character."[50] Taft retained membership in other organizations, including the Hampton Normal and Agricultural Institute for Negroes. Even this became embarrassing in 1926, when the Virginia legislature passed legislation separating the races in public assemblies. Ranking officials of Hampton Institute pressed the Chief Justice, as member of the Board of Trustees, to urge Governor Byrd to veto the measure. Taft vehemently denounced the "unsanity of race prejudice"; but he refused to write a letter. "One of the reasons why I dislike to be connected with any institution, other than the Supreme Court," he explained, "is that in one way or another, . . . my colleagues always seek to use the influence of my position to affect measures in which the institution is interested. It is this which makes me very anxious to break off association with everything."[51]

One organization he never eliminated from his life was the American Bar Association. Too closely linked to his professional career, too vitally related to the attainment of the legal reforms he had long espoused, the Bar Association remained a magnet for Taft's unwavering allegiance. At numerous annual conventions the gregarious Chief Justice threw himself into the task of promoting judicial reform. "I had spoken at the meeting of the affiliated Bar association," he wrote after the 1923 convention, "then at the meeting of the Minnesota State Bar Association in the afternoon and then at the dinner of the Judicial section in the evening. At noontime I had to go to a Harvard Law School luncheon and make a speech."[52]

A day of pumping hands, making small talk, alerting the delegates to the necessity of supporting this or that reform, and endless large and small meals left the Chief Justice exhausted.[53] Originally he had hoped to escort a large contingent of his colleagues to these meetings and thus win the bar's endorsement of measures his Court sponsored.[54] Querying the propriety of this course of action, his Associates were strongly opposed. Even the Chief's participation came under fire. Preparing to preside at a meeting of the Committee for the Improvement of Law, he noted with chagrin that "some of my brethren are kicking about it, notably McKenna, who thinks it is a reflection on the court, which shows how childish he is growing."[55] Encouraging the Chief Justice's own inclinations, Elihu Root noted that Taft was the "first Chief Justice to fully appreciate the dynamics of the Bar as an organization."[56] The Bar was a force for reform Congress could not safely ignore. "There is no reason why," he wrote in 1923, "the Bar should not exert a tremendous influence through the country. Its organization is necessary to bring about such a result. I want, so far as I can, to organize the Bench and Bar into a united group in this country dedicated to the cause of the improvement in judicial procedure and in the defense of the constitutional provisions for the maintaining, through the judiciary, of the guarantees of the Constitution."[57]

The Bar Association's technical resources and its usefulness as a pressure group loomed so importantly that Taft was unable to resist taking on even trivial tasks. Despite a slight heart attack in the spring of 1924, he busied himself as head of an American Bar Association committee in search of a site for the statue of Blackstone in the Hall of the Law Court in England. Outraged, Elihu Root asked:

> . . . why in the devil should you be bothering yourself about the site for that statue of Blackstone. Unless you prevent it, a succession of little things of that kind will prevent you from being a real Buddha. Turn all these little things over to Mischler. He can locate statues just as well as you can. But he can't be a Buddha. That is your business and it is of primary importance.[58]

The solid considerations motivating his generosity became evident three years later when the Conference of Bar Association Delegates met with its chairman, Charles Evans Hughes, to discuss the need for an improved organization of the bar. In a letter read by Hughes, Taft blasted local bar associations, "which in the past had been formed too often for merely social enjoyment and fraternization, with but a subordinate purpose to secure needed self-discipline and to influence legislative bodies to real reform measures of legal procedure."[59]

Interest in judicial reform, and the Bar Association as an instrument for promoting it, antedated his Chief Justiceship. He had publicized his views at Chautauquas and in magazines and newspapers. After coming to the bench, Taft was deluged with invitations to give addresses and write articles. He pleaded overwork and the "traditional silence which wisdom has imposed on judges, lest they be led into expressions that will rise to confront them in some issue that comes before the Court."[60] Yet arguments and opinions of an earlier day continued to be published. In extenuation, he insisted that "if in any phase such issues were to come before the Court . . . my 'curbstone' opinions would not have the slightest weight with me."[61]

One way of avoiding embarrassment was to exercise discretion in his public comments. A guiding rule was that the ultimate purpose be public service. In 1925 he and Van Devanter wrote an article describing the "Judges' Bill."[62] "I am generally not in favor of Judges writing articles," he explained, "but as this is a new subject, I think it will help us to have the Bar get clearly in their minds what our power is with this act."[63]

Nevertheless, offhand remarks continued to plague the Chief Justice. On one occasion he declared that "the administration of criminal law in the United States is a disgrace to our civilization. . . ."[64] When the chairman of the $5,000,000 Harvard Law School Endowment Drive announced his intention to use this statement for promotional purposes, William D. Guthrie, president of the New York City Bar Association, objected vehemently. Guthrie charged that Taft's statement, reflecting on the character of lawyers and judges, had "done more harm than any other single utterance . . . made during the last thirty years."[65] The Chief Justice's derogatory comment vanished from the Harvard booklet, but Taft urged the editor of the New York *World* to "continue . . . to emphasize the necessity for public attention to this matter of strengthening our machinery for the prosecution of crimes and arousing legislators and the Bar to their responsibility in the matter."[66]

The year was 1926; the nation was in the grip of a crime wave. Agitated by the increasing audacity of mobsters and the feeble reaction of law-enforcement agencies, Taft granted an interview to Oliver P. Newman of *Collier's* magazine. Newman's "Stop Helping the Criminal" inveighed against clumsy state police methods and cumbersome judicial practice. Later Taft wondered about the propriety of the interview. "I presume it is unusual for a Chief Justice to submit to an interview like this," he wrote the *Collier's* editor, "but it seems to me the circumstances are exceptional, and that those who criticize the propriety will not be blind to the necessity for emphasizing in every possible way the duty of the Legislatures of the States and the Executives to assume and exercise more responsibility in respect to this most serious menace to the usefulness of our Government."[67]

Publication of Newman's feature article continued to stir doubts.[68] "I shrink from the publicity that you are giving to the article," the Chief wrote the editor. "It is not of sufficient importance, and I can not help doubting the propriety of my having given you the interview."[69]

Such misgivings did not curb his activities. Three years later he granted an interview to Basil Manly of the Washington *Star*, again attacking lax law enforcement. "Our police forces," he declared, "our prosecuting organizations, and our court system must all be improved until we are able to subdue these criminal organizations. . . . If we can perfect our police systems and our court procedures, I have no doubt that within a reasonable time we can bring under control even the most aggressive gangs which are now preying upon our cities and States."[70] That such statements threw the spotlight on those primarily responsible—state and Federal agents and judges—did not matter. Nor did the knowledge that by implication he was passing judgment on the policies of relatively autonomous state government organizations and on those guiding Federal executive departments deter him.

Partisan politics was not off limits for Chief Justice Taft. Right-thinking Republicans could usually look to him for a helping hand. Always alert to the danger of Progressive uprisings, he decided that plunging in was sometimes the better part of valor. The night of President Harding's funeral he tried to gauge Coolidge's political strength, sounding out the 1916 presidential hopeful Charles Evans Hughes on the possibility of his running again. Hughes declared, the Chief Justice reported, that "he would not run for the Presidency and that was final."[71] With Hughes's unqualified negative, the former President wrote Charles D. Hilles that "my own impression is that Coolidge is the one upon whom more people can agree for nomination than anybody else."[72]

Later the Chief Justice became increasingly apprehensive about the President's chances, not for the nomination but for election. The Senate was apparently determined to pull the nails out of the tax-reduction plank in Coolidge's platform.

Still other aspects of the G.O.P. program enlisted his active concern. No measure jeopardized Mellon's tax plan so much as the bonus bill raid. To induce the two wayward Connecticut Senators to vote against it, Taft appealed to Charles Clark, editor of the influential Hartford *Courant:* "I think you ought to get going and do what you can to straighten the situation out."[73] "Of course," he noted somewhat sheepishly, "I have no right to take any part in this business, being on the Bench, but you and I are such close friends that I can trust you not to betray me."[74] Two weeks later a Taft-inspired editorial graced the pages of the *Courant,* evoking the Chief Justice's not wholly disinterested comment "that Charley Clark is nearing the right view on the subject."[75] All this extrajudicial maneuvering proved unavailing. Both Senators added their votes to the majority in favor of the bonus.

The surest means of preventing "disloyalty" was to elect loyal Republicans. He had begun his term determined to stay out of partisan politics. In 1921 Cyrenus Cole, running for the seat in Iowa's Fifth Congressional District, requested his endorsement. Taft resolutely turned him down. "As I have been appointed and qualified as Chief Justice, I feel that the proprieties prevent my taking any part whatever in a political contest. . . ."[76] As it turned out, Cole won the election anyway.

Much more crucial was the 1924 presidential race. Despite strong resolutions, the Chief Justice could not remain on the sidelines. As the year rolled on, it became apparent that Robert La Follette and his followers would bolt the Republican party, repeating the 1912 debacle, perhaps throwing the entire election into the House of Representatives. After La Follette's attack on the Court, and after the Progressive party's platform was released, the Chief Justice found it hard to remain cloistered. Rejecting a request from the Chicago *Daily News* for an article on campaign issues, he reminded the editor that ". . . it had never been the custom for judges of our Court to take part in political discussion in a presidential campaign, and certainly I would not be the first to initiate a departure from that rule, which is so necessary to the maintenance of the independence of our Court."[77] Self-restraint could not last. On the eve of the 1924 Republican Convention, he communicated with New York Republican Charles Hilles, Vice-Chairman of the party's Executive Committee as well as a member of the Convention's Credentials Committee. A zealous supporter of the World Court, Taft bluntly told Hilles to pack the Resolutions Committee with the Court's friends. This would ensure a strong platform plank approving America's participation in it.[78] After Henry Taft called on the delegates to pledge the party's support to the protocol establishing the Permanent Court of International Justice, a terse endorsement appeared in the platform.[79]

By 1924 the Chief Justice was preoccupied less with the fate of the World Court than with Western insurgency. Dissident Republicanism was of continuing concern. Battle-hardened himself, knowing exactly how to deal with these "Yahoos," he directed Hilles to "give authority to the Executive Committee to run an independent ticket in any case in which a Republican candidate regularly selected for the Senate, or for the House, shall be found supporting a third-party candidate."[80] To no one's surprise, La Follette headed a third-party slate, and Coolidge emerged as the Republican standard-bearer. No sooner had the convention ended than the Chief Justice wrote Louis Wiley of *The New York Times*, showering praise on the G.O.P. nominee, hailing his courage and steadfastness in the face of radical threats. Wiley endorsed Taft's appraisal of the President, but cautiously noted that "the position the *Times* will take in the presidential campaign cannot be determined until after the Democrats have acted."[81]

In the ensuing campaign Taft kept more or less within bounds. But when Charles Evans Hughes enlivened the campaign with a fighting speech at Cincinnati, he acclaimed it warmly. To his delight, Hughes had torn apart La Follette's platform with a vengeance, hammering especially at the plank attacking the Supreme Court.[82] "If the proposal of the Third Party were adopted," Hughes warned, "everything you have, the security of your person and life, would be held at the mercy of Congress."[83] The ex-President hailed Hughes's fighting words as "far and away the best speech of the campaign."[84] "The greatest thing you could do," he urged one die-hard Republican, "would be to circulate the last part of Mr. Hughes' speech on the third party among the people of California, Washington, Iowa, Minnesota, West Virginia and Maryland."[85]

During the Presidency of Calvin Coolidge, Taft was a frequent White House visitor. Known as the *fidus Achates* of the administration, the Chief Justice went to see Coolidge in the interest of causes related to the Court, but not exclusively so. Taft was among those who took the famous "I do not choose to run" pronouncement with the proverbial grain of salt. "He is the strongest man we have and he is safe,"[86] Taft commented hopefully. Coolidge was credited with "giving more body to the Republican party than it had had for a long time, the representative of prosperity."[87] The skyrocketing bull market was God's good and perfect gift to the Chief Justice's class and to his party. Nor were there any clouds darkening this silver lining. In early 1927, after a pleasant White House visit, "general business seemed to be settling itself into wise progress without feverish speculation."[88] Blocking realization of the brightest prospects in the country's history were six little words—"I do not choose to run"—the laconic Vermonter had uttered in the Black Hills. Though frequently Coolidge's guest, affording the President ample opportunity to express himself, the Chief Justice was never able to squeeze one word of elaboration, much less a hint that the President might yield to a draft. By late spring 1927, it became certain that Herbert Hoover would control the National Convention. In June, Taft sadly accepted this cruel fate.

It is difficult to square Taft's partisan political activity with the canons formulated by the Bar Association's Committee on Judicial Ethics, which Taft himself headed. "Judges should not take an active part in political campaigns," the 1922 code declared, "either by appearing on the platform for public discussion of partisan issues or by publishing their political sentiments for the benefit of candidates or in aid of a political faction or party."*[89] Cherishing victory for Coolidge and a resounding defeat for La Follette, Taft played a partisan political role unmatched by any Chief Justice of the United States since Salmon P. Chase.

Taft's political activities spread beyond domestic politics. Early in his tenure, he visited England, a pilgrimage designed to "strengthen the bond between the two countries"; foster a spirit of amity and cooperation between lawyers and judges of the two nations; enhance the stature of the American Bar Association; and, most importantly, permit him to study at first hand the more efficient English court procedure.[90] Arriving in the summer of 1922, the Chief Justice stepped into a boiling European financial crisis. Every nation, including Great Britain, owed the United States tremendous sums of money for supplies purchased during and after World War I. The entire repayment structure rested on the sagging foundations of a prostrate Germany. An inflationary holocaust was sweeping the country. France, whose reparation demands had been steadily trimmed, was preparing to exert pressure; England was clamoring for war debt cancellation.

Into this economic-political tangle, Taft plunged imme-

* Ethics canon Number 23 expressly endorsed Taft's reform activities. "A judge has exceptional opportunity to observe the operation of statutes, especially those relating to practice, and to ascertain whether they tend to impede the just disposition of controversies; and he may well contribute to the public interest by advising those having authority to remedy defects of procedure, of the result of his observation and experience."

diately. Speaking at a 10 Downing Street luncheon, the Chief Justice stood squarely behind George Harvey, United States Ambassador to the Court of St. James. Harvey's plan was to make the United States and Great Britain responsible for debt payments by jointly issuing bonds.[91] Soon after the conference, Taft informed President Harding and Secretary of State Hughes of his approval, leaving to Harvey the task of transmitting details.[92] Consternation enveloped the executive branch when Taft's letter reached the President before any communication was received from the Ambassador. Harding frantically contacted Hughes, only to discover that his intelligence also came from the Chief Justice. In a quandary, the President wrote:

> Your letter to the Secretary of State, as the one to me, has set the Secretary and myself wondering a bit as to what sort of a plan the Ambassador is suggesting. . . . I have asked the Secretary to make inquiry for information. I think any workable plan, other than cancellation, would be given pretty ready consideration by the members of our Debt Commission.[93]

The World War Foreign Debt Commission, established by Congress, provided a constant thorn in the side of debtor nations; it was legislatively prohibited from canceling any debts or accepting interest rates below 4½ per cent. Yet after Taft's meeting with Lloyd George, the embarrassing rumor spread that he and Harvey "had promised the English that they should get a reduction of the debt to a 2½ per cent basis."[94] Aware of the storm of protest such a report would arouse in Congress, he vigorously denied it, contending that Harvey had unmistakably insisted "that there was no hope of forgiving the debt . . . , and that they had better get ready to make the best arrangement they could."[95] Ambassador Harvey had told Lloyd George's successor, Bonar Law, that the British debt might be settled at a 2 per cent interest rate,[96] an intimation of policy that dismayed Hughes and puzzled the Chief Justice. Not responsible for foreign affairs, and unfamiliar with Hughes's policy and with Harvey's unauthorized debt diplomacy, Taft was left to ponder the intricacies of American international relations—a responsibility not entrusted to the head of the judiciary. In letters to both Harding and Hughes, Taft guessed that Lloyd George, a leading practitioner of personal diplomacy, had given the luncheon "for the purpose of making an appeal to me, which should filter through me to you. . . ."[97] If that was his purpose, Lloyd George's expectations were entirely successful.

More closely allied to his role as judicial leader were Taft's earnest efforts on behalf of America's participation in the Permanent Court of International Justice. Since approval of its creation, in December 1920, by the Assembly of the League of Nations, the Chief Justice had agitated for Senate acceptance. By 1922 the League and Court had become fatally embroiled in partisan politics. Thereafter, the *American Bar Association Journal* reported, Taft remained tactfully silent on the issue.[98] Yet he went on a confidential mission, approved by Secretary of State Hughes. Before departing, Hughes requested Taft to "see if the League of Nations could not so modify the statute establishing the Court as the United States might become a participant in respect to the Court, without assuming any of the obligations of the League."[99] In England, the Chief Justice explained the two conditions for America's membership on the Court: freedom from all other League obligations and equal opportunity to vote in the selection of its members.[100] After sounding out British opinion, the Chief Justice assured Hughes: "I found all of them much interested in the suggestions and favorable to it. . . ."[101]

Confidence strengthened, he opened negotiations with Lord Robert Cecil, at the latter's request. Cecil, Britain's representative at Geneva, informed him that any alteration in the statute creating the Court necessitated approval of the League's Assembly and that the change could be hastened if

Taft solicited the State Department's Court policy.[102] From Hughes, he learned that this country merely demanded "that the United States should have a vote for judges of the International Court although the United States is not a member of the League of Nations. . . ."[103] This was no help at all.

To reassure Cecil, Taft cast about for an alternative, finally discovering a weak substitute for a nonexistent American policy. Noting that the American Bar Association had passed a resolution advocating America's participation in the Court, Taft proudly recalled that "on my motion, the Committee on International Law was directed . . . to report the best procedure by which this object could be effected."[104] The one man who could get the project under way was Elihu Root, who together with Lord Phillimore had written the Court statute. Full of hope, Taft wrote him: "You ought to be able to draft a provision which would secure the object and make the difficulty of getting it through the Senate as little as possible."[105]

Six months later, President Harding sent to the Senate several proposed amendments incorporating conditions for membership on the Court. Foremost among them were the two contingencies which had guided Taft on his trip.[106] Fearing loss of sovereignty because of the Court's compulsory jurisdiction, the Senate balked. Finally in 1926 it approved a Court protocol, but with a fatal reservation—no American case should go to the World Court without the consent of two-thirds of the Senate. By that time Taft had severed his connection with the movement. After laboring four years to win American acceptance of both the Court and the League, the danger of public indignation aroused by his loose concept of the proprieties induced restraint. "This question of the World Court and of the League of Nations has become so distinctly political that being on the Bench, I must avoid activity in it. . . ."

Although Taft's trip to England involved nonjudicial matters, it also promoted a primary aim—to cement Anglo-American legal relations. The first fruits of Taft's expansive concept of his duties ripened the following year. Two thousand American and Canadian lawyers set sail for England—fountainhead of the Common Law. But once again the experience did not mean unalloyed pleasure. To his consternation, they embarked on the Cunard liner *Berengaria.* Since foreign ships were then able to serve alcoholic beverages outside the Prohibition zone, Taft feared charges that the bar had deliberately ignored the financially hard-pressed American shipping industry solely to quench its members' thirst for safe gin.[107] His apprehensions, doubtless stimulated by the knowledge that the year before he too had sailed on a British ship, were well founded. On the Senate floor Senator Norris queried: "I should like to ask . . . whether Chief Justice Taft did not likewise go on a British ship. . . . I think it ought to be said that the American Bar Association certainly have a legitimate right to follow a precedent established by the Chief Justice of the highest court in the land."[108]

"The Chief Justice," Taft had remarked in 1921, "goes into a monastery and confines himself to his judicial work."[109] He made this statement a month after his appointment, but he was unable to follow this rigid canon. As a result, the Chief Justiceship turned out to be less free from worry than he had anticipated. Naturally gregarious, eager to promote worthy causes, Taft exerted enormous influence on legislators, Presidents, Cabinet members, editors, lawyers, and friends—all this in spite of a host of tradition-ridden limitations imposed by judicial proprieties. His actions evoked a mixed chorus of condemnation and praise. While hearing the former, he turned an almost deaf ear to the latter. "A man who is never attacked," he rationalized, "is never useful, and one of the results of a long life's experience is to minimize the importance of such attacks. Circumstance and human nature give a pseudo importance to assaults upon one's character or one's motive, but it is reassuring to look back upon such attacks . . . and then note how soon their effect passed away and how quickly they are forgotten. . . ."[110] Critics were against progress and the Constitution, blind to the larger requirements of statesmanship. Moreover, Taft had the satisfaction of knowing that certain highly placed persons endorsed his action. Hailing Taft for his work in fostering Anglo-American solidarity, Ambassador George Harvey wrote: "You are the first Chief Justice to take the initiative in a great constructive programme, outside of and beyond the technical requirement of your exalted judicial position. You are thereby making an example . . . [for] all others in the public service to reach out in realization of the fact that any public office is only what the holder makes of it."[111]

Taft made the most of it. For him the Chief Justiceship became a veritable watchtower on the Potomac. From it he scanned the political horizons from Capitol Hill to the White House, from Costa Rica to London.

CHAPTER XII

FOREBODINGS

THE LIFE OF William Howard Taft is amazing both for the length of his public service (1881 to 1930) and for the variety of his activities: public prosecutor in his home state of Ohio, Solicitor General of the United States, Federal court judge, Governor General of the Philippines, Cabinet member, President of the United States, professor of law, and Chief Justice of the United States.

His years as Chief Justice span the "fabulous twenties," a period of economic expansion, political corruption, and high finance. The gospel of material prosperity—make the goods, get the goods, sell the goods—dominated American life. Industrial leaders, exultant with victory in World War I, encouraged by the political glory implicit in Harding's triumphant election, were certain that prosperity must be unending. "We want a period in America with less government in business and more business in government," President Harding announced. After Harding's untimely death came Calvin Coolidge, a man "whose essential qualities of mind and soul, and whose unswerving attachment to the fundamentals of free government" could not be questioned. Accepting the Republican nomination in 1928, Herbert Hoover averred that "no one can deny the fundamental correctness of our economic system." "We have not yet reached the goal," he commented hopefully, "but, given the chance to go forward with the policies of the last eight years, and we shall soon, with the help of God, be in sight of the day when poverty will be banished from this nation." The prospects for substantially unregulated enterprise were never so bright.

Taft never shared this unqualified optimism. The sheer force of numbers—popular power, whether organized in legislatures or in the ranks of trade unions—had long been a major preoccupation. Unruly forces, privileged and underprivileged, placed a high premium on law and judicial administration.[1] Early in his career he fixed his eye on the Supreme Court as the ultimate goal; his determination to reach it never wavered.

Law, the rock of civilization, made for certainty and order amid inevitable economic and social flux. Individual rights might be qualified to meet social needs,[2] but such changes, even when made "slowly and with deliberation,"[3] were palliatives invoked in default of "moral uplift"—the only genuine basis for a sound society.[4] Courts were society's assurance that the sober second thought of the community would prevail. "The leviathan, the People," he declared, "cannot . . . be given a momentum that will carry them in their earnestness and just indignation beyond the median and wise line."[5]

Taft came to the high bench determined to "preserve the form of government prescribed by our fathers."[6] Courts were best qualified to adjust judicial machinery and legal rules to current needs. During all the years prior to his Chief Justiceship, much thought and energy were devoted to hammering out specific revisions and promoting their enactment. Needed, above all, was the "executive principle." The Chief Justice should have an adequate administrative staff to keep watch over the dispatch of judicial business in all the districts and circuits. A periodic estimate of personnel needs should be made, and someone empowered to make the requisite assignments where the case load was heavy. On September 14, 1922, a year after he became Chief Justice, the Judicial Conference of Senior Circuit Judges came to fruition. Vainly Taft labored long and hard to secure revision of the outmoded Federal Rules of Civil Procedure. He backed construction of a Supreme Court building and played a leading role in selecting the site.

The groundwork for Taft's major achievement—the "Judges' Bill" of 1925—was laid as a Circuit Court judge. On March 17, 1892, soon after the Circuit Court of Appeals became fully organized under the act of March 4, 1891, President Harrison appointed him junior judge in the Sixth Circuit. Within a few months, he became presiding judge. Circuit Courts of Appeals were an experiment. Having participated in the trial period of these intermediate Federal courts, he saw the structure through to completion. Under the Act of February 13, 1925, nearly all the appellate jurisdiction which a defeated party can demand as of right was vested in the lower Federal courts.

For Taft a soundly constituted political society was almost a work of art; America's greatest institutional achievement was the judiciary, capped by the Supreme Court. It was not judicial power *per se,* but "the character of judicial power" that represented "the greatest advantage of our plan of government."[7] Taft believed with Plato that the propaedeutic for judicial guardianship of the republic lay not in mingling with the masses or in soiling one's hands in the grime of politics. It consisted rather in high-level contemplation of political values and in the development of an appropriate temper. A certain attitude—judicial temperament—was of the thew and sinew of a judge's moral fiber.[8]

The considerations moving him to oppose Brandeis in 1916 and enter the presidential campaign of 1920 went deeper than those motivating the beneficiary of any *ancien régime.* Scrupulous respect for property rights remained the core of his ideology. In the 1920's he became obsessed with the belief that these rights were jeopardized by those bent on the destruction of the institution designed for their protection. A major plank in La Follette's Progressive platform of 1924 aimed directly at judicial integrity. This threat had long been lurking on the political horizon. In 1893 and again in 1895, he had made this the subject of major pronouncements. In a presidential veto message of 1910, he had deplored the judicial recall as among the worst of all evils. The Supreme Court remained what it had been from the beginning—the bulwark of American society.

Under Chief Justice Taft's leadership, a firmly united judicial majority envisioned itself in the van of national progress. The laissez-faire dogma, glorified in the writings of Herbert Spencer and William Graham Sumner, was the principal avenue to wealth and social happiness. Spencer's measure of liberty—"the relative paucity of restraints imposed by government"—was raised to an ideal. Mr. Justice Sutherland sounded the dominant judicial keynote: "To sustain the individual freedom of action contemplated by the Constitution is not to strike down the common good but to exalt it; for surely the good of society as a whole cannot be better served than by the preservation against arbitrary restraint of the liberties of its constituent members."[9] Without the judicial check, popular action would more than likely be hasty and ill considered. "It is better to endure wrongs than to effect disastrous changes in which the proposed remedy may be worse than the evil."[10]

Responsibility for upholding time-tested values and for safeguarding society from the consequences of unwise legislative meddling rested primarily on the courts. Taft's wing of the Supreme Court wielded the authority of a "superlegislature." To protect property interests, the Justices indulged in what Dean Pound described as a "carnival of unconstitutionality." Before 1925 only fifty-three congressional acts were set aside. In the 1920's twelve, or nearly one fourth as many adverse rulings, were handed down. Between 1890 and 1937, 228 state statutes were nullified.

"Since 1920," Professor Frankfurter noted in 1930, "the Court has invalidated more legislation than in fifty years preceding. Views that were antiquated twenty-five years ago have been resurrected in decisions nullifying minimum-wage laws for women in industry, a standard-weight-bread law to protect buyers from short weights and honest bakers from unfair competition, a law fixing the resale price of theater tickets by ticket scalpers in New York, laws controlling exploitation of the unemployed by employment agencies, and many tax laws. . . ." "Merely as a matter of arithmetic," Frankfurter went on, "this is an impressive mortality rate. But a numerical tally of the cases does not tell the tale. In the first place, all laws are not of the same importance. Secondly, a single decision may decide the fate of a great body of legislation. . . . Moreover, the discouragement of legislative efforts through a particular adverse decision and the general weakening of the sense of legislative responsibility are destructive influences not measurable by statistics."[11]

The Chief Justice carried his Court to such dizzy heights that Holmes could see "hardly any limit but the sky" against the veto of state laws under the Fourteenth Amendment.[12] Excoriating judicial aggrandizement, Brandeis proclaimed: "The Court has the power to prevent an experiment. . . . But in the exercise of this high power, we must be ever on our guard, lest we erect our prejudices into legal principles. If we would guide by the light of reason we must let our minds be bold."[13]

The handy labels "liberal" and "conservative" obscure rather than define fundamental differences among the Justices. Taft and his majority of six believed there are certain rights beyond the reach of experimentation; it was the business of the Court to stay all such effort. The minority, on the other hand, held that change is essential to orderly advance. When the Court interrupts this vital process, it is, Brandeis declared, "an exercise of the powers of a superlegislature—not the performance of the constitutional function of judicial review."[14] "It is our judges who formulate our public policies and our basic law," a North Dakota judge commented in 1924. "We are governed by our judges and not by our legislatures."[15]

Taft's triumphant march continued to the end, but the future was clouded with uncertainty. By 1929, the world he had known and the people on whom he had come to rely were in eclipse. Even his own Court seemed engulfed in a whirlpool of radicalism. The noisy remnants of 1912 Progressives, among whom he sometimes numbered President Hoover, threatened the citadel of constitutionalism. As the economy slid rapidly toward the abyss, government intervention was openly advocated as an appropriate and essential remedy. To combat these forces, Taft's determination to hold on stiffened: "As long as things continue as they are, and I am able to answer in my place," he resolved to "stay on the Court in order to prevent the Bolsheviki from getting control."[16]

With the opening of the 1929 term, Taft had a presentiment of his own physical collapse. He felt "older and slower," less acute and more confused.[17] Everywhere he looked a red tide seemed to be flooding the pillars of the Republic. A dying man, he became obsessed with the necessity of maintaining the Court's conservative composition. In a senile rage he lashed out: "Brandeis is of course hopeless, as Holmes is, and as Stone is."[18] The most he could hope for was "continued life of enough of the present membership . . . to prevent disastrous reversals of our present attitudes."[19] ". . . We have a dissenting minority of three in the Court," he noted hopefully. "I think we can hold our six to steady the Court."[20]

Earlier doubts and misgivings had been kept within rational bounds. Following a lengthy conference in 1923, he had expressed displeasure over dissents, but commented philosophically: "I suppose I must expect to take my medicine."[21] Five years later the Chief Justice's attitude had changed. When outvoted, his unhappiness bordered on desperation. "We held a conference yesterday," he wrote his daughter, early January 1928, "in which the Court did something that I did not like, but which resulted in bringing before us a question which I hope a majority of the Court can be induced to decide the right way. I find it odd how absorbed one becomes in the merits or demerits of a question, and that old as I am and long as has been my experience, defeat colors the rest of the day which follows and one despairs of the Republic."[22]

From December 1929 on, the Chief Justice's mental deterioration became a matter of growing concern to his family. Gone was that essential quality—recognized as the earmark of a great judge—disinterestedness and self-knowledge. Earlier he had been willing to weigh divergent views and reach common ground. Now, feeling personally involved, he looked upon the conference as a battleground, a struggle between right and wrong, between virtue and vice, between constitutionalism and communism. Humor and tact lost their relevance; the goal of teamwork and harmony eluded him; influence over his colleagues dwindled.

As during his own Presidency and in 1920, judicial replacements loomed as the greatest danger. The advanced age of several Justices made vacancies imminent. Herbert Hoover now inspired no confidence at all. "The truth is," the Chief Justice confided to brother Horace, "that Hoover is a Progressive just as Stone is, and just as Brandeis is and just as Holmes is."[23] The former Relief Administrator's crusading zeal was frightening. "I think that Hoover is a new man and thinks that everything ought to be new."[24] The Quaker President's innovations included even the Court. To accomplish ends forbidden by the Constitution, he harbored dark plans to reduce the average age of the nine old men. "My feeling with respect to the Court is that if a number of us die, Hoover would put in some rather extreme destroyers of the Constitution. . . ."[25] "An attempted revolution" might occur. "Indeed, I have understood from pretty reliable sources that Hoover has announced his purposes in this regard."[26]

But Taft had not entirely lost his capacity for balanced

judgment. In more rational moments he realized the situation was not completely hopeless. Both Holmes and Brandeis would soon be replaced.[27] He reflected, moreover, that "the good luck of the Court in times past has been marked, and changes of a radical character have not been made all at once." Recalled also was the sobering effect of power even on starry-eyed George W. Norris when the Nebraska Senator became Chairman of the Judiciary Committee. "Men visited with the responsibility of change often find themselves rendered conservative by a fuller realization of the effect of the changes which when they haven't the responsibility they think they would make." Hoover might "learn a good deal before he gets through."[28] Meanwhile, the President would do well "to remember the warning in the Scriptures about removing landmarks."[29]

Among the landmarks, the Chief Justice numbered himself; he winced nervously every time he contemplated his probable successor. In Hoover's exclusive "Medicine-Ball Cabinet" was Associate Justice Stone. Knowing that Hoover's attachment to him was "very great," Taft feared the worst. "I have no doubt that if I were to retire or die, the President would appoint Stone as head of the Court."[30] Once in the Chief Justice's good graces—indeed his choice for the bench—Stone had fallen into profound disfavor. "He definitely has ranged himself with Brandeis and with Holmes in a good many of our constitutional differences."[31] Nor was Stone's "herding" with the Court's "kickers" his only shortcoming. He was "not a great leader and would have a great deal of trouble in massing the Court. . . ."[32] If Hoover's desire to elevate the Associate Justice were realized, Stone's inability to enlist followers might turn out to be a disguised blessing. It would not be easy to replace the solid constitutional structure erected under Taft's leadership. "With Van and Mac and Sutherland and you and Sanford," he wrote Justice Butler in 1929, "there will be five to steady the boat, and while the appointment of Stone to be Chief

Justice would give a great advantage to the minority, there would be a good deal of difficulty in working through reversals of present positions, even if I either had to retire or were gathered to my fathers, so that we must not give up at once."[33]

Stone's inadequacies must be made known. Though no longer enjoying easy access to the White House, the Chief Justice could expound his views to others. From his good friend Fred Starek, veteran Cincinnati newspaperman and politician, Taft received welcome reassurances. "Since my visit with you," Starek wrote, "I spent a day with Senator Root at Clinton [New York]. One of the things we discussed was the aspiration of a certain Associate Justice. . . . The Senator was deeply interested in the situation and is of the conviction that the gentleman in question is seriously lacking in the proper qualifications. I am sure he will cooperate earnestly in preventing a mistake in this connection."[34]

Though there is some evidence to support the belief that Stone was President Hoover's first choice, the Associate Justice was not elevated.* Taft resigned on February 3, 1930.

---

* For nearly three decades the story has persisted that Hoover had made up his mind to appoint Stone when someone (supposedly Joseph P. Cotton, his Undersecretary of State) reminded the President of the "deep political debt" the party owed Charles Evans Hughes for his help in the 1928 election campaign. It would be a fine political gesture, this strategist reasoned, to offer Hughes the post on the theory that he would decline. Acting on this hunch, Hoover is supposed to have telephoned Hughes and tendered him the Chief Justiceship. As the conversation proceeded, Hoover blanched; his jaw dropped. The President hung up, visibly shaken. "Well, I'll be damned. He accepted."

This story did not come to Chief Justice Hughes's attention until 1937. He was profoundly aroused; so was Herbert Hoover. The former President wrote Hughes an indignant denial, but his long letters of explanation went no further than to condemn the authors (Pearson and Allen) who spread "a purported [telephone] conversation of mine with Joe Cotton." For the full story, see my *Harlan Fiske Stone: Pillar of the Law*, pp. 276–283.

John Bassett Moore's memorandum, written less than three weeks after Hughes's appointment, sheds significant light on this episode:

"I met Mr. Justice Stone at the Century Club, New York, at half-past two today. About a week before the resignation of Chief Justice Taft was announced, the President asked Stone to breakfast with him, and, when they

continued on page 298

Replacing the stricken Chief Justice was the eminent Wall Street lawyer, Charles Evans Hughes.[35]

The man President Hoover appointed filled out Taft's image of what a Chief Justice should be. Two decades earlier, President Taft himself had mentioned the possibility of Hughes's promotion to the Chief Justiceship. More than once, he endorsed the New Yorker in the highest terms. Hughes singled out and deplored the very trends Chief Justice Taft had long combated. "We have entered," Hughes wrote in 1928, "upon an era of regulation with a great variety

---

continued from page 297
met, opened a conversation by saying that Taft would not resume his duties as Chief Justice. He asked Stone's advice as to Taft's successor. Stone replied that the successor should be a man of liberal tendencies and should be comparatively young so as to give assurance of length of service. In giving his reasons for these recommendations, he described the present condition of the Court not only in respect of age but also in respect of the limited range of intellectual interests of a majority of the members. He afterwards gave the President a short list of names, and particularly spoke of Chief Judge Cardozo of the New York Court of Appeals. He mentioned the facts that Cardozo was a Jew and a Democrat, but said he did not consider them to be objectionable, especially in view of the present personnel of the Court. The President asked him what he thought of ex-President Coolidge. Stone replied that that question perhaps should be put to someone else, as he owed his appointment as Attorney General and then as an Associate Justice to President Coolidge; but he intimated that because of Coolidge's want of a distinctly legal background, the strain on him would be very great, if he should consent to accept the office. The President indicated that he was thinking of Coolidge for the post of Associate Justiceship rather than for that of Chief Justice, and asked what he thought of Hughes for the latter position. Stone's response was altogether unfavorable, on the grounds of age and of the nature of Hughes's continual professional employments, and also on the ground of Hughes's having resigned his place on the Supreme Court to run for political office. He said he thought a place on the Supreme Court should not be for purposes of political or professional advancement and profit.

"Before Hughes's appointment was made, the Attorney General, Mitchell, had two conversations with Stone. They amounted to little beyond showing that Mitchell apprehended that the President had it in mind to appoint Hughes; but Mitchell was not taken into the President's confidence.

"It is perfectly evident that the appointment of Hughes was the result of direct prearrangement between the President and persons outside his Cabinet, and that it was prompted by political considerations. It seems equally clear that the President did not want a man of 'liberal tendencies.'" Memorandum of John Bassett Moore, February 20, 1930. *Moore Papers*, Library of Congress. This memorandum came to my attention through the kindness of my friend Professor David J. Danelski.

of legislative proposals, constantly multiplying governmental contacts with the activities of industry and trade." Hughes predicted that these developments would likely make judicial review "of increasing value."[36] Anticipated was the showdown in the crucial term, 1935–36, when the New Deal foundered on the shoals of constitutionality. One can only speculate on how Taft would have measured up if he, rather than Hughes, had sat in the center chair.

Where does Taft rank in the roster of our Chief Justices? Generally thought of as representing merely *primus inter pares,* the office is as demanding as it is highly prized. The qualifications necessary for pre-eminence have been rarely combined in one person. Excluding the present incumbent, thirteen men have occupied the office; only John Marshall has been universally acclaimed "the great Chief Justice." "When I consider his might, his justice, and his wisdom," Holmes observed, "I do fully believe that if American law were to be represented by a single figure, skeptic and worshiper alike would agree without dispute that the figure could be one alone, and that one, John Marshall."[37] In this estimate, Taft wholeheartedly concurred.

For success the Chief must be a good administrator. He must be capable of accommodating the clash of personalities inevitable in a group of nine often able and sometimes strong-willed men. A great Chief Justice must be a leader and, above all, a statesman. Never has he been consumed, as was Taft, with an unconquerable desire to refashion judicial organization and procedure.

Measuring our Chief Justices by these tests yields surprising results. The Court's most effective administrators have been Fuller, Taft and Hughes. Henry L. Stimson, who served under every President from Theodore Roosevelt to Harry Truman, gave President Taft top rating as an administrator.[38] Taft also demonstrated marked administrative talent as Chief Justice.

Taft's first three years were extraordinarily successful. Of the four Chief Justices under whom he served, Holmes gave Fuller and Taft highest praise. Fuller "had the business of the Court at his finger ends"; he was "perfectly courageous, prompt, decided,"[39] able to turn "off matters that daily called for action easily, swiftly, with the least possible friction, with inestimable good humor and with a humor that relieved tension." Holmes applauded Taft's "way of disposing of executive detail," and admired his ability "to take them easily and get through without friction."[40] The factor that may give Taft a rating somewhat higher than Fuller is the enlarged docket the former President had to handle. Hughes also got the work done, but certain of his colleagues complained that, in comparison with Taft, this was achieved at the expense of adequate consideration of the cases.[41]

Efficient dispatch of the Court's business is not only a matter of good judicial housekeeping. It depends also on the Chief's ability to lead his colleagues without driving them or hurting their egos. Whatever the group, Cabinet or Court, Taft had a remarkable gift for "welding them together and making them harmonious."[42] Good humor, willingness to compromise, and instinctive understanding of practical psychology, helped by certain colleagues who shared his respect for the Court as an institution—all this contributed to his success. At the end of the 1921–22 term, Justice Clarke believed that Taft had even succeeded in taking Brandeis into camp.

Also essential to leadership is familiarity with technical matters of procedure and jurisdiction. On this score, Hughes stands pre-eminent. Taft, on the other hand, confessed his inadequacy. In comparison, Justice Van Devanter's knowledge of authorities, procedure, and practice made the Chief Justice "feel quite small." Van Devanter's assistance was invaluable. Keeping the Court "consistent with itself" is, however, but a single aspect of the job of guiding and directing. A task no Chief Justice can delegate is the role of moderator. In 1927, after the cleavage had deepened, Taft realized that

"I must work along until I get to the end of my ten years, content to aid in the deliberation when there is difference of opinion."[43] By smoothing troubled waters, the Chief Justice may prevent the conference from degenerating into a row. Fuller did this with marked success. So did Taft; even for Brandeis, the colleague most likely to be critical, Taft was a "cultivated man." Usually capable of transcending the narrow bounds of self-defeating prejudice, he, like John Marshall, sometimes yielded to views he did not endorse. The effect was contagious, redounding to the good of all.

As a judicial architect, Taft is without peer. Oliver Ellsworth, his closest competitor, drafted the famous Judiciary Act of 1789, as a United States Senator, not as Chief Justice. Fuller and Hughes engaged in limited legislative activities; but Fuller had the help of a cooperative Congress, while Hughes built on foundations laid by Taft. On his own initiative, the tenth Chief Justice pressed for revisions in the judicial system. To win enactment, he stalked the halls of Congress, enlisted the support of newspapers, bar groups, and others. A year before he was elected President, Taft cited "the administration of exact justice . . . as the . . . highest ideal," adding that "appeals to judicial remedies should be limited in such a way that parties will not use them merely to delay and so clog efficient and just executive or legislative action."[44] The "Judges' Bill" of 1925 enables the Court to approximate this ideal. The palatial Supreme Court Building must be credited to Taft's planning and persistence. It may be that one man, Senator Thomas J. Walsh, aided by sympathetic colleagues, kept him from winning the revised Federal rules of civil procedure.

Greatness depends on the man: his standards and style, his values and vitality, his insights and outlook—on creativity, the capacity to find proximate solutions to enduring problems, to see the matter immediately at hand without losing sight of distant horizons.

"A great man," Holmes wrote in an essay on Chief Justice

Marshall, "represents a great ganglion in the nerves of society, . . . a strategic point in the campaign of history, and part of his greatness consists in his being *there*."[45] But a position of power is not enough. "The greatest statesmen," Woodrow Wilson observed, "are always those who attempt their tasks with imagination, with a large vision of things to come. . . . And so, whether by force of circumstance or by deliberate design, we have married legislation with adjudication and look for statesmanship in our courts."[46]

At every stage and in every major development in our history the Court has been *there*. As the national focus has shifted, so, sooner or later, has our constitutional law. Preliminary skirmishes in Taft's Court forecast tougher issues, deeper cleavages, and narrower margins. Dark shadows on the future filled him with foreboding, inclined him to resist. Yet his constitutional jurisprudence furnished substantial foundations for accommodating oncoming events. His interpretation of national power under the commerce clause goes back to Chief Justice Marshall. In a series of major decisions, he enforced the sweeping construction of the commerce power that the Hughes Court endorsed only *after* F.D.R.'s threat to pack it.* Chief Justice Taft sometimes broke away from his recalcitrant colleagues in due-process cases. In the minimum-wage decision of 1923, he protested the negation of regulatory measures "simply because they are passed to carry out economic views which the Court believes to be

---

* In the Jones-Laughlin case, the high-water mark of Chief Justice Hughes's liberal interpretation of the national commerce power, the Chief Justice declared that the Federal government may not be pushed "to such an extreme as to destroy the distinction which the Commerce Clause itself establishes between commerce 'among the several States,' and the internal concerns of the State. That distinction between what is national and what is local in the activities of commerce is vital to the maintenance of our Federal system." Cited as authority was "the explicit reservation of the Tenth Amendment." *N.L.R.B.* v. *Jones-Laughlin,* 301 U.S. 1, 30 (1937). Taft, on the other hand, declared that "the power of Congress in this respect [under the Commerce Clause] is . . . exactly what it would be in a government without States." WHT to Harlan F. Stone, Aug. 31, 1928. Pringle, *Life and Times of William Howard Taft,* II, 1015.

unwise or unsound." The 1923 decision also remained in good standing in the Hughes Court, despite intervening cases seriously undermining it. Once again the judicial backtrack came *after* President Roosevelt's audacious assault.

Meanwhile, Taft endorsed decisions, sometimes writing the majority opinion, that seemed to fasten both the national government and the states in a constitutional strait jacket. He spoke for a majority of eight in vetoing the national taxing statute designed to regulate child labor. He wrote for a unanimous Court in setting aside the Kansas Industrial Court act, making pronouncements that rank high in the annals of judicial conservatism. In both of these seemingly reactionary decisions, however, he had the support of the so-called liberals. Lacking was "a large vision of things to come."

An explanation of Taft's apparent inconsistency may be his high respect for judicial stability, to be achieved through the continuity of judicial decisions, especially the most recent rulings. Refusing in *Stafford* v. *Wallace* to revert to the Sugar Trust case of ancient memory, he built on Justice Holmes's intervening opinion in *Swift* v. *United States*. Similarly with the moss-covered Lochner case of 1905. Overruled *sub silentio* by the *Bunting* decision of 1917, it could thereafter be forgotten. On the other hand, Taft could not forget *Hammer* v. *Dagenhart*. The child labor tax could not stand, because only four years earlier the Court had set aside a similar statute enacted under the commerce power. Stability in judicial decisions and reliance on the most recent precedents were essential to the maintenance of respect for the Court's work.

Taft's overriding concern with the Court's prestige and his passion to "mass the Court" suggest that in the Court crises following his death he might have sought a "middle ground" on which the Justices could unite and thus avoid the near-catastrophe that befell the Hughes Court. Taft threw down a caveat against the obscurantist temptation to which the

Court yielded in 1936. Adumbrated was the danger of substituting judicial supremacy for judicial review. In strongest terms, he declared that in passing on legislation enacted under the commerce clause the Court "would not substitute its judgment for that of Congress . . . unless the relations of the subject to interstate commerce and its effect upon it are clearly nonexistent." Implied is the principle of judicial self-restraint which did not become the Court's watchword until after February 5, 1937.

None of Taft's predecessors, with the possible exception of Marshall, entertained such an expansive view of the Chief Justiceship or made such effective use of it on so many different fronts. Taft was a "great" administrator and a "great" judicial architect. For a while he demonstrated remarkable gifts for harmonizing human relations. Yet he is not commonly considered a great Chief Justice.

Surely he was no John Marshall either in intellect, style, or statesmanship. Marshall's unparalleled impact may be explained not merely in terms of natural endowments, great as these were, but also by the fact that his gifts, thanks to the dominance of Democratic-Republicans in the political branches of the government, could only be exploited in the judiciary. He wrote on practically a clean slate; such precedents as he inherited were remodeled in his own image. Completely overshadowed, few of his colleagues were his equals in any respect whatsoever. In questions of national power, "the great Chief Justice" went far beyond the necessities of the case, staking out claims for national authority not fully reaffirmed until our own time. He did this, however, without precluding opportunity for the exercise of creative genius of a different stamp. Chief Justice Taney and his successors remained free to make their own discoveries, without destroying the foundations laid by John Marshall.

Nor was Taft a Charles Evans Hughes, whose chief contribution lay in the civil liberties field. Even as his Court, disregarding Marshall's nationalistic jurisprudence, blocked the power to govern the economy, Hughes led in restoring the belief that certain rights—freedom of speech, press, and religion—must be preserved "in order to maintain the opportunity for free political discussion, to the end that government may be responsive to the will of the people and that changes, if desired, may be obtained by peaceful means." "Therein," the Chief Justice declared emphatically, "lies the security of the Republic, the very foundation of constitutional government."[47] Hughes's refusal, however, to recognize—until F.D.R. threatened to pack his Court—that energy is a leading characteristic of good government blemishes his record. Hoover's expectations in appointing Hughes Chief Justice had not been completely disappointed.

Exercise of the judicial function requires in its very nature "the sober second thought of the community." The Court can block legislative experimentation. But the Justices must not lose sight of the fact that government means action, that power to promote the general welfare is inherent in governing. "We must never forget," Chief Justice Marshall warned, "that it is a *Constitution* we are expounding," a document "intended to endure for ages to come and, consequently, to meet the various crises of human affairs." More than any other organ, the Supreme Court can enforce as law personal predilections not shared by the electorate. Sometimes, as in race relations and in the rotten-borough scandal, it has taken a stand in advance of the political branches. Needed is ability to weigh realistically the strength of the popular will and its claims to prevail. Taft, along with a host of Supreme Court Justices, did not meet this test. This may explain his failure, despite substantial achievements, to win a higher place in the roster of our Chief Justices.

BIBLIOGRAPHIC NOTES

I. YEARNINGS

1. WHT to Gus Karger, Mar. 20, 1916. Quoted in Henry F. Pringle, *Life and Times of William Howard Taft,* 2 vols. (New York: Farrar and Rinehart, 1939), II, 951.
2. WHT to Alphonso Taft, Aug. 24, 1889. Pringle, *op. cit.,* I, 107.
3. Pringle, *op. cit.,* I, 111.
4. WHT to H. D. Peck, Apr. 26, 1890. Pringle, *op. cit.,* I, 115.
5. Mrs. W. H. Taft, *Recollections of Full Years* (New York: Dodd, Mead, 1914), p. 24. Cited hereafter as "*Recollections.*"
6. Joseph B. Foraker to WHT, Jan. 31, 1890. Quoted in Julia B. Foraker, *I Would Live It Again* (New York: Harper, 1932), pp. 307–308.
7. Archibald Butt, *Taft and Roosevelt: The Intimate Papers of Archie Butt* (New York: Doubleday, Doran, 1930), II, 756.
8. Address to the Pocatello, Idaho, Chamber of Commerce in 1911, New York *Evening Post,* Oct. 6, 1911.
9. Joseph B. Foraker, *Notes of a Busy Life* (Cincinnati: Stewart & Kidd, 1916), I, 237.
10. WHT to Joseph B. Foraker, Jan. 31, 1887. For a full account of the circumstances surrounding Taft's appointment, see Joseph B. Foraker, *op. cit.,* I, pp. 236–240.
11. WHT to Joseph B. Foraker, Feb. 11, 1900. Quoted in Julia B. Foraker, *op. cit.,* p. 308.
12. *Recollections,* pp. 21–22.
13. *Ibid.,* pp. 30–31.
14. Mrs. W. H. Taft to WHT, July 18, 1891. Letters cited in these notes are, unless otherwise stated, from the Taft Papers, Library of Congress.
15. *Recollections,* p. 30.
16. *Ibid.*
17. *Ibid.,* p. 33.
18. Pringle, *op. cit.,* I, 161.
19. *Recollections,* p. 35.
20. *Ibid.,* p. 263.
21. *Ibid.,* p. 264.
22. *Ibid.,* p. 269.
23. Butt, *op. cit.,* II, 440–441.
24. *Recollections,* p. 269.
25. A. T. Mason, *Brandeis: A Free Man's Life* (New York: Viking, 1946), p. 521.
26. Pringle, *op. cit.,* I, 252.
27. WHT to Milton A. McRae, Nov. 12, 1904.
28. Quoted in *Recollections,* p. 303.
29. *Ibid.,* p. 304.
30. *The Outlook,* Sept. 21, 1901, p. 166.
31. *Recollections,* p. 222.
32. *Ibid.*
33. Remarks of Judge Arthur C.

Denison, 285 U.S., p. XII (1931).

34. *Recollections,* p. 223. See, in this connection, "Judge Taft's Decisions Affecting Labor Organizations." Remarks of F. W. Stevens, June 30, 1908. 7 *Ohio Law Bulletin and Reporter* (1908), 217–261; A. T. Mason, "The Labor Decisions of Chief Justice Taft," 78 *University of Pennsylvania Law Review* (1930), 585–625.
35. Pringle, *op. cit.,* I, 256.
36. *Ibid.,* p. 107.
37. *Ibid.,* p. 217.
38. *The Bench and Bar,* Vol. 18 (June, 1908), p. 88.
39. H. H. Kohlsaat, *From McKinley to Harding* (New York: Scribner, 1923), pp. 161–162. Archie Butt (*op. cit.,* II, 736) recalls the President's great confidence in Kohlsaat, as indicated by his willingness to give the newspaperman almost limitless time. But the details of Kohlsaat's delightful story are apocryphal. "I read that story," Taft commented many years later, "but the incident did not occur." *New York Times,* July 1, 1921, p. 13, col. 5. Evidence of the conflicting motivations prompting the story is present in great abundance.
40. Willard L. King, *Melville Weston Fuller* (New York: Macmillan, 1950), p. 303.
41. *Ibid.*
42. *Ibid.,* p. 305.
43. Charles Henry Butler, *A Century at the Bar of the Supreme Court of the United States* (New York: Putnam, 1942), pp. 165–166.
44. Quoted in King, *op. cit.,* pp. 305–306.
45. Pringle, *op. cit.,* I, 265.
46. *Ibid.*
47. WHT to Mrs. W. H. Taft, Apr. 15, 1904. Pringle, *op. cit.,* I, 265.
48. WHT to Mrs. W. H. Taft, Aug. 3, 1904. Pringle, *op. cit.,* I, 265.
49. Pringle, *op. cit.,* I, 313–314.
50. Butler, *op. cit.,* p. 184.
51. *War Secretary's Diaries,* p. 128. Quoted in Pringle, *op. cit.,* I, 315.
52. Pringle, *op. cit.,* I, 315.
53. *Ibid.,* p. 316.
54. King, *op. cit.,* p. 307.
55. WHT to Giles Taintor, Dec. 1, 1905. Pringle, *op. cit.,* I, 312.
56. *Recollections,* p. 304.

56a. Alphonso Taft to Salmon P. Chase, Dec. 7, 1864. Chase Manuscripts, Library of Congress.

56b. WHT to H. A. Morrill, Dec. 2, 1908.

57. *Recollections,* p. 332.
58. King, *op. cit.,* p. 309. See also WHT to Horace D. Taft, Oct. 6, 1921. Pringle, *op. cit.,* II, 966.
59. King, *op. cit.,* p. 308.
60. Butt, *op. cit.,* II, 433.
61. *Ibid.,* p. 794.
62. *Ibid.,* p. 492.
63. *Ibid.,* p. 850.
64. WHT to Mr. Justice W. H. Moody, July 8, 1910. Quoted in Butt, *op. cit.,* II, 439.
65. WHT to Chauncey M. Depew, Oct. 15, 1910. Pringle, *op. cit.,* I, 534.
66. Pringle, *op. cit.,* I, 534.
67. Butt, *op. cit.,* I, 223.
68. *Ibid.,* pp. 335–337 *passim.*
69. Quoted in Merlo J. Pusey, *Charles Evans Hughes* (New

York: Macmillan, 1951), I, 271–272.
70. C. E. Hughes to WHT, Apr. 24, 1910. Pusey, *op. cit.*, I, 273.
71. Butt, *op. cit.*, I, 310.
72. July 5, 1910. *Ibid.*, II, 433.
73. *Ibid.*, p. 434.
74. *Ibid.*, pp. 566–567.
75. C. E. Hughes, "The Supreme Court, 1910–1916." Unpublished chapters prepared for the use of his biographer. One notes a discrepancy between Archie Butt's account and Hughes's as to the date of the telephone calls to the White House.
76. Butt, *op. cit.*, II, 438.
77. Hughes's unpublished biographical notes.
78. George W. Wickersham to Henry F. Pringle, Jan. 23, 1935. Quoted in Pringle, *op. cit.*, I, 535. The same sentiments are recorded in Butt, *op. cit.*, II, 439.
79. Butt, *op. cit.*, II, 757.
80. Julia B. Foraker, *op. cit.*, p. 327.
81. Butt, *op. cit.*, II, 754–755.
81a. WHT to Walter Lenoir Church, July 10, 1924.
82. Butt, *op. cit.*, I, 294.

II. PLATFORM

1. Address of President John E. Edgerton, Oct. 14, 1929. *Proceedings of Thirty-fourth Annual Meeting of the National Association of Manufacturers,* p. 16.
2. Edmund Burke, *Reflections on the French Revolution* (Maynard's English Classic Series), p. 3.
3. Charles Henry Butler, *A Century at the Bar of the Supreme Court of the United States* (New York: Putnam, 1942), p. 208.
4. David J. Brewer, "The Nation's Safeguard," *Proceedings of the Sixteenth Annual Meeting of the New York State Bar Association,* Vol. 16, pp. 37–47 *passim.*
5. James Bradley Thayer, "The Origin and Scope of the American Doctrine of Constitutional Law," *Harvard Law Review,* VII (Oct. 1893), 129.
6. *Ibid.*, p. 136.
7. *Ibid.*, p. 137. (Emphasis added.)
8. *Ibid.*, p. 144.
9. *Ibid.*, p. 148. (Emphasis added.)
10. *Ibid.*, p. 152.
11. "The Right of Private Property," 3 *Michigan Law Journal* (Aug. 1894), 215–233 *passim.*
12. *Pollock* v. *Farmers' Loan & Trust Co.,* 158 U.S. 601 (1895).
13. *United States* v. *E. C. Knight,* 156 U.S. 1 (1895).
14. *In re Debs,* 158 U.S. 564 (1895).
15. *Lochner* v. *New York,* 198 U.S. 45 (1905).
16. "Criticisms of the Federal Judiciary," Annual Address delivered before the American Bar Association, Aug. 28, 1895. *American Law Review,* XXIV (1895), 641–674 *passim.*
17. "Administration of Criminal Law," address to the graduating class of the Law School of Yale University, June 26, 1905. William Howard Taft,

Present Day Problems: A Collection of Addresses Delivered on Various Occasions (New York: Dodd, Mead, 1908), pp. 333–355 *passim.*

18. *Four Aspects of Civic Duty* (New York: Scribner, 1906), pp. 11–53 *passim.*
19. "Delays and Defects in the Enforcement of Law in This Country," based on an address delivered before the Civic Forum, New York City, at Carnegie Hall, Apr. 28, 1908. *North American Review,* CLXXXVII (1908), 851–861 *passim.*
20. "Address of William Howard Taft in Response to Notification Speech at Cincinnati, Ohio, July 28, 1908," p. 20. *Addresses of William H. Taft,* Vol. 4.
21. "The People Rule: Mr. Taft's Reply to Mr. Bryan at Hot Springs, Virginia, August 21, 1908." *Ibid.,* pp. 7–8.
22. "Inequalities in the Administration of Justice," address delivered before the Virginia Bar Association at Hot Springs, Virginia, August 6, 1908. *New Jersey Law Journal,* XXXI (Sept. 1908), 269–277. Published also as "The Delays of the Law," *Yale Law Journal,* XVIII (Nov. 1908), 28–39 *passim.*
23. Remarks of W. H. Taft, Proceedings of the Judicial Section, 41 *American Bar Association Reports* (1916), 741.
24. 208 U.S. 412. See A. T. Mason, *Brandeis: Lawyer and Judge in the Modern State* (Princeton, N.J.: Princeton University Press, 1933), Chapter VI.
25. A. T. Hadley, "The Constitutional Position of Property in America," *The Independent,* LXIV (Jan.–June 1908), 838.
26. Language of Louis D. Brandeis. See A. T. Mason, *Brandeis: A Free Man's Life* (New York: Viking, 1946), p. 104.
27. "Message of the President of the United States communicated to the two Houses of Congress at the beginning of the second session, Sixty-first Congress, December 7, 1909" (Washington: Government Printing Office, 1909), *Addresses of William H. Taft,* Vol. 4, pp. 27–28. (Emphasis added.)
28. "Message of the President of the United States communicated to the two Houses of Congress at the beginning of the third session, Sixty-first Congress, December 6, 1910" (Washington: Government Printing Office, 1910), *Addresses of William H. Taft,* Vol. 4, pp. 41–43.
29. Inter-Mountain rate cases, 234 U.S. 476, 491 (1913). (Emphasis added.)
30. 47 *Congressional Record,* 62d Cong., 1st Sess., p. 3964.
31. Archibald Butt, *Taft and Roosevelt* (New York: Doubleday, Doran, 1930), II, 742.
32. *Popular Government: Its Essence, Its Permanence, and Its Perils* (New Haven: Yale University Press, 1913), pp. 152–153.
33. *Ibid.,* p. 233.
34. *Ibid.,* p. 180.
35. *Ibid.,* pp. 184–185.
36. New York *Evening Post,* Oct. 6, 1911, p. 1.

37. Senate Doc. No. 98, 61st Cong., 1st Sess. 2 (1909).
38. "An Appreciation of General Grant," May 30, 1908. *Present Day Problems,* pp. 63–64.
39. *Popular Government,* p. 167.
40. W. H. Taft, *The Anti-Trust Act and the Supreme Court* (New York: Harper, 1914), p. 33.
41. *Popular Government,* pp. 222–223.
42. *Ibid.,* p. 174.
43. *Ibid.,* pp. 235–238 *passim.* See also "The Social Importance of Proper Standards for Admission to the Bar," 38 *American Bar Association Reports* (1913), pp. 924, 936.
44. *The Anti-Trust Act and the Supreme Court,* pp. 33–43 *passim.*
45. *Our Chief Magistrate and His Powers* (New York: Columbia University Press, 1916), pp. 12–13. Originally delivered in 1915 at Columbia University as the Blumenthal Lectures under the general title "The Presidency, Its Powers, Duties, Responsibilities and Limitations." For similar views, see "The Address of Ex-President Taft at the American Bar Association," *Oklahoma Law Journal,* Vol. 13 (Jan. 1915), pp. 288–290.
46. "Ethics of the Law," an address in the Hubbard Course on Legal Ethics, delivered before the students of the Albany Law School, May 21, 1914, p. 3. *Addresses of William H. Taft,* Vol 4.
47. "The Attacks on the Courts and Legal Procedure," 5 *Kentucky Law Journal,* No. 2, pp. 3–24. Taft made similar recommendations for judiciary reforms to the Judiciary Committee of the Constitutional Convention at Albany, New York, June 11, 1915. See "Ex-President Taft on the Courts," *New Jersey Law Journal,* XXX-*VIII* (June 1915), 164–166.
48. *Liberty Under Law* (New Haven: Yale University Press, 1922), pp. 42–43.
49. *Mixed Essays, Irish Essays and Others* (New York: Macmillan, 1899), pp. 4–5.
50. *Four Aspects of Civic Duty,* p. 8.
51. Thomas W. Shelton, "Chief Justice Taft," *Central Law Journal,* Vol. 93 (Aug. 1921), p. 94.
52. "The Boundaries between the Executive, the Legislative and Judicial Branches of the Government," 25 *Yale Law Journal* (June 1916), 599, 616.

III. ENTERING THE TEMPLE

1. Quoted in A. L. Todd, *Justice on Trial: The Case of Louis D. Brandeis* (New York: McGraw-Hill, 1964), p. 28.
2. *Holmes–Pollock Letters,* Mark De Wolfe Howe, ed. (Cambridge: Harvard University Press, 1941), I, 211.
3. Quoted in Todd, *op. cit.,* p. 33.
4. *Ibid,* p. 34.
5. *Ibid.*
6. *Ibid.,* p. 29.
7. *New York Times,* Jan. 4, 1916, p. 12.
8. Quoted in Todd, *op. cit.,* p. 27.
9. Woodrow Wilson Papers. Li-

brary of Congress.
10. *Ibid.*
11. *Ibid.*
12. Quoted in Todd, *op. cit.*, pp. 27–28.
13. *Ibid.*, p. 28.
14. *Ibid.*, p. 32.
15. *Ibid.*
16. Woodrow Wilson Papers. Library of Congress.
17. WHT to Gus Karger, Jan. 31, 1916.
18. Quoted in Todd, *op. cit.*, p. 81.
19. See Mason, *Bureaucracy Convicts Itself* (New York: Viking, 1941).
20. Quoted in Todd, *op. cit.*, p. 78.
21. *Ibid.*, p. 79.
22. *Ibid.*, p. 81.
23. Mason, *Brandeis: A Free Man's Life* (New York: Viking, 1946), p. 489.
24. Todd, *op. cit.*, p. 132.
25. Mason, *Brandeis: A Free Man's Life*, pp. 489–490.
26. Woodrow Wilson Papers. Library of Congress.
27. *Ibid.*
28. Charles L. Swem Transcripts. Woodrow Wilson Papers. Library of Congress.
29. WHT to Henry W. and Horace D. Taft, Jan. 28, 1900. Quoted in Pringle, *op. cit.*, I, 148.
30. WHT to Sir William Pakenham, July 23, 1921.
31. *Ibid.*
32. Archibald Butt, *Taft and Roosevelt* (New York: Doubleday, Doran, 1930), II, 768.
33. WHT to H. H. Kohlsaat, July 19, 1921. Pringle, *op. cit.*, II, 960.
34. *Ibid.*
35. *New York Times*, Mar. 29, 1921, p. 1.
36. Charles D. Hilles, "The Unique Career of William Howard Taft," Taft Correspondence, Dec. 1929, Misc., Library of Congress.
37. WHT to Mrs. W. H. Taft, Mar. 1, 1921.
38. WHT to J. M. Dickinson, Apr. 25, 1921.
39. *Ibid.*
40. *Ibid.*
41. WHT to Mrs. W. H. Taft, Mar. 1, 1921.
42. Gus Karger to WHT, Jan. 14, 1921. Pringle, *op. cit.*, II, 956.
43. Warren G. Harding to WHT, Jan. 4, 1921.
44. WHT to Mrs. W. H. Taft, Dec. 26, 1920. Pringle, *op. cit.*, II, 955.
45. *Ibid.*
46. W. G. Harding to WHT, Jan. 14, 1921.
47. WHT to H. D. Taft, Jan. 18, 1921.
48. WHT to Helen H. Taft, Mar. 11, 1921.
49. Max Pam to WHT, Mar. 21, 1921.
50. WHT to Helen H. Taft, Mar. 14, 1921.
51. W. G. Harding to WHT, Mar. 28, 1921.
52. WHT to Helen H. Taft, Mar. 1, 1921.
53. *Ibid.*
54. WHT to G. Karger, Mar. 26, 1921.
55. G. Karger to WHT, Mar. 28, 1921. Karger wrote: "I put myself in touch today with Dr. Richardson and cautioned him as to the confidential nature of your conversation with him. He agreed to govern himself accordingly."
56. WHT to Helen H. Taft, Apr. 4,

1921; Gus Karger to WHT, Apr. 1, 1921.

57. WHT to C. Sidney Shepard, Apr. 11, 1921. Pringle, *op. cit.*, II, 957.
58. WHT to Helen H. Taft, Aug. 3, 1922.
59. WHT to C. S. Shepard, Apr. 11, 1921. Pringle, *op. cit.*, II, 957.
60. *Ibid.*
61. J. J. Richardson to WHT, May 18, 1921.
62. WHT to G. Karger, May 19, 1921.
63. G. Karger to WHT, Jan. 14, 1921. Pringle, *op. cit.*, II, 956.
64. M. Pam to WHT, Sept. 24, 1920.
65. WHT to Helen H. Taft, Dec. 26, 1920.
66. Frank B. Brandegee to WHT, May 30, 1921.
67. G. Karger to WHT, May 25, 1921.
68. WHT to Mabel Boardman, May 31, 1921.
69. Frank B. Brandegee to WHT, May 23, 1921.
70. WHT to Mabel Boardman, May 31, 1921.
71. WHT to F. B. Brandegee and G. Karger, May 30, 1921. Pringle, *op. cit.*, II, 958–959.
72. *New York Times,* July 1, 1921. p. 13, col. 5.
73. WHT to G. Karger, May 19, 1921. Quoted in Pringle, *op. cit.*, II, 958.
74. See Cortez A. M. Ewing, *The Judges of the Supreme Court, 1789–1937: A Study of Their Qualifications* (Minneapolis: University of Minnesota Press, 1938).
75. Felix Frankfurter, "The Supreme Court in the Mirror of Justice," *University of Pennsylvania Law Review,* 1957, p. 786.
76. WHT to Mabel Boardman, May 31, 1921.
77. G. Karger to WHT, May 24, 1921.
78. G. Karger to WHT, June 3, 1921.
79. G. Karger to WHT, June 30, 1921.
80. WHT to H. D. Taft, June 7, 1921.
81. Luther A. Brewer to WHT, June 9, 1921.
82. WHT to H. D. Taft, June 7, 1921.
83. G. Karger to WHT, June 14, 1921. Pringle, *op. cit.*, II, 959.
84. G. Karger to WHT, June 21, 1921. *Ibid.*
85. G. Karger to WHT, June 23, 1921.
86. G. Karger to WHT, June 29, 1921.
87. WHT to Helen H. Taft, June 29, 1921.
88. WHT to G. Karger, May 19, 1921. Pringle, *op. cit.*, II, 957.
89. WHT to Helen H. Taft, June 30, 1929.
90. Charles E. Barker to WHT, July 1, 1921.
91. Oliver Wendell Holmes to Harold Laski, May 27, 1921. *Holmes–Laski Letters,* M. De Wolfe Howe, ed. (Cambridge: Harvard University Press, 1953), I, 339.
92. O. W. Holmes to Frederick Pollock, July 11, 1911. *Holmes–Pollock Letters,* II, p. 72.
93. O. W. Holmes to H. Laski, July 12, 1921. *Holmes–Laski Letters,* I, p. 346.
94. O. W. Holmes to H. Laski, Nov. 13, 1925. *Ibid.,* p. 797.

95. Quoted in "Chief Justice Taft," *Literary Digest*, Vol. 70 (July 16, 1921), 13.
96. H. D. Taft to WHT, July 11, 1921.
97. WHT to Helen H. Taft, July 2, 1921.
98. WHT to Helen H. Taft, July 5, 1921.
99. *Ibid.*
100. Julia B. Foraker, *I Would Live It Again* (New York: Harper, 1932), p. 325.
101. *Ibid.*, p. 328.
102. *Ibid.*, p. 326.
103. W. H. Taft, *Popular Government: Its Essence, Its Permanence, Its Perils* (New Haven: Yale University Press, 1913), pp. 113–114.

IV. JUDICIAL REFORMER

1. Felix Frankfurter and James M. Landis, *The Business of the Supreme Court* (New York: Macmillan, 1928), p. 220.
2. *Ibid.*, p. 222.
3. "The Causes of Popular Dissatisfaction with the Administration of Justice," 29 *American Bar Association Reports* (1906) 395.
4. "Delays and Defects in the Enforcement of Law in This Country," *North American Review*, Vol. 187 (June 1908), 851–861.
5. 39 Stat. 726–727, C. 448, Sec. 2.
6. WHT to Theodore Roosevelt, May 26, 1910. Henry F. Pringle, *Theodore Roosevelt* (New York: Harcourt, Brace, 1931), p. 531.
7. "Adequate Machinery for Judicial Business," address delivered at the Forty-fourth Meeting of the American Bar Association, at Cincinnati, Ohio, Aug. 30, 1921, 7 *American Bar Association Journal* (Sept. 1921), p. 453.
8. WHT to Thomas W. Shelton, Nov. 9, 1926.
9. "Adequate Machinery for Judicial Business," *loc. cit.*
10. WHT to Elihu Root, May 12, 1922.
11. Robert M. La Follette, "Child Labor and the Federal Courts," *American Federationist*, XXIX (July 1922), 471.
12. "The Supreme Court and the Public Welfare," *Outlook*, June 20, 1923.
13. W. H. Taft, "Criticisms of the Federal Judiciary," 29 *American Law Review* (Sept.–Oct. 1895), 642–643.
14. WHT to Clarence H. Kelsey, Sept. 9, 1922.
15. WHT to Harlan Fiske Stone, Jan. 27, 1925.
16. WHT to George W. Wickersham, Mar. 29, 1928.
17. WHT to Horace D. Taft, May 7, 1922. Quoted in Henry F. Pringle, *Life and Times of William Howard Taft* (New York: Farrar and Rinehart, 1939), II, 967.
18. WHT to Henry W. Taft, May 18, 1926.
19. WHT to Robert A. Taft, Apr. 5, 1924.
20. WHT to R. A. Taft, Apr. 5, 1924.
21. WHT to Casper S. Yost, Apr. 16, 1928.

22. WHT to Jacob M. Dickinson, Nov. 2, 1922.
23. WHT to H. D. Taft, Mar. 30, 1922.
24. WHT to H. D. Taft, Dec. 7, 1924.
25. WHT to Louis D. Brandeis, July 25, 1922.
26. 62 *Congressional Record* 5, 67th Cong., 2d Sess., pp. 5107–08.
27. *Ibid.*, p. 5108.
28. WHT to H. F. Stone, Jan. 27, 1925. See also WHT to H. D. Taft, Dec. 7, 1924. Taft Papers, Library of Congress.
29. WHT to Elihu Root, Apr. 5, 1922.
30. WHT to H. F. Stone, Jan 27, 1925.
31. WHT to Frank B. Brandegee, Jan. 23, 1922.
32. WHT to Henry Cabot Lodge, Jan. 17, 1922.
33. WHT to H. D. Taft, Dec. 14, 1926.
34. Quoted in Walter F. Murphy, *Elements of Judicial Strategy* (Chicago: University of Chicago Press, 1964), pp. 132–133.
35. See 46 *American Bar Association Reports* 561; 9 *Proceedings Canadian Bar Association* 138; "Adequate Machinery for Judicial Business," *loc. cit.;* "Three Needed Steps of Progress," 8 *American Bar Association Journal* (1922), 34; "Possible and Needed Reforms in the Administration of Justice in the Federal Courts," 8 *American Bar Association Journal* (1922), 601. See also 57 *American Law Review* 1; and 6 *Journal of the American Judicature Society* 36.
36. "Adequate Machinery for Judicial Business," *loc. cit.*, p. 457.
37. "Three Needed Steps of Progress," *loc. cit.*, p. 35.
38. WHT to Angus W. McLean, Dec. 1, 1924.
39. Statement of Harry M. Daugherty, "Additional Judges, United States District Courts," *Hearings before the Committee of the Judiciary*, U.S. Senate, 67th Cong., 1st Sess. (Oct. 5, 1921), p. 20.
40. The members were: Judge John E. Sater of the Sixth Circuit; Judge John C. Pollock of the Eighth Circuit; Judge William I. Grubb of the Fifth Circuit; William H. Hayward, U.S. Attorney for the Southern District of New York; and Charles F. Clyne, U.S. Attorney for the Northern District of Illinois.
41. WHT to H. D. Taft, July 2, 1921.
42. Statement of H. M. Daugherty, "Additional Judges . . . ," *loc. cit.*
43. WHT to H. D. Taft, July 2, 1921.
44. WHT to Helen H. Taft, July 15, 1922.
45. H. M. Daugherty to WHT, July 22, 1922.
46. "Additional Judges . . . ," *loc. cit.*, pp. 11–12.
47. *Ibid.*, p. 15.
48. "Three Needed Steps of Progress," *loc. cit.*, p. 34.
49. See "Additional Judges . . . ," *loc. cit.*, p. 10.
50. WHT to H. D. Taft, Apr. 9, 1922.
51. *Ibid.*
52. 62 *Cong. Rec.* 5, 67th Cong., 2d Sess., p. 4853.

53. *Ibid.*, pp. 4853, 4855.
54. *Ibid.*, p. 5098.
55. WHT to Frank H. Hiscock, Apr. 12, 1922.
56. WHT to H. D. Taft, Apr. 3, 1922.
57. 62 *Cong. Rec.* 5, 67th Cong., 2d Sess., pp. 4861–62.
58. *Ibid.*, p. 4863.
59. *Ibid.*, p. 4853.
60. *Ibid.*, p. 4849.
61. *Ibid.*, p. 4853.
62. *Ibid.*, pp. 4851–52.
63. *Ibid.*, p. 5097.
64. Act of Sept. 14, 1922. 42 Stat. 837, 839.
65. "Possible and Needed Reforms in the Administration of Civil Justice in the Federal Courts," 8 *American Bar Association Journal*, p. 601.
66. See Sections 2 and 3, H.R. 9103, 67th Cong., 2d Sess.; Section 2, S. 2433, 67th Cong., 1st Sess.
67. WHT to H. D. Taft, Apr. 3, 1922.
68. 62 *Cong. Rec.* 5, 67th Cong., 2d Sess., pp. 5113–14.
69. *Ibid.*, p. 4857.
70. *Ibid.*, p. 4858.
71. *Ibid.*, p. 4863.
72. *Ibid.*, p. 4857.
73. *Ibid.*, p. 4858.
74. 62 *Cong. Rec.* 1, 67th Cong., 2d Sess., p. 202.
75. 62 *Cong. Rec.* 5, 67th Cong., 2d Sess., pp. 4863–64.
76. *Ibid.*, p. 4853.
77. "Additional Judges . . . ," *loc. cit.*, p. 14.
78. John K. Shields, 62 *Cong. Rec.* 5, 67th Cong., 2d Sess., p. 4863.
79. 62 *Cong. Rec.* 1, p. 203.
80. "After Dining Oratory at Cincinnati," 7 *American Bar Association Journal* (Nov. 1921), 605, 606.
81. WHT to W. T. Allen, Jan. 16, 1922.
82. WHT to H. M. Daugherty, Nov. 28, 1923.
83. WHT to William B. Gilbert, May 1, 1929.
84. WHT to H. M. Daugherty, Nov. 28, 1923.
85. *Ibid.*
86. Frankfurter and Landis, *op. cit.*, p. 242.
87. John H. Clarke to Woodrow Wilson, Sept. 9, 1922, Woodrow Wilson Papers, Library of Congress.
88. "Three Needed Steps of Progress," *loc. cit.*, pp. 35–36.
89. Willis Van Devanter to WHT, May 11, 1927.
90. *Hearings before the Committee on the Judiciary*, U. S. Senate, 67th Cong., 2d Sess., on H.R. 10479, Mar. 30, 1922, p. 1.
91. WHT to Albert B. Cummins, Nov. 25, 1921.
92. H.R. Report, No. 1075, 68th Cong., 2d Sess., Jan. 6, 1925, p. 2.
93. *Ibid.*, p. 8.
94. WHT to Charles P. Taft, Jan. 27, 1924.
95. Thomas W. Shelton to WHT, Jan. 31, 1924.
96 WHT to J. B. Woodward, Mar. 3, 1924.
97. See 16 Richardson: *Messages and Papers of the Presidents*, 7431, 7534, quoted in Frankfurter and Landis, *op. cit.*, p. 259; and also W. H. Taft, "The Attacks on the Courts and Legal Procedure," 5 *Kentucky Law Journal*, No. 2, p. 18.
98. 66 *Cong. Rec.* 3, 68th Cong., 2d Sess., p. 2753.

99. "Jurisdiction of Circuit Courts of Appeals and of the Supreme Court," *House Reports on Public Bills,* Vol. 1, Report No. 1075, 68th Cong., 2d Sess., Jan. 6, 1925, on H. R. 8206, p. 8.
100. Address by Thomas J. Walsh delivered at Lynchburg, Virginia, June 18, 1922, "The Overburdened Supreme Court," in 62 *Cong. Rec.* 8, 67th Cong., 2d Sess., p. 8547.
101. *Ibid.*
102. WHT to W. Van Devanter, Feb. 4, 1922. For this reference I am indebted to Mr. Leon I. Salomon.
103. T. W. Shelton to WHT, Apr. 4, 1924.
104. WHT to T. W. Shelton, May 2, 1924.
105. WHT to R. A. Taft, Nov. 30, 1924.
106. WHT to A. Owsley Stanley, Dec. 5, 1924.
107. T. W. Shelton to WHT, Dec. 19, 1924.
108. WHT to Helen Taft Manning, Dec. 7, 1924.
109. WHT to H. D. Taft, Dec. 7, 1924.
110. "Procedure in Federal Courts," *Hearings before a Subcommittee of the Committee on the Judiciary,* U.S. Senate, 68th Cong., 1st Sess., Feb. 2, 1924, on S. 2060 and S. 2061.
111. WHT to H. D. Taft, Feb. 2, 1925.
112. 66 *Cong. Rec.* 3, 68th Cong., 2d Sess., p. 2926.
113. WHT to H. D. Taft, Feb. 2, 1925.
114. 66 *Cong. Rec.* 3, p. 2928. See Act of Feb. 13, 1925, Sec. 14, 43 Stat. 936, 942.
115. *Hearings before a Senate Subcommittee of the Committee on the Judiciary,* 68th Cong., 1st Sess., Feb. 2, 1924, p. 26.
116. "The Jurisdiction of the Supreme Court under the Act of February 13, 1925," 35 *Yale Law Journal* 1.
117. *Senate Journal,* 61st Cong., 3d Sess., p. 13.
118. "Three Needed Steps of Progress," *loc. cit.,* p. 35.
119. *Ibid.*
120. Statement before the Committee of the Judiciary, U.S. Senate, 67th Cong., 1st Sess., p. 16.
121. "Three Needed Steps of Progress," *loc. cit.*
122. *Ibid.*
123. WHT to Charles H. Paul, Aug. 28, 1925.
124. "President's Address," *Senate Journal,* 61st Cong., 3d Sess., p. 13.
125. WHT to C. H. Paul, Aug. 28, 1925.
126. *Ibid.* See also W. H. Taft Address, 41 *American Bar Association Reports,* Proceedings of the Judicial Section, Aug. 30, 1916, p. 741.
127. "Possible and Needed Reforms in Federal Courts," *loc. cit.,* p. 604.
128. "Three Needed Steps of Progress," *loc. cit.*
129. S. 477, 69th Cong., 1st Sess.
130. WHT to H. F. Stone, May 18, 1926.
131. WHT to T. W. Shelton, May 23, 1926.
132. *Ibid.*
133. *Ibid.*
134. WHT to T. W. Shelton, Mar. 5, 1928.
135. Statement before the Committee of the Judiciary, U.S. Sen-

ate, Oct. 5, 1921, pp. 18–19.

136. See "Reform of Federal Procedure," Address delivered by Thomas J. Walsh, *Senate Misc. Doc.*, Vol. II, Doc. No. 105, 69th Cong., 1st Sess.
137. *Ibid.*, p. 13.
138. WHT to T. J. Walsh, May 12, 1926.
139. "Declaratory Judgments," *Hearings before Subcommittee of the Committee on the Judiciary*, U.S. Senate, 70th Cong., 1st Sess., Apr. 27 and May 18, 1928, on H.R. 5623.
140. *Ibid.*, p. 4.
141. Address by W. H. Taft, "Three Needed Steps . . . ," *loc. cit.*

    In presenting his three-pronged program, the Chief Justice had taken a realistic stance:

    The reforms that I have been advocating involve some increase in the power of the Judges of the Courts, either in the matter of the assignment of judges, the matter of the enlargement of the *certiorari* power or in the adoption of more comprehensive rules of procedure. I am well aware that they will be opposed solely on this ground, and that the objection is likely to win support because of this. It is said that judges are prone to amplify their powers—that this is human nature, and therefore the conclusion is that their powers ought not to be amplified, however much good this may accomplish in the end. The answer to this is that if power is abused, it is completely within the discretion—indeed within the duty—of the legislature to take it away or modify it.

    "Possible and Needed Reforms in the Federal Courts," *loc. cit.*, p. 607.
142. *The National Corporation Reporter*, Vol. 41 (Dec. 15, 1910), pp. 568–569.
143. *Central Law Journal*, Vol. 78 (May 1914), p. 388.
144. Act of June 19, 1934, 48 Stat., 1064.
145. 82 L. ed., 1565.
146. Felix Frankfurter, "Chief Justices I Have Known," 39 *Virginia Law Review* 883 (1953), 987. Reprinted in Frankfurter, *Of Law and Men* (New York: Harcourt, 1956).

V. LOBBYIST

1. S. 2060, 68th Cong., 1st Sess.
2. S. 2061, 68th Cong., 1st Sess.
3. WHT to Thomas W. Shelton, Mar. 23, 1924.
4. T. W. Shelton to WHT, Mar. 25, 1924.
5. *Ibid.*
6. WHT to Louis D. Brandeis, Dec. 3, 1923.
7. 66 *Congressional Record* 13, Feb. 3, 1925, 68th Cong., 2d Sess., p. 2920; WHT to Senator Royal S. Copeland, Dec. 9, 1924.
8. WHT to Robert A. Taft, Feb. 8, 1925.
9. WHT to Harry M. Daugherty, Aug. 8, 1921.

10. *Ibid.*
11. H. M. Daugherty to WHT, Aug. 11, 1921.
12. WHT to H. M. Daugherty, Sept. 29, 1921.
13. See WHT to Joseph Walsh, Nov. 21, 1921; WHT to Arthur C. Denison, Nov. 27, 1921.
14. James F. Smith to WHT, Oct. 19, 1921.
15. 62 *Cong. Rec.* 1, 67th Cong., 2d Sess., p. 166.
16. George S. Graham to WHT, Feb. 20, 1925.
17. W. H. Taft, "Three Needed Steps of Progress," 8 *American Bar Association Journal* (Jan. 1922), p. 36.
18. 62 *Cong. Rec.* 5, 67th Cong., 2d Sess., p. 4858.
19. *Ibid.*
20. 67 *Cong. Rec.* 10, 69th Cong., 1st Sess., p. 10942.
21. *Ibid.*, p. 10943.
22. "Procedures in Federal Courts," *Hearings, Subcommittee of the Senate Judiciary Committee,* 68th Cong., 1st Sess., Feb. 2, 1924, on S. 2060 and S. 2061, p. 25.
23. *Ibid.*, p. 42.
24. "Additional Judges, United States District Courts," *Hearings of the Senate Judiciary Committee,* 67th Cong., 1st Sess., on S. 2432, S. 2433, S. 2523 on Oct. 5 and Nov. 21, p. 18.
25. L. D. Brandeis to WHT, Dec. 23, 1923.
26. WHT to L. D. Brandeis, Dec. 3, 1923.
27. "Jurisdiction of Circuit Courts of Appeals and of the Supreme Court of the United States," *Hearings of the House Judiciary Committee,* 68th Cong., 2d Sess., on H.R. 8206, Dec. 18, 1924, p. 29.
28. WHT to Charles P. Taft II, Feb. 8, 1925.
29. WHT to Horace D. Taft, Mar. 30, 1922.
30. See also House Judiciary Committee *Hearings,* 67th Cong., 2d Sess., Mar. 30, 1922, on H.R. 10479, p. 12.
31. See 62 *Cong. Rec.* 5, 67th Cong., 2d Sess., Mar. 31, 1922, p. 4845.
32. WHT to Albert B. Cummins, Dec. 3, 1925.
33. "Adequate Machinery for Judicial Business," 7 *American Bar Association Journal* (Sept. 1921), p. 453.
34. "Additional Judges . . . ," *loc. cit.*, p. 14.
35. WHT to J. M. Dickinson, Nov. 2, 1922.
36. 62 *Cong. Rec.* 5, 67th Cong., 2d Sess., Mar. 31, 1922, p. 4858.
37. WHT to H. D. Taft, Apr. 9, 1922.
38. WHT to C. P. Taft II, Jan. 27, 1924.
39. WHT to T. W. Shelton, Jan. 31, 1924.
40. WHT to Willis Van Devanter, Jan. 29, 1924.
41. WHT to Harlan Fiske Stone, Oct. 7, 1924.
42. WHT to George W. Anderson, May 12, 1926.
43. *Appropriation Budget Estimates,* etc., Senate Doc. No. 159, 69th Cong., 1st Sess., H.R. 13040, p. 92.
44. See "Limiting the Jurisdiction of District Courts of the United States," Senate Reports

on Public Bills, Vol. 2, 70th Cong., 1st Sess., Report No. 626, Mar. 27, 1928, on S. 3151.
45. "Possible and Needed Reforms in the Administration of Civil Justice in the Federal Courts," 8 *American Bar Association Journal* (1922), p. 604.
46. WHT to Casper S. Yost, Apr. 5, 1928.
47. *Ibid.*
48. WHT to C. S. Yost, Apr. 16, 1928.
49. WHT to Henry W. Taft, Apr. 5, 1928.
50. *New York Times,* Apr. 22, 1928, Sec. III, p. 4; May 10, 1928, p. 26.
51. From the *Florida Times-Union,* Apr. 28, 1928, in 69 *Cong. Rec.* 7, 70th Cong., 1st Sess., p. 7422.
52. WHT to H. W. Taft, Apr. 7, 1928.
53. WHT to Charles P. Taft, Sept. 10, 1922.
54. *Ibid.*
55. WHT to R. A. Taft, July 29, 1922. Pringle, *Life and Times of William Howard Taft,* II, 1041.
56. WHT to C. P. Taft, Sept. 10, 1922.
57. "American Law Institute Holds Fourth Meeting," 12 *American Bar Association Journal* (May 1926), p. 300.
58. WHT to Clarence H. Kelsey, Aug. 17, 1923.
59. 69 *Cong. Rec.* 6, 70th Cong., 1st Sess., p. 6379.
60. WHT to H. W. Taft, Apr. 7, 1928.
61. 69 *Cong. Rec.* 6, p. 6378.
62. *Ibid.*, p. 6379.
63. *Ibid.*
64. WHT to H. W. Taft, May 16, 1928.
65. WHT to T. W. Shelton, Nov. 9, 1926.
66. WHT to Charles Evans Hughes, Apr. 27, 1926, in 12 *American Bar Association Journal* (May 1926), p. 326.
67. S. 624, 68th Cong., 1st Sess.
68. WHT to T. W. Shelton, Apr. 13, 1924. H.R. 3260 in the House.
69. WHT to H. W. Taft, May 11, 1924.
70. *Ibid.*
71. For WHT's participation in the movement for Federal Uniform Procedure, see "Procedure in Federal Courts," *Hearings, Subcommittee of the Judiciary Committee,* U. S. Senate, 68th Cong., 1st Sess., Feb. 2, 1924, on S. 2060 and S. 2061, p. 76.
72. See S. 2860, 67th Cong., 2d Sess.; Address by WHT, "Bill to Unify Federal Courts," 5 *Journal of the American Judicature Society* (Aug. 1921), p. 37.
73. W. H. Taft, "Possible and Needed Reforms in the Administration of Civil Justice in the Federal Courts," 57 *American Law Review* (Jan.-Feb. 1923), pp. 21–22.
74. WHT to Wells Goodykoontz, Jan. 12, 1923. I am indebted to my colleague Walter F. Murphy for this reference.
75. "Authorizing Supreme Court to Make and Publish Rules in Common-Law Actions," *Senate Reports,* Vol. III, Report No. 1174, 69th Cong., 1st Sess., July 1, 1926, on S. 477, p. 13.

76. WHT to John C. Oldman, July 6, 1924.
77. WHT to Henry W. Rogers, July 26, 1923.
78. 65 *Cong. Rec.* 9, 68th Cong., 1st Sess., p. 8843.
79. WHT to C. E. Hughes, Mar. 25, 1925.
80. See H.R. 10821 passed June 8, 1926. 67 *Cong. Rec.* 10, 69th Cong., 1st Sess., p. 10959.
81. WHT to Charles Curtis, Feb. 26, 1923.
82. WHT to C. Curtis, Feb. 28, 1923.
83. C. Curtis to WHT, Mar. 1, 1923.
84. H.R. 6559. 69th Cong., 1st Sess.
85. WHT to Senator Reed Smoot, July 3, 1925.
86. 67 *Cong. Rec.* 8, 69th Cong., 1st Sess., p. 8670.
87. *Ibid.*, p. 8673.
88. WHT to Richard M. Elliott, May 11, 1926.
89. WHT to W. Van Devanter, May 11, 1926.
90. Senate Report 197, 69th Cong., 1st Sess.; House Report 1223, *ibid.*
91. P.L. 281.
92. WHT to George H. Moses, Oct. 3, 1926.
93. WHT to Henry W. Keyes, Apr. 26, 1928.
94. WHT to Arthur R. Gould, May 1, 1928.
95. WHT to Claude A. Swanson, May 1, 1928.
96. WHT to Henry F. Ashurst, May 1, 1928.
97. *Ibid.*
98. *Ibid.*
99. "A Building for the Supreme Court of the United States," House Report 1773, 70th Cong., 1st Sess., May 19, 1928, on H.R. 13665. See also H.R. 13242, *House Journal,* 70th Cong., 1st Sess., p. 740; H.R. 13665, *ibid.*, pp. 834, 913.
100. WHT to W. Van Devanter, Dec. 7, 1928.
101. H.R. 3864, 71st Cong., 2d Sess.
102. See Public Law 644, 70th Cong., 2d Sess.
103. WHT to C. Curtis, Sept. 4, 1925.
104. WHT to F. T. Manning, Feb. 1927.
105. WHT to C. Curtis, Sept. 4, 1925.
106. WHT to Mrs. Charles P. Taft, Dec. 9, 1929.
107. Public Law 26, 71st Cong., 2d Sess.
108. WHT to R. A. Taft, Dec. 22, 1929.
109. WHT to C. P. Taft II, Feb. 27, 1927.
110. "Corner Stone of New Home of Supreme Court of the United States is Laid," 18 *American Bar Association Journal* (Nov. 1932), pp. 723, 728.

VI. PRESIDENTIAL ADVISER

1. WHT to Gus Karger, June 19, 1920.
2. *Ibid.*
3. WHT to G. Karger, July 30, 1920.
4. WHT to Horace D. Taft, July 12, 1921.
5. "President's Address," *Senate Journal,* 67th Cong., 2d Sess., p. 391.

6. *Ibid.*, p. 390. See also *New York Times*, Aug. 19, 1922, p. 1.
7. WHT to Warren G. Harding, Aug. 27, 1922.
8. WHT to James M. Beck, Dec. 18, 1921.
9. WHT to J. M. Beck, Jan. 18, 1922.
10. WHT to H. D. Taft, Oct. 6, 1921.
11. WHT to Norton L. Upson, Aug. 21, 1921.
12. WHT to Isaac M. Ullman, July 18, 1921.
13. WHT to W. G. Harding, July 20, 1921.
14. W. G. Harding to WHT, Oct. 17, 1922.
15. WHT to Niles Mosely, Nov. 28, 1921.
16. WHT to Harry M. Daugherty, Nov. 28, 1921.
17. *Ibid.*
18. Charles Evans Hughes to WHT, Apr. 22, 1924.
19. WHT to H. D. Taft, Sept. 29, 1923, in Pringle, *Life and Times of William Howard Taft* (New York: Farrar and Rinehart, 1939), II, 1019.
20. WHT to Charles P. Taft II, Dec. 16, 1923.
21. WHT to Mrs. William C. Herron, Aug. 14, 1923.
22. WHT to St. G. R. Fitzhugh, Aug. 14, 1923, in Pringle, *Taft*, II, 1019.
23. WHT to H. D. Taft, Sept. 27, 1923.
24. WHT to H. D. Taft, Sept. 29, 1923, in Pringle, *Taft*, II, p. 1019.
25. WHT to Henry W. Taft, Sept. 27, 1923.
26. See "To Limit the Power of United States Courts to express opinion as to the credibility of witnesses or weight of testimony," *House Reports* on *Public Bills*, Vol. II, Report No. 365, 68th Cong., 1st Sess. on H.R. 3260; also see: S. 624, 68th Cong., 1st Sess.; S. 455, 69th Cong., 1st Sess.
27. S. 455, 69th Cong., 1st Sess. WHT to H. W. Taft, May 18, 1926.
28. WHT to C. E. Hughes, Mar. 19, 1926.
29. WHT to Joseph Buffington, Mar. 18, 1926.
30. WHT to C. E. Hughes, Mar. 19, 1926.
31. Calvin Coolidge to WHT, Nov. 30, 1923.
32. *Craig* v. *Hecht*, 263 U.S. 255, 268 (1923).
33. *Ibid.*, pp. 255, 278.
34. *Ibid.*, p. 279.
35. *Ibid.*, p. 281.
36. WHT to Calvin Coolidge, Nov. 29, 1923.
37. *Ibid.*
38. *New York Times*, Dec. 4, 1923.
39. WHT to H. D. Taft, Mar. 6, 1924.
40. *Ibid.*
41. H. D. Taft to WHT, Mar. 7, 1924.
42. WHT to H. D. Taft, May 6, 1924.
43. WHT to H. D. Taft, Apr. 28, 1924, in Pringle, *Taft*, II, 1061.
44. WHT to Andrew W. Mellon, Apr. 28, 1924.
45. WHT to H. D. Taft, Apr. 26, 1924.
46. WHT to A. W. Mellon, Apr. 28, 1924; H.R. 7959, 68th Cong., 1st Sess.
47. *Ibid.* See: S. 5, 68th Cong., 1st Sess.

48. WHT to A. W. Mellon, Apr. 28, 1924.
49. WHT to A. W. Mellon, May 5, 1924.
50. S. 1898, 68th Cong., 1st Sess.
51. WHT to A. W. Mellon, May 5, 1924.
52. *Ibid.* See: S. 3555, 68th Cong., 1st Sess.
53. See *Senate Journal,* 70th Cong., 1st Sess., p. 508.
54. WHT to R. A. Taft, May 27, 1928.
55. WHT to A. W. Mellon, Apr. 28, 1924.
56. *Ibid.*
57. A. W. Mellon to WHT, Apr. 29, 1924.
58. WHT to A. W. Mellon, May 1, 1924.
59. WHT to Willis Van Devanter, Dec. 27, 1926.
60. Van Devanter's reply was put on Taft's letter of Dec. 27, 1926.
61. WHT to Charles Moore, Jan. 2, 1927.
62. "Communication from the President of the United States: United States Supreme Court Site," *House Misc. Documents,* Vol. II, Doc. No. 655, 69th Cong., 2d Sess.
63. See Senate Doc. 251, p. 41; also Public Law 660, H.R. 16462, 69th Cong., 2d Sess.
64. C. 249, 42 Stat. 1448.
65. WHT to H. D. Taft, May 15, 1924.
66. WHT to Harlan Fiske Stone, May 29, 1924.
67. *Ibid.*
68. WHT memorandum, May 31, 1924.
69. *Oklahoma* v. *Texas,* 265 U.S. 513, 517 (1924).
70. Everett Sanders (Secretary to President Coolidge) to WHT, Sept. 24, 1927. *New York Times,* Dec. 1, 1927, p. 29.
71. John W. Weeks to WHT, July 23, 1921.
72. WHT to J. W. Weeks, Aug. 6, 1921.
73. Conversation with Arthur Page, March 18, 1955. Elting E. Morison, *Turmoil and Tradition: A Study of the Life and Times of Henry L. Stimson* (Boston: Houghton, Mifflin, 1960), p. 302.
74. WHT to Caspar W. Hodgson, Mar. 6, 1929.
75. WHT to H. L. Stimson, Apr. 5, 1929.
76. *Ibid.*
77. See *New York Times,* Feb. 26, 1929, p. 26, col. 8; Mar. 10, 1929, p. 12, col. 7.
78. See *New York Times,* May 16, 1929, p. 1.
79. WHT to H. D. Taft, Oct. 11, 1925. Pringle, *op. cit.,* II, 1063.
80. WHT to H. D. Taft, Mar. 23, 1920.
81. WHT to H. D. Taft, Jan. 28, 1928.
82. WHT to H. D. Taft, Oct. 31, 1928.
83. *Ibid.*
84. *Ibid.*
85. *Ibid.*
86. *Ibid.*
87. *Ibid.*
88. WHT to Robert A. Taft, Jan. 20, 1929.
89. *Ibid.*
90. WHT to Helen Taft Manning, Jan. 13, 1929.
91. Herbert Hoover, "The Cabinet and the Presidency, 1920–33,"

in *Memoirs* (New York: Macmillan, 1952), p. 267.
92. WHT to Helen Taft Manning, Mar. 17, 1929.
93. *Ibid.*
94. *Ibid.*
95. *Ibid.*
96. WHT to R. A. Taft, Mar. 17, 1929.
97. *Ibid.*
98. *Ibid.*
99. *Ibid.*
100. *Ibid.*
101. *Ibid.*
102. *Ibid.*
103. WHT to Helen Taft Manning, Mar. 17, 1929.
104. WHT to R. A. Taft, Apr. 7, 1929.
105. *Ibid.*
106. Herbert Hoover to WHT, Apr. 7, 1929.
107. WHT to Herbert Hoover, Apr. 8, 1929.
108. WHT to R. A. Taft, May 12, 1929.
109. *Ibid.*
110. WHT to R. A. Taft, Mar. 31, 1929.
111. WHT to Charles P. Taft II, Nov. 3, 1929.
112. WHT to I. M. Ullman, Dec. 2, 1929.

VII. PACKING THE COURT

1. Judge Arthur C. Denison, Dec. 13, 1930, speaking as representative of the circuit and district judges. 285 U.S., XIII (1931).
2. Archie Butt, *Taft and Roosevelt* (New York: Doubleday, Doran, 1930), I, 15.
3. WHT to Charles P. Taft, Sept. 10, 1910.
4. WHT to William H. Moody, Oct. 4, 1910. Pringle, *Life and Times of William Howard Taft,* I, 536.
5. Pringle, *op. cit.*, I, 536–37.
6. WHT to Robert Winslow, Oct. 21, 1916. Pringle, *Taft,* II, 899.
7. *Ibid.*, p. 898.
8. W. H. Taft, "Mr. Wilson and the Campaign," *Yale Review,* X, Oct. 1920, pp. 19–20.
9. "Justice and Freedom for Industry" (pamphlet), address before the National Association of Manufacturers, May 26, 1915, p. 4.
10. W. H. Taft, Address of the President, 39 *American Bar Association Reports* (1914), at 368: ". . . the momentum that such a popular movement acquires prevents its stopping at the median line, and we are in danger of excessive regulation which will really interfere with that freedom of trade and unrestricted initiative which has helped so much the material progress of the country heretofore."
11. WHT to Horace D. Taft, Sept. 17, 1922.
12. Eleven are listed for the eight years between 1912 and 1920 in Fred A. Maynard, "Five to Four Decisions of the Supreme Court of the United States," 54 *American Law Review* (Jul.–Aug. 1920), 481, at 513. This constituted more than 15 per cent of all 5–4 decisions reported in Maynard's survey,

covering the entire period from 1800 onward. Maynard's article was written to unite the bar against the continued agitation of Gompers for legislative recall of judicial decisions, and served to point up the crisis in which a split Court found itself.

13. Remarks of W. H. Taft, Proceedings of the Judicial Section, 41 *American Bar Association Reports* (1916), 741.
14. W. H. Taft, "Mr. Wilson and the Campaign," *loc. cit.*, p. 19.
15. WHT to H. D. Taft, Sept. 17, 1922.
16. WHT to Charles D. Hilles, Oct. 19, 1922.
17. WHT to Clarence H. Kelsey, July 21, 1921.
18. WHT to C. D. Hilles, Nov. 4, 1923.
19. WHT to Warren G. Harding, Nov. 4, 1922.
20. W. G. Harding to WHT, Nov. 2, 1922.
21. WHT to H. D. Taft, Oct. 8, 1922.
22. WHT to C. D. Hilles, Oct. 19, 1922.
23. WHT to H. D. Taft, Oct. 8, 1922.
24. WHT to C. D. Hilles, Sept. 9, 1922.
25. WHT to C. D. Hilles, Oct. 19, 1922.
26. WHT to Charles P. Taft II, May 3, 1925; WHT to Robert A. Taft, May 17, 1925.
27. Quoted in W. F. Murphy, "Chief Justice Taft and the Lower Court Bureaucracy," *Journal of Politics*, Vol. 24 (1962), 461.
28. WHT to Edward Colston, Feb. 21, 1923.
29. WHT to H. D. Taft, July 10, 1924.
30. Butt, II, 645.
31. WHT to George Sutherland, July 2, 1921. Quoted in W. F. Murphy, "In His Own Image: Mr. Chief Justice Taft and Supreme Court Appointments," *The Supreme Court Review*, 1961, p. 162.
32. W. F. Murphy, "In His Own Image," *loc. cit.*, p. 180.
33. WHT to H. D. Taft, Dec. 20, 1922.
34. WHT to Henry W. Taft, Jan. 16, 1923.
35. WHT to C. D. Hilles, Dec. 3, 1922.
36. WHT to Elihu Root, Dec. 21, 1922.
37. WHT to Willis Van Devanter, Aug. 19, 1922.
38. WHT to G. Sutherland, Sept. 10, 1922.
39. WHT to W. Van Devanter, Sept. 22, 1922.
40. WHT to C. D. Hilles, Sept. 9, 1922.
41. WHT to Max Pam, Oct. 28, 1922.
42. WHT to W. Van Devanter, Sept. 16, 1922.
43. WHT to Pierce Butler, Nov. 2, 1922.
44. WHT to P. Butler, Nov. 17, 1922. Maneuverings and pressures that went into Butler's appointment are detailed in D. J. Danelski, *A Supreme Court Justice Is Appointed* (1964).
45. WHT to P. Butler, Nov. 17, 1922.
46. 64 *Congressional Record* 1, 67th Cong., 4th Sess., Dec. 21, 1922, p. 813.
47. WHT to Helen Taft Manning, Nov. 26, 1922.

48. George W. Wickersham to WHT, Nov. 23, 1922.
49. WHT to P. Butler, Nov. 7, 1922.
50. WHT to W. G. Harding, Dec. 4, 1922.
51. WHT to M. Pam, Oct. 28, 1922.
52. WHT to E. Root, Nov. 19, 1922.
53. WHT to W. G. Harding, Nov. 8, 1922.
54. W. G. Harding to WHT, Nov. 6, 1922.
55. WHT to W. G. Harding, Dec. 4, 1922.
56. *Ibid.*
57. *Ibid.*
58. *Ibid.*
59. *Ives* v. *South Buffalo Railway Co.*, 201 N.Y. 271 (1911).
60. WHT to H. W. Taft, Nov. 29, 1922.
61. WHT to C. D. Hilles, Dec. 3, 1922.
62. WHT to Charles C. Burlingham, Jan. 16, 1923. Quoted in W. F. Murphy, "In His Own Image," *loc. cit.*, p. 182.
63. WHT to Helen Taft Manning, Jan. 11, 1925.
64. WHT to R. A. Taft, Jan. 10, 1925.
65. WHT to R. A. Taft, July 2, 1925. Pringle, *op. cit.*, II, 1043.
66. *Ibid.*
67. See A. T. Mason, *Harlan Fiske Stone: Pillar of the Law* (New York, Viking, 1956), p. 184.
68. Language of Judge A. C. Denison, Dec. 13, 1930. 285 U.S., XIII (1931).
69. H. W. Taft to WHT, Oct. 26, 1922.
70. *Ibid.*
71. Walter Bagehot accorded these rights to the British monarch in the mid-nineteenth century. See *The English Constitution* (New York: Appleton, 1914), p. 143.
72. WHT to C. D. Hilles, Dec. 31, 1922.
73. WHT to C. D. Hilles, Jan. 14, 1923.
74. *Ibid.*
75. WHT to C. D. Hilles, Dec. 31, 1922.
76. Remarks of Martin J. Wade, Proceedings of the Judicial Section, 41 *American Bar Association Reports* (1916), 746.
77. "Taft and the Supreme Court," *The New Republic*, Oct. 27, 1920, pp. 208–209.

VIII. THE LOWER FEDERAL COURTS

1. Walter F. Murphy, "Chief Justice Taft and the Lower Federal Court Bureaucracy," *Journal of Politics*, Vol. 24 (1962), p. 459.
2. WHT to Charles D. Hilles, Jan. 20, 1923.
3. WHT to Joseph N. Teal, Oct. 5, 1926.
4. WHT to Horace D. Taft, Apr. 5, 1924.
5. WHT to C. D. Hilles, Mar. 21, 1927.
6. See George Wharton Pepper, *Family Quarrels: The President, the Senate, the House* (New York: Baker, Voorhis, 1931), p. 90.

7. WHT to Helen Taft Manning, Nov. 30, 1924.
8. 285 U.S., XIII, 1931.
9. WHT to Henry W. Taft, May 31, 1925.
10. WHT to F. T. Murphey, Nov. 30, 1923.
11. *New York Times,* Mar. 9, 1921, p. 3.
12. WHT to Clarence H. Kelsey, July 21, 1921.
13. WHT to H. D. Taft, Jan. 7, 1922.
14. WHT to H. D. Taft, Sept. 28, 1923.
15. WHT to Harry M. Daugherty, June 5, 1922.
16. WHT to Charles P. Taft, Jan. 2, 1923.
17. WHT to Robert A. Taft, Jan. 27, 1924.
18. WHT to H. D. Taft, Apr. 10, 1924.
19. WHT to Loyal E. Knappen, Mar. 12, 1924.
20. WHT to L. E. Knappen, Mar. 23, 1924.
21. WHT to Arthur C. Denison, Apr. 17, 1924.
22. WHT to Harlan Fiske Stone, Apr. 22, 1924.
23. WHT to H. F. Stone, Aug. 1, 1924.
24. WHT to H. F. Stone, Dec. 17, 1924.
25. H. F. Stone to C. D. Hilles, Dec. 10, 1924. Quoted in A. T. Mason, *Harlan Fiske Stone: Pillar of the Law* (New York: Viking, 1956), p. 162.

25a. WHT to C. D. Hilles, Dec. 3, 1924.

26. *Ibid.*
27. WHT to Helen Taft Manning, Nov. 30, 1924.
28. WHT to R. A. Taft, Feb. 1925. Quoted in William Allen White, *A Puritan in Babylon: The Story of Calvin Coolidge* (New York: Macmillan, 1938), p. 321.
29. WHT to Charles P. Taft II, Feb. 14, 1926.
30. WHT to C. P. Taft II, May 29, 1927.
31. *Ibid.*
32. Quoted in W. A. White, *op. cit.*, pp. 348, 413.
33. WHT to M. Woolsey Stryker, Sept. 23, 1924.
34. See WHT to R. A. Taft, Mar. 15, 1924, in William Allen White, *op. cit.*, p. 286.
35. WHT to H. D. Taft, Aug. 12, 1923.
36. WHT to Warren G. Harding, Jan. 6, 1923; WHT to Fred T. Murphey, Nov. 30, 1923.
37. WHT to F. T. Murphey, Nov. 30, 1923.
38. WHT to H. D. Taft, Aug. 12, 1923.
39. Gus Karger to WHT, Sept. 11, 1923.
40. WHT to F. T. Murphey, Nov. 30, 1923.
41. WHT to Casper S. Yost, Sept. 20, 1923.
42. WHT to G. Karger, Sept. 14, 1923.
43. *Ibid.*
44. WHT to C. S. Yost, Sept. 20, 1923.
45. WHT to H. D. Taft, Sept. 27, 1923.
46. WHT to Calvin Coolidge, Oct. 19, 1923.
47. WHT to Calvin Coolidge, Mar. 19, 1924.
48. WHT to R. A. Taft, May 3, 1925. Quoted in W. A. White, *op. cit.*, p. 288.
49. WHT to C. D. Hilles, Apr. 24, 1925. *Ibid.*, p. 288.

50. WHT to A. C. Denison, Nov. 22, 1928.
51. WHT to C. D. Hilles, Dec. 3, 1924.
52. WHT to R. A. Taft, May 3, 1925. W. A. White, *op. cit.*, p. 288.
53. WHT to C. P. Taft II, Aug. 11, 1928.
54. WHT to Charles Evans Hughes, Apr. 26, 1927.
55. WHT to Learned Hand, Apr. 30, 1927.
56. WHT to L. Hand, Apr. 27, 1927.
57. WHT to L. Hand, Apr. 30, 1927.
58. WHT to C. E. Hughes, Apr. 26, 1927.
59. WHT to L. Hand, May 25, 1927.
60. WHT to A. C. Denison, July 21, 1927.
61. WHT to R. A. Taft, Nov. 4, 1928.
62. WHT to R. A. Taft, Nov. 11, 1928.
63. *Ibid.*
64. WHT to C. P. Taft II, Feb. 14, 1926.
65. WHT to John G. Sargent, Apr. 21, 1925.
66. WHT to George W. Wickersham, Dec. 27, 1928.
67. *Ibid.*
68. WHT to Helen Taft Manning, Jan. 13, 1929.
69. WHT to Charles C. Burlingham, Feb. 11, 1929.
70. Address, Apr. 26, 1929. Quoted in 72 *Congressional Record* 1, 71st Cong., 2d Sess., Dec. 17, 1929, p. 787.
71. *Ibid.*
72. WHT to C. P. Taft II, Apr. 20, 1929.
73. WHT to William D. Mitchell, July 30, 1929.
74. WHT to W. D. Mitchell, Oct. 24, 1929.
75. WHT to Helen Taft Manning, Oct. 20, 1929.
76. *Ibid.*
77. Herbert Hoover, *Memoirs: The Cabinet and the Presidency, 1920–33* (New York: Macmillan, 1952), p. 269.
78. WHT to H. D. Taft, Dec. 30, 1921. Quoted in W. F. Murphy, *op. cit.*, p. 454.
79. Felix Frankfurter and James M. Landis, *The Business of the Supreme Court* (New York: Macmillan, 1928), p. 218.
80. WHT to Judge John Peters, Oct. 11, 1927. Quoted in W. F. Murphy, "Chief Justice Taft and the Lower Federal Court Bureaucracy," *loc. cit.*, p. 459.
81. WHT to G. W. Wickersham, Nov. 23. 1929.

IX. AT THE HELM

1. Charles Evans Hughes, *The Supreme Court of the United States* (New York: Columbia University Press, 1928), pp. 56–58.
2. Harlan Fiske Stone to Irving Dilliard, June 7, 1941. The Stone Papers, Library of Congress.
3. Quoted in Felix Frankfurter, "Chief Justices I Have Known," *Virginia Law Review*, Nov. 1953, pp. 899–900. Reprinted in Frankfurter, *Of Law and*

Men (New York: Harcourt, 1956), pp. 111–138.

4. Oliver Wendell Holmes to Frederick Pollock, Oct. 2, 1921. *Holmes-Pollock Letters* (Cambridge: Harvard University Press, 1941), II, 79.
5. WHT to Helen H. Taft, Aug. 3, 1921.
6. *Ibid.*
7. WHT to Gus Karger, July 17, 1921.
8. WHT to Andrew J. Volstead, Mar. 1, 1922.
9. Editorial, *Christian Science Monitor,* Feb. 5, 1930.
10. O. W. Holmes to Harold Laski, Dec. 22, 1921. *Holmes-Laski Letters* (Cambridge: Harvard University Press, 1953), I, 389–390.
11. O. W. Holmes to H. Laski, Oct. 22, 1922. *Ibid.,* I, 457.
12. *United Mine Workers of America* v. *Coronado Coal Company,* 259 U.S. 344 (1921).
13. WHT to Horace D. Taft, June 16, 1922.
14. WHT to H. F. Stone, Sept. 4, 1925.
15. WHT to Louis D. Brandeis, July 25, 1922.
16. WHT to H. D. Taft, Apr. 27, 1922.
17. WHT to Robert A. Taft, Mar. 4, 1928.
18. *Ibid.*
19. WHT to R. A. Taft, Apr. 15, 1928.
20. William Stansbury to WHT, July 3, 1923.
21. WHT to Charles P. Taft II, Mar. 18, 1923.
22. WHT to R. A. Taft, June 3, 1928.
23. WHT to R. A. Taft, Nov. 28, 1926. See also WHT to Brethren, Memorandum, May 11, 1928.
24. WHT to H. D. Taft, Nov. 13, 1925.
25. W. Stansbury to WHT, Feb. 16, 1922.
26. James M. Beck to WHT, Sept. 25, 1923.
27. WHT to J. M. Beck, Sept. 25, 1923.
28. WHT to L. D. Brandeis, Dec. 18, 1926.
29. L. D. Brandeis to WHT, Nov. 3, 1923.
30. WHT to L. D. Brandeis, Nov. 4, 1923.
31. WHT to L. D. Brandeis, Mar. 12, 1923.
32. WHT to William Lyon Phelps, May 30, 1927.
33. WHT to R. A. Taft, June 7, 1925.
34. WHT to W. L. Phelps, June 7, 1925.
35. WHT to Arthur C. Denison, Dec. 16, 1927.
36. WHT to A. C. Denison, Dec. 29, 1927.
37. John H. Clarke to WHT, July 1, 1921.
38. James C. McReynolds to WHT, July 1921.
39. O. W. Holmes to F. Pollock, Feb. 24, 1923. *Holmes–Pollock Letters,* II, 114.
40. O. W. Holmes to H. Laski, Oct. 9, 1921. *Holmes–Laski Letters,* I, 373.
41. O. W. Holmes to F. Pollock, May 21, 1922. *Holmes–Pollock Letters,* II, 96.
42. WHT to R. A. Taft, May 3, 1925.
43. WHT to Learned Hand, Mar. 3, 1923.
44. WHT to W. K. Hutchinson, Dec. 29, 1925. Pringle, *Life*

and Times of William Howard Taft (New York: Farrar and Rinehart, 1939), II, 960.
45. WHT to L. D. Brandeis, July 24, 1921. Pringle, *op. cit.*, II, 995.
46. H. D. Taft to WHT, July 6, 1921. Alexander M. Bickel, *The Unpublished Opinions of Mr. Justice Brandeis: The Supreme Court at Work* (Cambridge: Harvard University Press, 1957), pp. xix–xx.
47. WHT to H. D. Taft, July 6, 1921.
48. L. D. Brandeis to Felix Frankfurter. Manuscript of conversation in Library of Harvard Law School. Bickel, *op. cit.*, p. 203.
49. *Ibid.*, p. 18.
50. WHT to L. D. Brandeis, Mar. 30, 1922.
51. L. D. Brandeis to WHT, Mar. 30, 1922.
52. L. D. Brandeis to F. Frankfurter conversations. Bickel, *op. cit.*, p. 18.
53. *Board of Trade of City of Chicago* v. *Olsen,* 262 U.S. 1 (1923).
54. *McKee* v. *Gratz,* 260 U.S. 127 (1922).
55. L. D. Brandeis to WHT, Dec. 23, 1922.
55a. See Alexander M. Bickel, *The Unpublished Opinions of Mr. Justice Brandeis* (Cambridge: The Belknap Press, 1957).
56. *Southwestern Telephone Co.* v. *Public Service Commission,* 262 U.S. 276 (1923).
57. Brandeis–Frankfurter conversations. Bickel, *op. cit.*, p. 199.
58. WHT to O. W. Holmes, March 30, 1922.
59. *United Mine Workers of America* v. *Coronado Coal Co.*, 259 U.S. 344 (1921).
60. L. D. Brandeis to WHT, May 28, 1922.
61. WHT to L. D. Brandeis, May 29, 1922.
62. Brandeis–Frankfurter conversations. Bickel, *op. cit.*, p. 97.
63. *Ibid.*
64. *Sonneborn Bros.* v. *Cureton,* 262 U.S. 506 (1923).
65. Brandeis–Frankfurter conversations. Bickel, *op. cit.*, p. 113.
66. WHT to Charles D. Hilles, June 9, 1925. A. T. Mason, *The Supreme Court from Taft to Warren* (Baton Rouge: Louisiana State University Press, 1958), p. 58.
67. *United Mine Workers of America* v. *Coronado Coal Co.*, 259 U.S. 344 (1921).
68. *Sonneborn Bros.* v. *Cureton,* 262 U.S. 506 (1923).
69. *Bailey* v. *Drexel Furniture Co.*, 259 U.S. 20 (1921).
70. WHT to L. D. Brandeis, Nov. 19, 1926.
71. *Burke* v. *Sanitary District of Chicago,* 280 U.S. 585 (1924).
72. WHT to Pierce Butler, Jan. 7, 1929.
73. Memorandum. P. Butler to WHT, May 19, 1928.
74. P. Butler to WHT, Apr. 11, 1923.
75. H. F. Stone to WHT, Dec. 7, 1925.
76. WHT to R. A. Taft, Feb. 2, 1929.
77. Willis Van Devanter to WHT, Aug. 27, 1923.
78. WHT to Helen H. Taft, Apr. 13, 1924.
79. J. H. Clarke to WHT, Mar. 7, 1922.
80. WHT to George Sutherland,

Oct. 3, 1927. J. Francis Paschal, *Mr. Justice Sutherland: A Man Against the State* (Princeton: Princeton University Press, 1951), p. 154.

81. O. W. Holmes to H. Laski, June 15, 1929. *Holmes–Laski Letters,* II, 1158.
82. WHT to Harry A. Hollzer, Feb. 14, 1928.
83. H. F. Stone to Marshall and Lauson Stone, Nov. 24, 1939. A. T. Mason, *Harlan Fiske Stone: Pillar of the Law* (New York: Viking, 1956), p. 316.
84. WHT to H. D. Taft, Feb. 1, 1923.
85. WHT to R. A. Taft, Mar. 25, 1928.
86. WHT to H. D. Taft, Feb. 1, 1923.
87. WHT to R. A. Taft, Dec. 18, 1927.
88. WHT to P. Butler, Dec. 5, 1922.
89. WHT to R. A. Taft, Jan. 27, 1924.
90. WHT to Charles P. Taft, Feb. 18, 1923.
91. WHT to R. A. Taft, Mar. 25, 1928.
92. *Southern Railway* v. *Watts,* 260 U.S. 519 (1923).
93. WHT to L. D. Brandeis, Dec. 18, 1922.
94. Bickel, *op. cit.,* p. 204.
95. WHT to L. D. Brandeis, May 18, 1923.
96. 259 U.S. 44, 66.
97. O. W. Holmes to H. Laski, Feb. 22, 1929. *Holmes–Laski Letters,* II, 1035.
98. WHT to P. Butler, Dec. 5, 1922.
99. WHT to Joseph H. Jones, Feb. 4, 1926; WHT to W. L. Phelps, May 30, 1927.
100. Pringle, *op. cit.,* II, 1027.
101. WHT to R. A. Taft, May 3, 1925.
102. O. W. Holmes to H. Laski, Dec. 17, 1925. *Holmes–Laski Letters,* I, 806.
103. Holmes to Laski, Apr. 25, 1927. *Ibid.,* II, 938.
104. WHT to R. A. Taft, May 3, 1925.
105. *Ibid.*
106. WHT to Helen H. Taft, Apr. 28, 1924.
107. WHT to R. A. Taft, May 3, 1925.
108. WHT to Helen H. Taft, Apr. 28, 1924.
109. WHT to R. A. Taft, May 3, 1925.
110. WHT to Helen H. Taft, Apr. 28, 1924.
111. WHT to H. D. Taft, Jan. 17, 1927.
112. WHT to Helen H. Taft, May 3, 1927.
113. *Ibid.*
114. 274 U.S. 380 (1926).
115. WHT to Edward T. Sanford, Jan. 26, 1927.
116. W. Van Devanter to WHT, ca. June 1927.
117. WHT to W. Van Devanter, July 9, 1926.
118. *Ibid.*
119. *James C. Davis* v. *Commonwealth of Kentucky, Southern Railway* v. *Commonwealth of Kentucky,* 274 U.S. 76 (1926).
120. WHT to P. Butler, Jan. 28, 1927.
121. *St. Louis and O'Fallon Railroad Co.* v. *United States,* 279 U.S. 461 (1929).
122. WHT to C. P. Taft II, May 12, 1929.
123. WHT to E. T. Sanford, July 4, 1929. Pringle, *op. cit.,* II, 1077.

124. *Railroad Commission of California* v. *Southern Pacific Company,* 264 U.S. 331 (1924).
125. Brandeis–Frankfurter conversations. Bickel, *op. cit.,* p. 209.
126. *Ibid.,* pp. 209–210.
127. WHT to Helen H. Taft, Apr. 5, 1925.
128. *Ibid.*
129. Brandeis–Frankfurter conversations. Bickel, *op. cit.,* p. 210.
130. WHT to Helen H. Taft, Apr. 3, 1924.
131. WHT to Helen H. Taft, Apr. 5, 1924.
132. WHT to Helen H. Taft, Apr. 3, 1924.
133. WHT to R. A. Taft, Dec. 26, 1926.
134. WHT to C. P. Taft II, Nov. 1, 1925.
135. *American Steel Foundries* v. *Tri-City Central Trades Council,* 257 U.S. 184 (1921).
136. Max Pam to WHT, Dec. 16, 1921.
137. WHT to R. A. Taft, May 24, 1925.
138. WHT to Mahlon Pitney, Mar. 31, 1922.
139. WHT to Helen Taft Manning, Mar. 2, 1924.
140. WHT to H. D. Taft, Nov. 2, 1923.
141. WHT to H. D. Taft, Apr. 17, 1922.
142. *Ibid.*
143. *Ibid.*
144. WHT to Joseph McKenna, May 9, 1924.
145. WHT to J. McKenna, May 23, 1924.
146. WHT to J. H. Clarke, May 3, 1923.
147. WHT to Helen Taft Manning, June 11, 1923. Pringle, *op. cit.,* II, 969.
148. WHT to Helen H. Taft, May 8, 1924.
149. WHT to H. D. Taft, Nov. 2, 1923.
150. WHT to H. D. Taft, Apr. 17, 1922.
151. WHT to Helen Taft Manning, Mar. 2, 1924.
152. WHT to C. D. Hilles, Sept. 9, 1922. Pringle, *op. cit.,* II, 1059.
153. WHT to H. D. Taft, Nov. 2, 1923.
154. WHT to Helen H. Taft, Apr. 5, 1924.
155. WHT Memorandum to Brethren, Nov. 10, 1924.
156. WHT to George W. Wickersham, Jan. 8, 1925.
157. Pringle, *op. cit.,* II, 951.
158. WHT to R. A. Taft, Feb. 1, 1925.
159. WHT to R. A. Taft, April 20, 1924.
160. WHT to Helen Taft Manning, June 11, 1923. Quoted in W. F. Murphy, "In His Own Image," *Supreme Court Review* (1961), p. 166.
161. *Railroad Commission of Wisconsin* v. *Chicago B. and Q. R.R. Co.,* 257 U.S. 563 (1921).
162. J. C. McReynolds to WHT, ca. 1922.
163. WHT to R. A. Taft, Mar. 8, 1925.
164. J. C. McReynolds to WHT, Nov. 23, 1929.
165. WHT to R. A. Taft, Feb. 1, 1925.
166. WHT to Helen H. Taft, Feb. 1, 1926.
167. J. C. McReynolds to WHT, ca. Feb., 1922.
168. J. C. McReynolds to WHT, ca. Mar., 1924.
169. WHT to J. C. McReynolds, Mar. 28, 1924.

170. WHT to Elihu Root, Sept. 13, 1922.
171. J. H. Clarke to WHT, n.d.
172. WHT to R. A. Taft, Oct. 26, 1922.
173. WHT to C. D. Hilles, Sept. 9, 1922.
174. WHT to E. Root, Sept. 13, 1922.
175. WHT to H. D. Taft, May 15, 1922.
176. WHT to G. Karger, Jan. 3, 1916. Pringle, *op. cit.*, II, 952.
177. WHT to M. Pam, Sept. 12, 1924.
178. L. D. Brandeis to WHT, Nov. 30, 1924.
179. *Ibid.*
180. WHT to W. Van Devanter, Dec. 1, 1924.
181. WHT to R. A. Taft, Dec. 14, 1924.
182. WHT to C. P. Taft II, Nov. 3, 1929.
183. WHT to H. L. Stimson, May 13, 1928. Pringle, *op. cit.*, II, 969–970.
184. WHT to Helen Taft Manning, June 11, 1923. *Ibid.*, p. 969.
185. WHT to C. P. Taft II, Mar. 7, 1926. *Ibid.*
186. WHT to R. A. Taft, Mar. 7, 1926.
187. WHT to R. A. Taft, Mar. 4, 1928.
187a. Samuel J. Konefsky, "Holmes and Brandeis, Companions in Dissent," 10 Vanderbilt Law Review, 269, 270 (1957).
188. WHT to R. A. Taft, Jan. 25, 1925.
189. WHT to James Rowland Angell, Dec. 2, 1926.
190. WHT to W. L. Phelps, May 30, 1927.
191. WHT to R. A. Taft, Jan. 16, 1927.
192. F. Frankfurter, *Of Law and Men*, p. 129.
193. *Keokuk and Hamilton Bridge Co.* v. *Salem*, 258 U.S. 122 (1921).
194. W. Van Devanter to WHT, Feb. 9, 1922.
195. *Truax* v. *Corrigan*, 257 U.S. 312 (1921).
196. WHT to W. Van Devanter, Dec. 7, 1921.
197. 262 U.S. 522 (1923).
198. W. Van Devanter to WHT, ca. May 1923.
199. WHT to J. M. Dickinson, Dec. 12, 1928.
200. WHT to R. A. Taft, Oct. 23, 1927. Quoted in W. F. Murphy, "Marshalling the Court," *loc. cit.*, pp. 640, 643.
201. H. F. Stone to John Bassett Moore, May 17, 1943. A. T. Mason, *Harlan Fiske Stone*, p. 790.
202. WHT to Sir Thomas White, Jan. 8, 1922.
203. WHT to H. L. Stimson, May 18, 1928.
204. WHT to L. Hand, Sept. 7, 1927.
205. *Bluefield Water Works and Improvement Co.* v. *Public Service Commission of West Virginia*, 258 U.S. 622 (1921).
206. WHT to W. Van Devanter, Aug. 19, 1922.
207. WHT to C. P. Taft II, Dec. 28, 1924.
208. WHT to H. D. Taft, Dec. 12, 1926.
209. WHT to C. P. Taft II, Dec. 22, 1924.
210. WHT to W. Van Devanter, Dec. 23, 1924. Pringle, *op. cit.*, II, 984.
211. WHT to H. D. Taft, Dec. 26, 1924. *Ibid.*, p. 971.

212. WHT to H. D. Taft, Dec. 12, 1926.
213. *Ibid.*
214. *Myers* v. *United States,* 272 U.S. 52 (1926).
215. WHT to P. Butler, Nov. 7, 1925.
216. WHT to E. T. Sanford, Nov. 7, 1925.
217. WHT to W. Van Devanter, July 9, 1926.
218. WHT to H. D. Taft, Nov. 23, 1925.
219. *Ibid.*
220. *Ibid.*
221. WHT to R. A. Taft, Jan. 10, 1926.
222. WHT to L. D. Brandeis, Jan. 4, 1926.
223. WHT to H. D. Taft, Jan. 5, 1926.
224. WHT to R. A. Taft, Oct. 24, 1926.
225. WHT to H. D. Taft, Oct. 27, 1926. Pringle, *op. cit.,* II, 1025.
226. WHT to C. P. Taft II, Oct. 30, 1926.
227. 277 U.S. 438 (1928).
228. WHT to E. T. Sanford, May 31, 1928.
229. WHT to H. D. Taft, June 8, 1928.
230. WHT to H. D. Taft, June 12, 1928.
231. WHT to H. D. Taft, June 8, 1928.
232. WHT to H. D. Taft, June 12, 1928.
233. *Ibid.*
234. *Ibid.*
235. 277 U.S. 438, 485 (1928).
236. WHT to H. D. Taft, June 8, 1928.
237. *Ibid.*
238. W. Van Devanter to WHT, June 16, 1928.
239. 274 U.S. 380 (1926).
240. WHT to G. Sutherland, Jan. 25, 1927.
241. WHT to E. T. Sanford, Jan. 24, 1927.
242. WHT to H. F. Stone, Jan. 26, 1927. A. T. Mason, *Harlan Fiske Stone,* pp. 256–257.
243. J. C. McReynolds to H. F. Stone, n.d.
244. H. F. Stone to WHT, Jan. 26, 1927.
245. *Ibid.*
246. WHT to G. Sutherland, Jan. 25, 1927.
247. WHT to G. Sutherland, Mar. 11, 1927.
248. WHT to R. A. Taft, Apr. 10, 1927.
249. 274 U.S. 123 (1926).
250. 273 U.S. 70 (1926).
251. WHT to H. F. Stone, Apr. 24, 1927.
252. H. F. Stone to WHT, Apr. 25, 1927.
253. WHT to C. P. Taft II, Oct. 13, 1929.
254. Attorney General William D. Mitchell, 285 U.S., p. xxiv (1931).
255. WHT to L. Hand, Nov. 9, 1922. Pringle, *op. cit.,* II, 1057.
256. WHT to H. D. Taft, Nov. 14, 1922.
257. W. Stansbury to Robert Von Moschzisker, Dec. 23, 1929.
258. WHT to Clarence H. Kelsey, Feb. 14, 1924.
259. WHT to Helen H. Taft, May 4, 1924.
260. WHT to H. D. Taft, June 12, 1924.
261. WHT to R. A. Taft, Feb. 15, 1925. Pringle, *op. cit.,* II, 1074.
262. WHT to C. P. Taft II, Mar. 27, 1925.
263. WHT to R. A. Taft, Jan. 3, 1926.

264. WHT to J. M. Dickinson, Aug. 21, 1926.
265. WHT to H. D. Taft, Oct. 21, 1926.
266. Walter Tittle, "Glimpses of Interesting Americans," 110 *Century* (Sept. 1925), 570.
267. *Ibid.*
268. WHT interview with the Associated Press. *New York Times,* July 7, 1927, p. 8.
269. *Ibid.*
270. *Holmes–Laski Letters,* June 6, 1926, II, 848.
271. WHT typewritten manuscript, May 1921.
272. *Felix Frankfurter Reminisces* (New York: Reynal, 1960), p. 54.
273. WHT to J. H. Clarke, Sept. 5, 1922.
274. WHT to Frank H. Hiscock, Oct. 24, 1926.
275. WHT to John S. Seymour, Aug. 5, 1921.
276. WHT to J. H. Clarke, Sept. 5, 1922.
277. Compare the words of Judge A. C. Denison, 285 U.S., xiii (1931).
278. *Our Chief Magistrate and His Powers* (New York: Columbia University Press, 1916), p. 140.
279. 280 U.S., v. (1930).

X. CONSTITUTIONAL CREED

1. "Mr. Chief Justice Taft," *The New Republic,* Vol. 27 (July 27, 1921), pp. 230–231.
2. *Ibid.*
3. *Truax* v. *Corrigan,* 257 U.S. 312 (1921).
4. Edward S. Corwin, "Constitutional Law in 1921–1922," *American Political Science Review,* Vol. 16 (Nov. 1922), p. 632.
5. *Truax* v. *Corrigan, loc. cit.,* p. 328.
6. *Ibid.,* pp. 329–330.
7. *Ibid.,* p. 327.
8. *Ibid.,* p. 330.
9. *Ibid.,* pp. 335–336.
10. *Ibid.,* p. 338. (Emphasis added.)
11. WHT to Horace D. Taft, May 7, 1922. Pringle, *Taft,* I, 967.
12. "The Chief Justice–A Mistaken Appointment," *The Nation,* CXIII (July 13, 1921), 32.
13. *Truax* v. *Corrigan, loc. cit.,* pp. 342–344.
14. *Ibid.,* pp. 354–355.
15. *Ibid.,* p. 357.
16. *Ibid.,* p. 368.
17. *Ibid.,* p. 376. For a favorable critique of Taft's majority opinion as well as some barbed criticisms of the dissenting opinions of Holmes and Brandeis, see Corwin, "Constitutional Law in 1921–1922," *loc. cit.,* pp. 632–635.
18. *Stafford* v. *Wallace,* 258 U.S. 495 (1922).
19. *Ibid.,* pp. 514–515.
20. *Ibid.,* pp. 515–516.
21. *Swift* v. *United States,* 196 U.S. 375 (1905).
22. *Stafford* v. *Wallace, loc. cit.,* p. 517.
23. *Swift* v. *United States, loc. cit.,* p. 398.
24. *Stafford* v. *Wallace, loc. cit.,* pp. 518–519.
25. *Ibid.,* p. 521.
26. *Board of Trade of City of Chi-*

cago v. *Olsen*, 262 U.S. 1 (1923).

27. *Ibid.*, p. 35. Professor Corwin thought Taft paid mere lip service to congressional judgment in *Olsen*. The decision was based, he contended, not on a presumption of the validity of the act but on a finding of fact by the Court itself, viz., that the Court would be "unwarranted in rejecting the finding of Congress" as "unreasonable." See Corwin, "Constitutional Law in 1922–1923," *American Political Science Review*, Vol. 18 (Feb. 1924), p. 52.
28. *Bailey* v. *Drexel*, 259 U.S. 20 (1922).
29. *Hammer* v. *Dagenhart*, 247 U.S. 251 (1918).
30. *Bailey* v. *Drexel*, *loc. cit.*, p. 36.
31. *Ibid.*, p. 37.
32. *Ibid.*, p. 25. (Emphasis added.)
33. *Ibid.*, p. 37.
34. *Ibid.*, p. 38.
35. *Ibid.*, pp. 32–33. (Emphasis added.)
36. *Ibid.*, pp. 39–40.
37. *McCray* v. *United States*, 195 U.S. 27 (1904).
38. *Ibid.*, p. 56.
39. *Bailey* v. *Drexel*, *loc. cit.*, p. 42.
40. Corwin, "Constitutional Law in 1921–1922," *loc. cit.*, p. 615. (Emphasis added.)
41. *United States* v. *Kahriger*, 345 U.S. 22, 37–38 (1953).
42. *Atherton Mills* v. *Johnston*, 259 U.S. 13 (1922).
43. Alexander M. Bickel, *The Unpublished Opinions of Mr. Justice Brandeis* (Cambridge: Harvard University Press, 1957), pp. 18–19.
44. *McCray* v. *United States*, 195 U.S. 27 (1904).
45. *United States* v. *Doremus*, 249 U.S. 86 (1919).
46. *Adkins* v. *Children's Hospital*, 261 U.S. 525 (1923).
47. *Ibid.*, p. 546.
48. *Ibid.*, p. 562.
49. *Ibid.*
50. *Lochner* v. *New York*, 198 U.S. 45 (1905).
51. *Holden* v. *Hardy*, 169 U.S. 366 (1897).
52. *Muller* v. *Oregon*, 208 U.S. 412 (1908).
53. *Bunting* v. *Oregon*, 243 U.S. 426 (1917).
54. *Adkins* v. *Children's Hospital*, *loc. cit.*, pp. 563–564.
55. *Ibid.*, p. 564.
56. *Ibid.*, pp. 565–566.
57. *Ibid.*, p. 567.
58. *Ibid.*, p. 568.
59. *Wolff Packing Co.* v. *Court of Industrial Relations of Kansas*, 262 U.S. 522 (1923).
60. *Adkins* v. *Children's Hospital*, *loc. cit.*, p. 566.
61. *Wolff Packing Co.* v. *Court of Industrial Relations*, *loc. cit.*, p. 534. See also *Tyson* v. *Banton*, 273 U.S. 418 (1927), where Taft joined Sutherland's majority in voiding state regulation of ticket scalping. Prices and wages, Sutherland contended, were the very "heart of the contract" and were, therefore, relatively free from government regulation. Taft, of course, had railed against Sutherland's use of the same argument in *Adkins*.
62. *Munn* v. *Illinois*, 94 U.S. 113 (1877).
63. *Wolff Packing Co.* v. *Court of*

Industrial Relations, loc. cit., pp. 534–536.

64. *Ibid.*, p. 536.
65. *Ibid.*
66. *Ibid.*, p. 538.
67. *Ibid.*, p. 539.
68. *Wilson* v. *New*, 243 U.S. 332 (1916).
69. *Wolff Packing Co.* v. *Court of Industrial Relations, loc. cit.*, pp. 542–543.
70. Louis D. Brandeis to WHT; slip opinion in *Wolff*.
71. *Myers* v. *United States*, 272 U.S. 52 (1926).
72. Quoted in A. T. Mason, *Harlan Fiske Stone: Pillar of the Law* (New York: Viking, 1956), p. 222.
73. *Ex Parte Grossman*, 267 U.S. 86 (1925).
74. *Ibid.*, p. 122.
75. *Myers* v. *United States, loc. cit.*, p. 96.
76. *Ibid.*, p. 134.
77. WHT to A. L. Spaulding, July 23, 1891. For this reference I am indebted to Mr. Leon I. Salomon.
78. *Myers* v. *United States, loc. cit.*, p. 134.
79. *Ibid.*, p. 293.
80. See Robert H. Jackson, *The Struggle for Judicial Supremacy* (New York: Knopf, 1941), pp. 107–109.
81. *Humphrey's Executor* v. *United States*, 295 U.S. 602 (1935).
82. *Ibid.*, pp. 626–627.
83. *Olmstead* v. *United States*, 277 U.S. 438 (1928).
84. Pringle writes: "It sometimes seemed as though there were no lengths to which the Chief Justice would not go, and along which he would not attempt to lead the court, in his determination to uphold Prohibition enforcement." *The Life and Times of William Howard Taft*, II, 989.
85. *Olmstead* v. *United States, loc. cit.*, p. 464.
86. *Ibid.*, pp. 465–466.
87. *Ibid.*, p. 468.
88. *Ibid.*, pp. 467–468.
89. *Ibid.*, p. 470.
90. *Ibid.*, pp. 487–488.
91. Language of Chief Justice John Marshall, *McCulloch* v. *Maryland*, 4 Wheat. 316, 407 (1819).
92. *Olmstead* v. *United States, loc. cit.*, p. 487.
93. *Ibid.*, p. 472.
94. *Weems* v. *United States*, 217 U.S. 349, 373 (1909).
95. *Olmstead* v. *United States, loc. cit.*, p. 473.
96. *Ibid.*, p. 476.
97. *Ibid.*, p. 474.
98. *Ibid.*, pp. 478–479.
99. WHT to H. D. Taft, June 8, 1928.
100. WHT to H. D. Taft, June 12, 1928.
101. WHT to George Sutherland, Sept. 14, 1928.
102. Archibald Butt, *Taft and Roosevelt*, I, 293–294.
103. WHT to Harlan Fiske Stone, Aug. 31, 1928. Pringle, *op. cit.*, II, 1015.
104. *Gibbons* v. *Ogden*, 9 Wheat. 1, 197 (1824).
105. *McCulloch* v. *Maryland*, 4 Wheat. 316, 423 (1819).
106. *Ibid.*
107. *Ibid.*, p. 406.
108. Butt, *op. cit.*, I, 183.
109. "Mr. Chief Justice Taft," *loc. cit.*, p. 231.
110. Pringle, *op. cit.*, II, 129.
111. *Ibid.*, I, 165.

XI. PROPRIETIES

1. *Literary Digest,* Vol. 70 (July 16, 1921), 13.
2. Herbert Little, "The Omnipotent Nine," *American Mercury,* Vol. 15 (Sept. 1928), p. 49.
3. *Ibid.*
4. "Address by Chief Justice William Howard Taft," in A Report of the Annual Meeting, at Luncheon, of the Alumni of the Yale School of Law, June 18, 1928.
5. *Ibid.*
6. *New York Times,* Oct. 9, 1928, p. 7.
7. "Statement of Chief Justice William Howard Taft." *Hearings before the Committee on the Judiciary.* H. R., 68th Cong., 2d Sess., on H. R. 8206, Dec. 18, 1924, p. 26.
8. J. F. Essary, "The Human Side of the Supreme Court," *Scribner's Magazine,* Vol. 86 (Nov. 1929), p. 501.
9. WHT to Robert A. Taft, Apr. 19, 1925.
10. *Ibid.*
11. WHT to Charles P. Taft II, Apr. 19, 1925.
12. Francis McHale, *President and Chief Justice: The Life and Public Services of William Howard Taft* (Philadelphia: Dorrance, 1931), p. 300.
13. *Dillingham* v. *McLaughlin,* 264 U.S. 370, 372.
14. Oliver Wendell Holmes to Frederick Pollock, Apr. 6, 1924. *Holmes–Pollock Letters,* M. De Wolfe Howe, ed. (Cambridge: Harvard University Press, 1946), II, p. 132.
15. WHT to R. A. Taft, Apr. 8, 1928.
16. *New York Times,* Jan. 8, 1925, p. 5.
17. WHT to Charles Curtis, Sept. 4, 1925. Pringle, *op. cit.,* II, 1076. See also 67 *Congressional Record* 8, 69th Cong., 1st Sess., p. 8667.
18. WHT to H. D. Taft, Nov. 28, 1925.
19. WHT to H. D. Taft, Dec. 12, 1926.
20. WHT to C. Bascom Slemp, Dec. 30, 1924.
21. James C. McReynolds to WHT, Feb. 23, 1925.
22. WHT to J. C. McReynolds, Feb. 24, 1925.
23. Charles Evans Hughes to WHT, Mar. 2, 1925.
24. WHT to C. Curtis, Feb. 8, 1925.
25. *Ibid.*
26. Memorandum, Feb. 23, 1925.
27. Proceedings of the Judicial Section, 41 *American Bar Association Report* (Aug. 30, 1916), 743.
28. See *New York Times,* Aug. 28, 1921, p. 75.
29. WHT to Jonathan M. Wainwright, Aug. 6. 1921.
30. Merlo J. Pusey, *Charles Evans Hughes* (New York: Macmillan, 1951), II, 635.
31. WHT to H. D. Taft, Oct. 21, 1923.
32. *Papers Relating to the Foreign Relations of the United States,* 1914 (Washington: Government Printing Office, 1922), I, 1000–1015.
33. WHT to Helen H. Taft, Aug. 3, 1921.

34. John F. Hayford, Dean, College of Engineering, Northwestern University, and Ora Miner Leland, Cornell University. See *New York Times,* Aug. 25, 1921, p. 15; also C. E. Hughes to WHT, Aug. 25, 1921.
35. WHT to Pierce Butler, Aug. 29, 1929.
36. WHT to O. W. Holmes, Aug. 28, 1929.
37. WHT to H. D. Taft, Sept. 18, 1923.
38. WHT to Robert A. Taft, Apr. 7, 1929.
39. WHT to Franklin MacVeagh, Mar. 5, 1922.
40. 62 *Cong. Rec.* 5, 67th Cong., 2d Sess., 5113–5114.
41. WHT to Isaac M. Ullman, Apr. 6, 1922.
42. WHT to Frank H. Hiscock, Apr. 12, 1922.
43. WHT to George Stuart Patterson, Apr. 8, 1922.
44. WHT to Gus Karger, Aug. 30, 1916. Pringle, *The Life and Times of William Howard Taft,* II, 953.
45. WHT to Henry S. Pritchett, Apr. 25, 1923.
46. *Ibid.*
47. WHT to James Rowland Angell, Apr. 15, 1923.
48. WHT to Helen H. Taft, Sept. 25, 1923.
49. WHT to Samuel Gompers, Sept. 30, 1921.
50. WHT to Ralph M. Easley, Aug. 24, 1922.
51. WHT to Helen Taft Manning, Mar. 15, 1926.
52. WHT to H. W. Taft, Aug. 30, 1923.
53. *Ibid.*
54. WHT to Elihu Root, Aug. 18, 1922.
55. WHT to Henry W. Taft, Feb. 7, 1923.
56. Elihu Root to WHT, Sept. 9, 1922.
57. WHT to Clarence H. Kelsey, Aug. 17, 1923.
58. E. Root to WHT, June 7, 1924.
59. WHT to C. E. Hughes, Apr. 27, 1926. 12 *American Bar Association Journal* (May 1926), 326.
60. WHT to Howard W. Odum, Aug. 24, 1921.
61. WHT to George H. Tinkham, Sept. 1, 1922.
62. William Howard Taft, "The Jurisdiction of the Supreme Court under the Act of February 13, 1925," 35 *Yale Law Journal* (Nov. 1925), 2.
63. WHT to P. Butler, Sept. 16, 1925.
64. Quoted in New York *Evening World,* editorial, Nov. 6, 1926. See also WHT to Thomas W. Shelton, Apr. 6, 1924.
65. New York *Evening World,* editorial, Nov. 6, 1926.
66. WHT to Harold S. Pollard, Nov. 18, 1926.
67. WHT to William L. Chenery, Dec. 13, 1926.
68. See *Collier's,* Vol. 78 (Jan. 22, 1927), pp. 8–9.
69. WHT to W. L. Chenery, Jan. 15, 1927.
70. Washington *Star,* Jan. 9, 1929, in 70 *Cong. Rec.* 2, 70th Cong., 2d Sess., 1465.
71. WHT to Mrs. W. H. Taft, Aug. 11, 1923. Quoted in William Allen White, *A Puritan in Babylon* (New York: Macmillan, 1938), p. 245.

72. WHT to Charles D. Hilles, Sept. 8, 1923.
73. WHT to Charles H. Clark, Dec. 18, 1923.
74. *Ibid.*
75. WHT to I. M. Ullman, Jan. 2, 1924.
76. WHT to Luther A. Brewer, July 20, 1921.
77. WHT to C. S. Thompson, Sept. 21, 1924.
78. WHT to C. D. Hilles, June 5, 1924.
79. *Republican Campaign Text-Book, 1924,* Republican National Committee, p. 67.
80. WHT to C. D. Hilles, June 5, 1924.
81. Louis Wiley to WHT, June 6, 1924.
82. *New York Times,* Oct. 5, 1924, p. 1.
83. *Ibid.*
84. WHT to C. E. Hughes, Oct. 5, 1924. Merlo J. Pusey, *op. cit.,* II, 569.
85. WHT to George H. Paine, Oct. 9, 1924.
86. Quoted in W. A. White, *op. cit.,* p. 350.
87. *Ibid.,* p. 377.
88. *Ibid.,* p. 334.
89. *New York Times,* Nov. 14, 1922, p. 1.
90. WHT to H. W. Taft, Aug. 12, 1922; WHT to Horace D. Taft, Nov. 11, 1921.
91. See Pringle, *op. cit.,* II, 1003–1004.
92. WHT to George Harvey, July 21, 1922.
93. Warren G. Harding to WHT, July 27, 1922.
94. WHT to Helen Taft Manning, Feb. 3, 1923.
95. *Ibid.*
96. Memorandum of Interview, Jan. 21, 1923. Pusey, *op. cit.,* p. 585.
97. WHT to C. E. Hughes, July 21, 1927; see also similar letter, WHT to W. G. Harding, July 21, 1922.
98. "The Chief Justice Abroad," 8 *American Bar Association Journal* (Aug. 1922), 456.
99. WHT to E. Root, Aug. 18, 1922.
100. WHT to C. E. Hughes, July 21, 1922.
101. *Ibid.*
102. Robert Cecil to WHT, July 28, 1922.
103. C. E. Hughes to WHT, Aug. 1, 1922.
104. WHT to R. Cecil, Aug. 18, 1922.
105. WHT to E. Root, Aug. 18, 1922.
106. See *Foreign Relations,* I (1923), 10–17.
107. WHT to Frederick E. Wadhams, Dec. 3, 1923.
108. 65 *Cong. Rec.* 1, 68th Cong., 1st Sess., 442.
109. WHT to W. J. Moore, July 30, 1921. Pringle, *op. cit.,* II, 961.
110. WHT to C. P. Taft II, Mar. 25, 1923.
111. G. Harvey to WHT, Sept. 1, 1922.

XII. FOREBODINGS

1. Address of the President, 39 *American Bar Association Reports* (1914), 359, 368.
2. "The Social Importance of Proper Standards for Admission to the Bar," 38 *American Bar*

Association Reports (1913), 924, 933–934.
3. "To be valuable [social changes] must come slowly and with deliberation." *Ibid.*, p. 935. Cf. Taft, *Liberty under Law* (New Haven: Yale University Press, 1922), pp. 20–21.
4. "The Social Importance of Proper Standards for Admission to the Bar," *loc. cit.*, p. 934.
5. Taft, *The Anti-Trust Act and the Supreme Court* (New York: Harper, 1914), p. 34.
6. Taft, *Popular Government* (New Haven: Yale University Press, 1913), p. 184.
7. *Ibid.*
8. Remarks to the Judicial Section, 41 *American Bar Association Reports* (1916), 741.
9. *Adkins* v. *Children's Hospital,* 261 U.S. 525 (1923), 561.
10. *Liberty under Law*, p. 21.
11. Frankfurter, "The United States Supreme Court Molding the Constitution," *Current History*, May 1930, p. 239.
12. *Baldwin* v. *Missouri,* 281 U.S. 586 (1930), 595.
13. *New State Ice Company* v. *Liebman,* 285 U.S. 262 (1932), 311. Brandeis had used much the same language in *Jay Burns Baking Co.* v. *Bryan,* 264 U.S. 504 (1924), 520.
14. *Jay Burns Baking Co.* v. *Bryan,* 264 U.S. 504, 534.
15. Andrew A. Bruce, *The American Judge* (New York: Macmillan, 1924), pp. 6, 8.
16. WHT to Horace D. Taft, Nov. 14, 1929. Pringle, *Life and Times of William Howard Taft,* II, 967.
17. *Ibid.*
18. WHT to H. D. Taft, Dec. 1, 1929.
19. WHT to Pierce Butler, Sept. 14, 1929.
20. WHT to H. D. Taft, Dec. 1, 1929.
21. WHT to Robert A. Taft, Nov. 25, 1923.
22. WHT to Mrs. Helen Taft Manning, Jan. 8, 1928.
23. WHT to H. D. Taft, Dec. 1, 1929.
24. WHT to H. D. Taft, Dec. 8, 1929.
25. *Ibid.*
26. WHT to H. D. Taft, Dec. 1, 1929.
27. *Ibid.*
28. WHT to H. D. Taft, Dec. 8, 1929.
29. WHT to H. D. Taft, Dec. 1, 1929.
30. WHT to Charles P. Taft, May 12, 1929. Pringle, *op. cit.*, II, 1044.
31. *Ibid.*
32. *Ibid.*
33. WHT to P. Butler, Sept. 14, 1929.
34. Fred Starek to WHT, Sept. 25, 1929.
35. See, in this connection, Mason, *Harlan Fiske Stone: Pillar of the Law* (New York: Viking, 1956), pp. 276–283.
36. Charles Evans Hughes, *The Supreme Court of the United States* (New York: Columbia University Press, 1928), p. 96.
37. Oliver Wendell Holmes, *Collected Legal Papers* (New York: Harcourt, Brace and Howe, 1920), p. 270.
38. See Theodore H. White, *The Making of the President 1960* (New York: Atheneum, 1961), p. 366.
39. Holmes to Judge W. L. Put-

nam, July 12, 1910. Quoted in W. L. King, *Melville Weston Fuller* (New York: Macmillan, 1950), p. 334.

40. *Holmes–Pollock Letters* (Cambridge: Harvard University Press, 1941), II, 79.
41. See John P. Frank, "Harlan Fiske Stone: An Estimate," 9 *Stanford Law Review* (1957), 629, note 31.
42. Archie Butt, *Taft and Roosevelt* (New York: Doubleday, Doran, 1930), II, 656.
43. WHT to R. A. Taft, Oct. 23, 1927.
44. Taft, *Present Day Problems,* (New York: Dodd, Mead, 1908), pp. 167–168.
45. O. W. Holmes, *op. cit.,* pp. 267–268.
46. Woodrow Wilson, *Constitutional Government in the United States* (New York: Columbia University Press, 1917), p. 168.
47. *De Jonge* v. *Oregon,* 299 U.S. 353, 365 (1937).

INDEX

Date Due